Praise for The Startup Lottery

"*THE STARTUP LOTTERY* is a quick and enjoyable read for entrepreneurs, potential investors, and joiners alike! It is especially useful for people thinking about joining a startup. Over 25 percent of my students consider the startup path while at HBS, and 'Employee's Due Diligence Checklist' will help them make well-informed decisions as they embark on their careers."

– Kristen Fitzpatrick
Managing Director, Career and Professional Development
Harvard Business School

"*THE STARTUP LOTTERY* is the must-have read for anyone considering joining a startup or founding one without prior experience. With over three decades of experience in the startup world and a Harvard MBA, Gus goes through everything from what questions you should ask before joining a start-up, how to evaluate an offer, to what an exit looks like."

– Katharine Weymouth
Entrepreneur, Investor, Former Publisher
The Washington Post

"*THE STARTUP LOTTERY* offers core lessons for surviving and thriving in startup life. The insights in this book will help you evaluate opportunities, embrace change, and manage risk. It's not enough to work hard. You need a good navigation system to reach your destination. *THE STARTUP LOTTERY* is the GPS for your startup career."

– Stephen Kaufer
Co-Founder and former CEO, Tripadvisor

"*THE STARTUP LOTTERY* provides a great framework for evaluating the risk of a startup combined with practical advice on whether a startup is right for you. Easy-to-follow explanations of complicated compensation topics with a healthy dollop of realism useful to counterbalance typical startup hype. An invaluable resource for anyone considering a role in a startup!"

— Ted Niedermayer, President of Fitch Solutions
Board member of the Tuck School of Business at Dartmouth

"*THE STARTUP LOTTERY* is an excellent book. I have never come across anything so useful for people looking at joining a startup. The book condenses a lifetime of learnings and wisdom, offering practical advice, demystification, and great frameworks for evaluating career options. I highly recommend this book to anyone considering working at a startup."

— Alison Davis
Experienced public and private company board director
Venture capital investor in more than 800 early-stage companies

THE
STARTUP
LOTTERY

YOUR GUIDE TO NAVIGATING
RISK AND REWARD

GUS BESSALEL

THE

STARTUP

LOTTERY

YOUR GUIDE TO NAVIGATING
RISK AND REWARD

GUS BESSALEL

Jones Media Publishing

Jones Media Publishing
10645 N. Tatum Blvd. Ste. 200-166
Phoenix, AZ 85028
www.JonesMediaPublishing.com

Disclaimer:

The author strives to be as accurate and complete as possible in the creation of this book, notwithstanding the fact that the author does not warrant or represent at any time that the contents within are accurate due to the rapidly changing nature of the Internet.

While all attempts have been made to verify information provided in this publication, the Author and the Publisher assume no responsibility and are not liable for errors, omissions, or contrary interpretation of the subject matter herein. The Author and Publisher hereby disclaim any liability, loss or damage incurred as a result of the application and utilization, whether directly or indirectly, of any information, suggestion, advice, or procedure in this book. Any perceived slights of specific persons, peoples, or organizations are unintentional.

In practical advice books, like anything else in life, there are no guarantees of income made. Readers are cautioned to rely on their own judgment about their individual circumstances to act accordingly. Readers are responsible for their own actions, choices, and results. This book is not intended for use as a source of legal, business, accounting or financial advice. All readers are advised to seek the services of competent professionals in legal, business, accounting, and finance field.

Printed in the United States of America

ISBN: 978-1-948382-65-6 paperback

DEDICATION

To the employees
without whom no startup could succeed

Acknowledgments

In early September 2021, looking out over the water from the deck of the beautiful Nags Head, North Carolina home of Leslie Miles and Jayson Schwam, I was reflecting on my eight-year run at Fugue. With the company's sale looming, the stark imbalance between the prospective payouts to the investors and to the employees came into sharp focus. As my wife, our friends and I discussed how to level the playing field, I became convinced of the need to educate and empower startup employees by sharing the realities of the startup game. Inspired, I drafted the table of contents for this book.

My startup odyssey started in the summer of 1991 when my friend and co-worker Neal Simon introduced me to his uncle, the late Mel Chasen, founder of Transmedia Networks, Inc. (now Rewards Network). Mel's faith and support enabled me to follow my budding entrepreneurial dream. My friend Tom Gorman joined me, giving me the confidence to leave my job and start my first company. Numerous friends and family, including my wife's brother and sister-in-law, agreed to invest, and with the help of a small but mighty team anchored by Frank Rothgeb, the company flourished. Having left my conventional career behind, I never looked back.

Being an entrepreneur can be daunting and lonely at times. The Washington-area tech and angel community has been a constant source of energy, education, and support. I cannot quantify the value I took from countless pitch sessions and networking events run by organizations such as the University of Maryland's Dingman Center for Entrepreneurship, John May and Cal Simmons' Washington Dinner Club, and Tien Wong's CONNECTPreneur. I am indebted to the friends, mentors, and investors who provided wise counsel over the years, including Neal Simon, Peter Jaffe, Mark Joseph, Todd Klein, Ron Kaiser, Randy Domolky, and Jonathan Silver, the first VC whose fund we invested in.

For nearly nine years, I shared a mission and (until the pandemic) offices with a talented group of colleagues at Fugue. Special thanks to Josh Stella for trusting me to join him on Fugue's excellent adventure. Tim Webb, my partner in crime at Fugue, validated that Josh was on to something really important. Drew Wright, Fugue's co-founder, for all those late-afternoon, far-ranging conversations. My sincere appreciation also goes out to Phillip Merrick, from whom I learned more than I could have imagined. To my colleagues on the finance team, Mary Christine and Jenny Damiani, without whom I couldn't have done my job.

Thank you to Tom Knox and Dan Kahan of King & Spalding for helping me and Fugue navigate many thorny issues. And, thanks to the late Harry Weller of New Enterprise Associates (NEA), whose enthusiasm for Josh's vision was irrepressible. Harry's death in late 2016 shook the company and the entire DC-area tech community.

Writing a book is its own form of startup. You have an idea. You build a prototype. You test and iterate until it's ready to launch. I appreciate the early readers and thought partners who validated for me that there is value in the book's lessons–David Morris and Ankush Khurana from Fugue; Adam Dakin, Dreamit Ventures; Tom Kohn, American University; Andrew Sachs, Nobel Learning; Eric Schoenberg, CampusWorks and Columbia University, Whitley Cargile, Carlyle Group; Julia Beck; Roger Golden; Shelly Schoo; Lou Morsberger; and Kim Schulze, one of the savviest human resources professionals I know.

No founder can do it alone. That is also true of an author. I have been fortunate to have a committed group of talented collaborators by my side. A hearty thank you to Emily Owen, whom I distracted (briefly) from her own startup to pick apart the manuscript and help me with the visuals. My immense gratitude to my editor, Marilyn Freedman, who set the standard and challenged me to set my ego aside and put in the hard work, matching my efforts with her commitment and enthusiasm. To my publisher, Jeremy Jones, thank you for your positive energy, discipline, and mentorship along the way.

In 1963, my parents left Argentina and came to the United States. My father came first in a pure act of entrepreneurship. With limited resources and speaking no English, he took a risk, established a foothold, and later that year, brought my mother and me over to join him. Their courage and perseverance opened the door to the opportunities available in our new home. I didn't have a choice in the decision, but I'm its biggest beneficiary.

I would not be where I am without the love and support of my biggest fans, my amazing wife, Amena Ali, and our awesome children, Sonya and Jordan. Amena and I have navigated the startup path in parallel, supporting each other's careers, strategizing, negotiating, and learning from each other's triumphs and tribulations. After witnessing up close our decades-long startup roller coaster rides, it comes as no surprise that our kids chose to pursue careers with large, stable companies.

Table of Contents

List of Exhibits

Foreword

In 1991, an experienced management consultant helped a nervous recent college graduate transition into a new career. Eager and motivated but lacking the confidence and knowledge to be successful, the young man needed not just a manager but a caring guide who would take an interest in his development, offer critical advice and information, and set a high bar for his performance. I was that new hire. My manager and mentor was Gus Bessalel.

It is no exaggeration that I would not have survived and thrived in consulting without that early guidance from Gus. His mentorship helped lay the foundation for my business career. I learned to focus on what matters and tackle issues from the highest level to the most minor details. This is why I was so thrilled when Gus told me he was writing *The Startup Lottery*. After more than thirty years of experience as an entrepreneur, start-up executive, advisor, and investor, Gus' decision to share his wisdom through this book with anyone considering joining a start-up is a true public good. Full stop.

Our startup system provides structural and informational advantages on every aspect of company building and financing to those in charge—founders, executives, and investors. Many resources exist to help them understand how to leverage these advantages. But until now, there has not been a comprehensive guide to help the employees. Without a resource such as *The Startup*

Lottery, navigating startup life has been akin to sailing the oceans before the invention of the astrolabe.

Basking in the glow of an offer to join an exciting new company, potential employees may not think about the intricacies of startup risk and the complexity of options, RSUs, or at-will employment. They may not realize the impact of the equity waterfall, dilution, or investors' liquidation preferences on the value of their opportunity. But understanding these concepts is critical to assessing a company's prospects and the long-term consequences for the employee's career and compensation.

The Startup Lottery makes an essential distinction between the risks that investors and employees take. Venture capitalists spread their risk through multiple investments and increase the probability of a "hit" through a portfolio approach. On the other hand, employees suffer from concentration risk—they can't diversify by taking multiple startup jobs at once and are disproportionately affected if their employer fails. With the stakes so high, those considering startup careers require the best insight and counsel possible. This simple fact alone makes *The Startup Lottery* an essential resource.

Gus is not a cheerleader for risk or adventure for its own sake. Rather, he systematically lays out the pros and cons of startup life to help the reader make better decisions about their careers. *The Startup Lottery* takes the reader through a comprehensive journey that begins with an introspective approach to determining whether a startup career makes sense. It then delves into the levers and financial elements that can help make the startup experience more valuable and profitable and addresses when to leave a job. *The Startup Lottery* can be read cover to cover, but also will serve as a handy reference over time.

While no one has yet invented a foolproof predictive mechanism to determine the chances of success of a startup, *The Startup Lottery* provides a comprehensive, deeply reasoned, and accessible companion to address the informational disadvantage potential employees face. This book will help readers make informed decisions that benefit them, the companies they choose to help build, and the rest of us who value a fairer startup ecosystem.

As someone who has worked in two startups (one that worked out and the other that did not), I wish I had had this book when I joined my first new venture in 1999. It would have helped me be more clear-eyed in navigating the dot-com boom and bust and armed me with an understanding of the challenges I would face in the startup world.

Over the last fifteen years, as part of the team that has grown LinkedIn into the world's most successful professional network, I have had the privilege of coaching and advising many young people contemplating startup life. Going forward, for anyone considering such a move, my first piece of counsel will be "Read *The Startup Lottery*."

Enjoy!

Ariel Eckstein,
Vice President,
Talent Solutions, LinkedIn

Introduction

My goal in writing this book is to help startup employees benefit from the lessons I learned the hard way over three decades working in more than a dozen early-stage companies. I observed that people were often in the dark regarding the risks they were taking and how to maximize their chances of reaping the rewards of their startup careers.

Like most young professionals, I started out knowing nothing about startups. You would think an MBA from Harvard Business School and seven years of management consulting experience would have laid a solid foundation for my business career. Had I chosen to work in corporate America for large, established companies, that certainly would have been the case. However, nothing other than fighting in the startup trenches came close to preparing me for the intensity and unpredictability of working in early-stage ventures.

I started my first company at 29 and have spent over 30 years in and around early-stage companies. During that time, I played almost every role possible—founder, employee, consultant, advisor, board member, and angel investor. I have been CEO, COO, and CFO of several companies, and my wife and I have directly invested in over a dozen others. I led my first company onto the *Inc. 500* and have helped companies raise more than $100 million in venture capital. I have also endured the painful process of laying off over 100 respected colleagues and shutting down several companies.

xxvi   The Startup Lottery

For more than 30 years, I have also been married to Amena Ali, an accomplished startup executive. Amena, like me, began her career at Bain; she later joined MCI, a fast-growing telecommunications company, during the go-go years. Fortunately, she left MCI just before the WorldCom scandal and joined a hot technology company about to go public. She has spent over twenty years in senior management roles in tech companies, most recently as CEO of three venture-backed startups. Throughout my wife's career, I have been by her side, hearing countless startup stories and advising her as she negotiated her compensation and dealt with capricious founders and CEOs, mercurial investors and board members, and uncertain prospects for her companies.

Our companies have ranged in size from founders with ideas to later-stage companies that were collectively acquired for more than $1.5 billion. We have seen startups from nearly every angle imaginable. We have had to evaluate the likelihood that our companies would succeed, how long to stay, whether to invest our own money in the businesses, and when to call it quits. We had no manual to refer to that would make those decisions easier. We made it up as we went along and made more than our share of mistakes along the way.

Apart from being a startup veteran and junkie, I am also a golf nut and the father of an accomplished former college golfer. Many golfers suggest the game is a good analogy for life, and I agree. Playing golf is also a lot like working in a startup. The beginning of a round is full of hope and possibilities. You start at even par, having made no mistakes yet. Then you tee off on the first hole, and the outcome is subject to many factors out of your control.

When we join a startup, we show up with our skills, talent, education, experience, and capacity for hard work. We apply those assets hoping to help our company achieve a successful outcome. Each action involves risks and rewards, the possibility for greatness but the equal if not greater probability of imperfection and failure. Like in golf, neglecting to analyze the landscape, plan your strategy, and consider shifting conditions can lead to frustration and defeat. Even if you do everything right, there are still bad bounces.

The results we achieve are the culmination of a series of decisions, actions, and circumstances influenced by both luck and timing that lead to highly variable outcomes. The journey involves small victories and missed opportunities, frequently ending in disappointment. Yet, knowing we may experience failure and frustration, we play the game anyway.

Founders pursuing the startup dream need unwavering optimism and an obsessive belief in themselves and their vision. Overcoming the enormous inertia of turning vision into reality takes extraordinary commitment. Startup founders can't afford to admit the possibility of failure if they want to maintain their passion and convince others to come along for the ride.

We have a cult of the founder in this country. Volumes have been written about them. They are lauded as the drivers of innovation. They are the luminaries who grace the stages at tech conferences and the covers of *Inc., Entrepreneur,* or *Fast Company.* But all the hype about founders fails to capture the whole picture.

When startups succeed, founders get the headlines. Investors reap most of the financial returns. But the hidden story behind those successes is the invaluable contribution of the dozens, hundreds, and sometimes thousands of employees who make their companies great. These are the unsung heroes of the startup world.

Millions of people have bought into the dreams of startup founders. They show up every day, building, creating, and investing their lives, often without a clear understanding of what they are getting themselves into or even what's in it for them. Over my career, I have encountered countless colleagues who had no idea what they were in for when they strapped on their backpacks and joined their startups. Both my wife and I have been guilty of that at times as well.

We become enamored of an idea, a visionary founder, and a story and dive in head first. We become glitter-eyed when a top-tier VC throws money at a company, assuming they know something we don't. We throw caution and judgment out the window and hop on the train.

When my son was twelve and competing in a golf tournament, he found himself in a tough spot with a long, challenging shot with low odds of getting on the green. With the optimism of inexperience, he decided to try a low percentage shot to save par. He never considered the risks nor admitted the possibility of failure. Had he pulled off that shot, it would have been heroic. Unfortunately, he didn't. He made a mess of the hole, started a downward spiral that wrecked the rest of his round, and landed far down the leaderboard.

After the round, his coach questioned his understanding of how difficult that shot was and its low probability of success. At the end of the discussion, his coach said something everyone considering working at a startup should heed.

"The next time you have a shot like that, I want you to ask yourself, 'What am I thinking?' That's a lot better than making a bad decision and then later asking, 'What was I thinking?'"

Deciding to join a startup involves assessing risk. You are buying a lottery ticket. There is certainly a probability of life-altering success. But given the failure rates of startups and how startup economics favor investors, the odds of the ticket paying off are long.

One of the first lessons we learned at Harvard Business School was to gather as much data as possible to make decisions with the best information available. It was a running joke in class. When a professor asked students the first thing they would do in a situation that required a decision, the answer was often "gather more information."

Venture capitalists are always gathering information. They weed through hundreds of company pitches and turn down more than 90 percent before diving more deeply into a few. Before investing, they subject those companies to rigorous examination.

Prospective employees rarely ask even basic questions about the companies they are considering joining. You will never have perfect information about a startup you are excited about. That shouldn't stop you from asking hard questions to determine if the opportunity is right for you and if the company has a realistic chance of success. Do your homework and carefully evaluate what you are getting into and why, or you might regret it later.

There are many good reasons to invest your career in working for startups. Countless people, including my wife and I, have had fulfilling and lucrative careers starting, working for, and helping build exciting young companies. There are also many reasons it may not be such a good idea to join the particular startup you are interviewing with or any startup at all. We have joined ventures that languished, failed, or simply were the wrong fit. Each company is different. Each person's situation is unique.

We have many friends who have ridden the startup train to great wealth. We have also seen too many people, ourselves included, jump into startups without proper due diligence. Too often, startup employees fail to ask themselves what they expect to get out of the experience and inadequately weigh the risks and whether they are worth taking.

This book is for anyone considering working in a startup, determining how best to navigate the journey, or deciding whether to stay. Use its lessons to weigh the ins and out, the pros and cons of startup life. It may be most helpful to those just starting their careers. But the lessons and information in its chapters are also good reminders to mid-career professionals. If you are a startup founder or executive, I encourage you to use the lessons in this book to better deal with your VCs and board and help your employees share more fully in your success.

The Startup Lottery contains cautionary tales and success stories you can learn from to help make the most of your startup experience–personally, professionally, and financially. Its chapters can help you assess whether working at a startup is a good fit and whether now is the right time.

Part I: Understanding Startups (Chapters 1 through 3) provides background on startups and how they work, including the key players and the lifecycle of startups from founding to exit.

Part II: Should You Work for a Startup? (Chapters 4 through 7), explores whether you should work in a startup, considers the risks, uncertainties, and nature of startup life, addresses issues of timing, and discusses general issues around compensation.

Part III: How Stock and Options Work (Chapters 8 through 17) details the complicated nature of compensation and equity in startups and details considerations and strategies for optimizing the value of your stock and option grants.

Part IV: Should You Stay or Should You Go? (Chapters 18 through 20) helps you determine when it's time to leave and what to do when you exit to maximize your professional and financial returns from your time at your startup.

At the back of the book, the Glossary defines important terms, which are bolded when they first appear in the text. I recommend scanning the Glossary before reading the book to familiarize yourself with the terms and returning to it regularly.

Finally, throughout the book, I refer to sections of the IRS tax code when discussing examples of financial outcomes and decisions you may face regarding your incentive compensation. Tax regulations change, so it is always a good idea to verify the most current tax rates and regulations with a financial advisor when considering the information provided and how it affects your decisions.

The Bottom Line

When you commit to working in a startup, you make a huge investment and take a significant leap of faith. The day you join, and every day you go to work, you are investing the most precious resource you have, your time and career. You should regularly take stock of how things are going at the company, what it means for you, and how to optimize your outcome.

Wittingly or unwittingly, investors and senior managers rely on the naivete or ignorance of their employees to achieve their desired outcomes. I know I did. Information flows freely when things are going well, as managers want to pump up the team. But most startups regularly face existential threats. They live on the edge. They constantly scramble to build products and attract customers to impress investors and attract the capital needed to keep going. When times are tough, holding the team together often requires keeping alarming information within a small circle at the top.

The lessons in this book alone cannot fully level the playing field—investors and senior executives simply have too much information and power and are driven by strong incentives to look out for their vested interests. Even if you do everything right, there are no guarantees of success in the startup world. But my experiences and observations about how startups work provide key lessons to help you scrutinize startup opportunities and make better career decisions for yourself and your family.

Stay vigilant, ask hard questions, and recognize that it is up to you to look out for your own best interest at every stage of your startup career. If you don't, after a few years of frustration or unfulfilled expectations, you may find yourself asking, "What was I thinking?"

PART I

UNDERSTANDING STARTUPS

—— CHAPTER 1 ——

What Is a Startup?

The term "startup" is overused. It can mean anything from one or two founders housed in a garage to a venture-backed rocket ship with a **unicorn** valuation (i.e., more than $1 billion) that may have received tens or hundreds of millions of dollars in venture financing.

In venture capital, "startup" usually means a technology or technology-enabled company. Technology, in this case, usually means software or something related to information technology. Startups in different sectors are typically described with a modifier specifying their sector, for example, a life sciences or biotech startup in healthcare or a consumer goods startup in retail or e-commerce.

In my view, a startup does not mean a small business with an owner-operator (think independent restaurant, home contractor, or professional services firm like a law practice or accounting firm.) You can find plenty of professional opportunities working in small companies like that, but that's not what this book is about.

Startup Characteristics

Five fundamental characteristics drive the dynamics you need to understand to manage your career in startup ventures:

1. **The company is privately owned**. Once a company goes public, it is no longer considered a startup. There may be

3

exceptions when startups go public with limited revenue and unclear business models or via a **Special Purpose Acquisition Company (SPAC)** or **reverse merger.**[1] You're probably best avoiding those as they often end poorly for their investors and employees.

2. **The company does not measure its revenue by the hour or project**. The startups I'm referring to sell products, offer software-as-a-service, create marketplaces, apps, and new technologies (like blockchain-enabled solutions, automation, or generative artificial intelligence, for example), or in the case of healthcare, new therapeutic drugs or medical devices. There are undoubtedly many successful professional services organizations, even publicly traded ones. Professional services businesses, however, don't typically offer the explosive growth potential associated with selling products or subscriptions.

3. **The company needs outside investors to realize its vision**. These investors include **angels** and **venture capitalists** but could also include large corporations and government economic development funds or incentive programs. It may be that deep-pocketed founders continually fund a startup, but that is the exception, not the rule. Once later-stage companies attract private equity investment (after achieving substantial revenue and maybe becoming

---

[1] Investopedia defines a SPAC as "a company without commercial operations and is formed strictly to raise capital through an initial public offering (IPO) for the purpose of acquiring or merging with an existing company." This process whereby a shell public company merges with an operating company for the purpose of creating a publicly traded entity with business operations is known as a "reverse merger." Julie Young, Samantha Silberstein, and Katrina Munichiello, "Special Purpose Acquisition Company (SPAC) Explained: Examples and Risks", Investopedia.com, https://www.investopedia.com/terms/s/spac.asp, March 15, 2023,

profitable), they take on characteristics that may make them look more like large companies than startups.

4. **The company is addressing a meaningful market opportunity**. Companies going after large markets typically need outside capital to scale. Here I would distinguish between a small business and a startup. Small businesses may look from the outside like startups, but they often serve relatively small markets, hire a modest number of employees, and exhibit limited growth potential. They are **lifestyle businesses** that provide income, work-life balance, and flexibility for their owners but limited wealth or advancement opportunities for employees. Startups are conceived to address national or global problems. They seek to generate significant returns for shareholders and employees from **liquidity events** tied to the value of the **equity**, not from cash flows generated in the business.

5. **The company is controlled by the founder(s), a small group of executives, and an outside board of directors representing investors.** This group has enormous decision-making control, and their personalities influence or define the organizational culture. The interplay among these stakeholders creates complexity in governance and decision making that is distinct from the dynamics in most small businesses.

Many large companies that fit these characteristics still refer to themselves as startups even when their revenues hit eight or nine figures. This mindset represents continued expectations for high growth and a desire to convey to investors and recruits that there is still plenty of room for them to run. It may also reflect that, as private companies, how they approach their markets, seek growth funding, and attract, motivate, and retain talent remain similar to earlier-stage ventures.

The presence of outside investors in a startup has significant implications. They create more complexity in company governance. They require information. And the expectation for rapid growth creates pressure on the founders and the team to deliver results quickly and cost-effectively. In a 2008 article in *Harvard Business Review*, Noah Wasserman described the Founder's Dilemma of being "rich or king."[2] The need for outside capital to realize the company's potential usually requires founders to give up significant control to realize the wealth-creation potential of their businesses. The subsequent tug-of-war for control among founders and investors drives many startup dynamics.

Startup Stages and Venture Capital

Although all venture-backed startups share fundamental characteristics, the "founder with an idea" startup differs from a more established company that has attracted customers and generated significant revenue. Where a startup is in its lifecycle determines some of its dynamics, the focus of its activities, and the nature of risk and uncertainty it faces. As startups grow their market presence, some early risks, such as whether their technology works, give way to other concerns, including competitive and operational risks in delivering their offerings to customers.

Startups are defined by their developmental **stage** as well as their financing **rounds**, and sometimes the terms coincide. These stages generally are associated with operational milestones tied to product development and revenue levels. For example, a **pre-seed** or **seed-stage** company is usually building its first product and is pre-revenue. An **early-stage** company has annual revenue of up to $3 to $5 million. **Growth-stage** companies have minimum

---

[2] Wasserman, Noam "The Founders Dilemma." hbr.org, *Harvard Business Review*, https://hbr.org/2008/02/the-founders-dilemma

revenues of $5 to $10 million and **late-stage** companies grow rapidly toward revenues exceeding $25 million.

The stages also coincide with funding rounds. Founders and high-net-worth individual investors usually fund companies at the pre-seed and seed stages, while venture capitalists lead funding through the later stages. Venture capital firms define their investment focus in terms of the stages they aim to invest in—early, growth, or late. They buy **preferred stock** in a series of funding rounds defined alphabetically—Series A, Series B, Series C, etc. Collectively, these rounds are referred to as the **series preferred** and consist of tranches of **stock** sold by the company to outside investors that provide those investors with preferential financial and governance rights over the company.

To get an idea of the kinds of preferential treatment I'm discussing, think about startup financing primarily as a last-in, first-out inventory model. Each time a company raises money, the new investor tries to negotiate the terms so that they get paid first when the company is sold. The more rounds of investment a company takes on, the more investors must be paid before the common shareholders and option holders (i.e., the founders and employees). That cascading payout schedule based on priorities is called the **waterfall**. As an employee in a startup, you sit downstream from the outside and investors, which significantly impacts your ultimate reward for working in a startup.

Exhibit 1-1 shows how the stages of a startup coincide with funding rounds and identifies the kinds of investors who would most likely invest at each point in a company's journey. When they discuss a company's progress, people often use the terms in the different columns interchangeably. In most cases, startup funding typically runs parallel to a company's progress, but some companies raise funds well ahead of their corresponding operational milestones in the exhibit and vice versa.

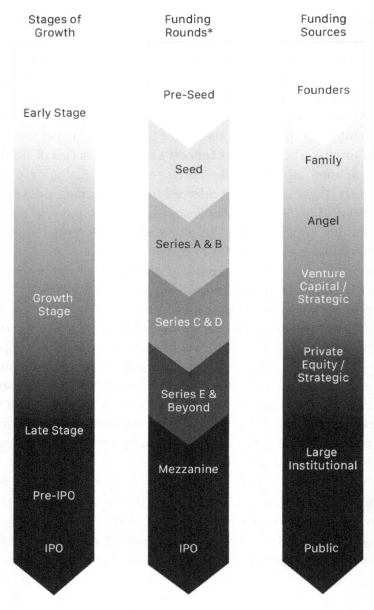

Stages of Growth	Funding Rounds*	Funding Sources
	Pre-Seed	Founders
Early Stage	Seed	Family
	Series A & B	Angel
Growth Stage	Series C & D	Venture Capital / Strategic
	Series E & Beyond	Private Equity / Strategic
Late Stage	Mezzanine	Large Institutional
Pre-IPO		
IPO	IPO	Public

*Company exit may happen via a sale at any point in the company's lifecycle.

Exhibit 1-1: Startup Stages and Funding Rounds

The Bottom Line

Venture-backed startups differ from other companies in concrete ways. They aim to address sizable market opportunities and require significant capital to hire their teams and build their offerings. Most of their capital comes from venture capitalists, whose job is to deliver high returns for their own outside investors.

Without venture capital, most startups going after large markets would not have the resources to innovate and reach their potential. However, the presence of outside investors complicates how these companies run and how financial returns are shared. Exploring the power dynamic and economic factors that arise from the presence of venture capital investors in startups and how those impact startup employees is what this book is about.

CHAPTER 2

The Cast

Every theater production has a playbill that lists the cast of characters. If it's a musical, the numbers to be performed are also listed. There is background on the show and pictures of the actors with their experience. All that information is designed to enhance the experience of the audience.

Some people walk into the theater and never crack open the program or just quickly flip through it. They might prefer to take in the action as it comes, figuring it out as the performance goes along. Though following this approach can still be an enjoyable experience, knowing in advance about the characters, the story, the actors, and the creators of the show helps you appreciate the action at a deeper level.

In 2019, three years after it came out, our family finally got around to seeing *Hamilton*, Lin-Manuel Miranda's masterpiece about the life of Alexander Hamilton. Apart from being an incredible show, *Hamilton* has more than 20,000 words in its libretto. The pace at which events unfold, the sheer complexity of the songs, and the veiled references in the dialogue and lyrics make it impossible for most first-time attendees to catch everything between the lines.

A friend recommended I do some homework before attending the show. First, he told me to read Ron Chernow's more than 700-page biography, *Alexander Hamilton*, the inspiration for the show. Then he suggested studying the nearly 300-page annotated libretto. I wouldn't normally spend months plowing through more than 1,000 pages just to get ready to see a three-hour production. But we purchased the tickets more than a year in advance (and at a very hefty price!), I had the time and felt the investment would be well worth it.

It took me a few months to get through the Chernow biography. Admittedly, I only made it through two-thirds of the libretto before running out of steam. Nonetheless, the effort to research the play and the players significantly enhanced my understanding and enjoyment of the show.

Working for a startup is a bit like going to see *Hamilton*. Both are fast paced, with a lot going on beneath the surface. Many people going to work for a startup spend very little time reading the playbill before they join. They just show up and try to figure it out when they get there. But before the show starts, it is valuable to at least understand who the characters are. Even if you are raptly paying attention once the show begins, you may catch only a fraction of what happens and what it means for you and your company.

The Cast (in Order of Appearance)

Every startup is unique, and the actors in different roles vary. However, a few consistent characters typically play parts throughout a company's life. In the beginning, the founder and co-founders appear on a dark stage with just a single spotlight shining on them as they toil away at their idea. Over time, they draw others onto the scene, including advisors, consultants, and angel investors, who help mold the initial idea into a sellable package to attract more capital and staff.

Founders play the leading roles initially. If the concept is sound, eventually, the company will attract more angel investors, venture capitalists, and seasoned executives with impressive resumes to help fuel and shape its future. As the company matures, the venture capitalists invest and assume board positions, and veteran executives gain power, while early players, sometimes including the founders, fade from the scene.

Understanding the relative power, motivations, constraints, and outside influences on these actors is invaluable in projecting where the company's future lies. Investors (angels and venture capitalists) all claim they are there to help founders build great companies, and their financing certainly greases the skids. But their primary goal is generating financial returns. They invest in early-stage deals hoping for home runs, recognizing that many startup investments fail. They take a portfolio approach, placing many bets and playing the odds that some pay off big.

Many startups tout themselves as flat organizations, but each has an established hierarchy. Control often resides with the investors and board of directors, who direct senior management (founders and executives), who in turn oversee the employees. Exhibit 2-1 shows the cast of characters and their relative positions in the company.

The solid lines with arrows represent reporting relationships, and dotted lines represent advisory relationships. For example, the board (often dominated by investors and independents) oversees the company and has the right to hire and fire the CEO. Advisors and angel investors, on the other hand, are resources available to help the company financially and provide advice, but have limited power and no oversight authority.

Founder

Every organization has a principal founder. Maybe they had the idea or had more time or resources to develop the concept. Founders are the driving force behind the company. They are the company's most visible face and voice, the visionary that others, from staff to

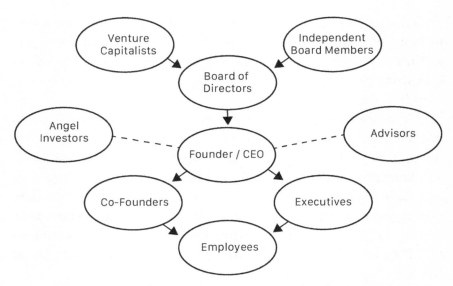

Exhibit 2-1: The Startup Cast Organizational Structure

funders, rally around and rely on to get the venture off the ground. Until outside investors come in, the principal founder is the largest shareholder in the company.

It is the rare founder who is motivated solely by money. The startup journey is challenging and risky, and there are more certain and direct ways to build wealth. Instead, founders are out to change the world. If they get rich in the process, great. They are evangelical in their zeal and obsessive in their commitment to turning their idea into reality.

The founder has a specific skill set, often technical, without the full breadth of experience building businesses. Successful founders are self-aware enough to recognize their limitations and find ways to attract talent with complementary skills to fill the gaps. They allow others to contribute, innovate, grow, and succeed. Dysfunctional founders exhibit territoriality, arrogance, and controlling behavior that impedes innovation, limits the potential of other employees, and poisons the work environment, spelling trouble for the organization in the long run.

Co-Founder(s)

Co-founders tend to be friends or colleagues of the principal founder. They join the founder to bring access to resources, networks, or even early money. They may have complementary skills such as technical talent to help build prototypes of the company's products.

Many founder/co-founder collaborations stand the test of time. Famous examples include Bill Gates and Paul Allen at Microsoft, Steve Jobs and Steve Wozniak at Apple, and Sergey Brin and Larry Page at Google (now Alphabet). Others, such as Mark Zuckerberg and Eduardo Saverin at Facebook (now Meta), have become imbalanced and fraught with resentment or petty rivalries that disrupt the organization.

The principal founder tends to assume a dominant role in the company, and co-founders can become increasingly marginalized over time, especially after outside investors and experienced executives come on stage. Going from being a co-founder with a seat in "the room where it happens," to quote *Hamilton*, to being just another employee in the company can give an ego significant bruising. How a co-founder handles the evolution of their power and role can significantly impact the organization.

At some point, the organization may outgrow its co-founders completely. The dynamic between the founder and co-founders can become increasingly uncomfortable. Co-founders often leave, are ousted, or are sometimes consigned to peripheral roles. My wife and I have worked and invested in several companies where co-founders have departed, and the process is emotionally and economically painful to navigate. Although the departure of a co-founder often destroys friendships among the founders, it can be necessary and healthy for the company. Having co-founders hang around past their "sell-by" date can be corrosive to the organization.

Advisor

When a company starts, the founder may enlist the assistance of advisors to enhance credibility and visibility or to address specific functional needs. Advisors represent a broad category of cast members, like the chorus in a Greek play. They include legal counsel, accountants, technical advisors, bankers, and experienced businesspeople.

Professional services organizations (lawyers, accountants, bankers) might engage the startup with discounted fees, hoping to win their business for the long term. They are banking on escalating engagement during funding rounds, mergers and acquisitions, and initial public offerings. Professional advisors play a critical role in keeping the company on the straight and narrow from a legal and compliance standpoint. Good professional advisors also bring deep experience and networks, becoming essential extended management team members handling critical administrative functions not necessarily related to building the product.

Other advisors come in two flavors. The first are often friends or former colleagues of the founders who are excited about the business idea and are willing to help, generally in exchange for being put on the company's **advisory board** (or **board of advisors**) and receiving stock or option grants. These advisors help with strategy, business development, or introductions to potential funders or customers. They play an active role early on and can provide invaluable guidance to the founding team, who may have limited business experience. Once the company gets off the ground, they quickly fade into the background and interact with the company only sporadically.

The second type of advisors carry big names in the industry and are willing to lend their star power to the organization to help it build credibility, mainly with potential funders. They may do very little to help the company actively, but they provide window-dressing the way endorsements from famous athletes help Nike or Under

Armour sell sporting goods. In exchange, they are compensated in **options** and can sit back and hope the company makes them a few bucks. If it doesn't, no big deal. A side note—if you get to the point where people want to throw stock in their company at you just to be able to put your name and photo on a PowerPoint slide in their pitch deck, do it! It's the closest thing I've seen in the business world to the Name, Image, and Likeness deals offered to star NCAA athletes.[3]

Except for professional advisors, such as lawyers and accountants, the role of advisors is most prevalent in the beginning and erodes over time. Unless advisors are also investors, they rarely reach out proactively to the company. As the company progresses, founders and executives get busy and rarely consult advisory board members. In addition, future investors focus on the company's progress and performance, and advisor relationships will play diminishing roles in a VC's decision to invest.

Angel Investor

The first outside investors in a company are high-net-worth individuals known as **angel investors** or **angels**. They usually know the founder, which stands to reason. Ideas are cheap, and execution ultimately drives value in a startup. When a company is first starting, it hasn't accomplished anything yet. Unless an angel knows and believes in the founders, they have no basis for believing the vision will become a reality other than knowing and trusting the founders. I am often approached by random founders asking me to invest. I rarely entertain those pitches.

The common phrase that describes angel investors is "friends, family, and fools." Without angel investors, most startups never get off the ground. Angels put capital in at the riskiest time and usually

---

[3] NIL - Name, Image, and Likeness. Refers to the endorsement deals college athletes are permitted to receive after the NCAA lifted restrictions on such compensation in June 2021 as a result of legal action.

at low **valuations**. When things go well, angels stand to earn excellent returns. But the road is long, with many twists and turns between when an angel first invests and when a company is sold, goes public, or shuts down. A lot can happen to derail a successful outcome.

The value of angel investors can also extend to non-monetary support. There is a category of angels called "**active angels**" who invest and serve as formal or informal advisors, as described above, while also providing credibility as the company seeks institutional funding. Angels can remain positive supporters as the company grows and help the management team address strategic needs.

Like co-founders and advisory board members, angel investors lose their influence over time. Funding rounds get larger as institutional investors come into the picture. Angels' pockets are often not deep enough to keep up with the more significant investments required as funding rounds get larger and institutional investors (i.e., VCs) come into the picture. So their ownership gets more and more diluted. In addition, later investors demand terms that give them priority payouts when the company is sold and significant governance rights over its affairs. These terms may diminish the value of the angels' holdings and their standing as investors to influence the company's direction.

Angels can also become a nuisance to the company, demanding attention and information from management while bringing little additional money or strategic value to the company in its later stages. Pragmatism dictates that the founders or management team focus on building the business and maintaining relationships with the major investors who serve on the board and influence the company's future. The earliest investors may find themselves sidelined without much voice in the company, especially if the time comes when an outside CEO replaces the founder, the angels' principal executive contact.

Employees

Before there are outside investors, there are a few hearty souls who drink the Kool-Aid and decide to join the founders on their excellent adventure. You can usually spot these employees. Like rock stars or soccer players, they are the one-namers whose email addresses are structured as firstname@companyname.com and take pride in their employee number at the company, which is usually in the single digits. These employees are generally folks with whom the founders have a prior relationship.

Just like angel investors, few will take a flier on an unfunded new venture unless they have supreme faith in the founders. With the chaos barely contained in a newly formed startup, early employees must show up and pitch in every day in unpredictable ways. They form the bedrock of the new team, and their flexibility and commitment are critical to kick-starting the venture.

Once the company has funding from angels and VCs, it can formally recruit additional staff. These later employees may have more specialized skills and experience and fill defined roles as the company matures and sets concrete goals. The newbies may use their last initials or last names in their emails to distinguish themselves from the early employees. They also expect to be paid reasonably competitive market compensation. At this point, the company may outgrow some of the early employees as the inevitable changing of the guard takes place.

Venture Capital

Venture capital is funding from institutional firms that have been formed for the purpose of investing in emerging growth businesses. "Venture capital" can refer to the funding itself or the general industry. Similarly, the terms "venture capitalist" or "VC" can refer to a firm or the individual who works at the firm. Venture capital firms invest money entrusted to them by **limited partners** or

LPs, institutional investors such as pension funds, and high net-worth individuals and families.

Only a tiny percentage of early-stage companies successfully attract VC funding. Those that do have innovative ideas targeted at markets with more than $1 billion in potential sales and have begun to prove their products can successfully serve a defined or emerging market need.

Venture capitalists have one goal: to make money for their LPs. They pursue that goal through an investment thesis that specifies the type of investments they make. They specialize by stage of company (early, growth, or late), sector or type of technology, check size, and target ownership percentage. One critical distinction is whether a VC leads a round by negotiating the details of the funding with the company or follows as a participant in rounds negotiated (i.e., led) by others.

VC firms often manage multiple funds out of which they invest in companies. Each fund invests in a portfolio of 15 to 30 companies. The VCs expect about 25 to 30 percent of the portfolio to deliver high enough returns to compensate for the companies that fail. The multitude of companies in a VC portfolio means a startup must have a strong relationship with the firm to compete for attention and funding against other portfolio companies.

The face of the VC firm to the startup is a **general partner** who champions the deal within the VC's investment committee. This partner shepherds the investment, often serving on the startup's board of directors and advocating on its behalf for further investment in later funding rounds. Without this partner's ongoing support, the startup becomes orphaned and loses the firm's backing. To exacerbate the problem, new investors often rely on the current VC's enthusiasm or lack thereof to decide whether to invest. Without strong support from existing investors, new investors may be scared off or seize the opportunity to drive aggressive funding terms.

The **lead VC** is the firm that negotiates the price and other legal terms of investment rounds. They are sophisticated and experienced investors and leading rounds allows them to shape the economics and governance rights associated with the investment. The **lead investor**, who usually provides the lion's share of funding in a given round, determines the composition of the startup's board of directors. They may also dictate who else can participate in the syndicate that forms the round (i.e., the **followers**) and how much they can invest. By controlling these discussions, the **lead VC**, in conjunction with the syndicate, has enormous power in dictating the startup's direction.

Partners in VC firms compete within their partnerships for recognition and advancement. Their firm's internal politics can play an outsized role in how an individual VC approaches the companies they are responsible for supporting. Individual partners commit time, effort, and capital to their companies until they decide (or their partners conclude) there is no payoff. They may then turn their attention elsewhere, stop funding the company, or push it toward a quick sale, sometimes with little warning.

The Board of Directors

The **Board of Directors** (the "Board") governs the major decisions a startup must make. The board's composition determines which of the various players holds sway over the startup's direction. In venture-backed startups, the board consists of individuals representing some or all of the following stakeholders:

1. The management team—usually represented by the principal founder/CEO, usually the largest holder of **common stock.**

2. The common shareholders, which include the founders, co-founders, employees, and sometimes early investors.

3. The preferred investors, who are the venture capitalists and angels if they invested in **preferred shares**.

4. Independent board members unaffiliated with other stakeholders and whose role is to provide objectivity and

balance the power of the other board members in making significant decisions for the company.

Control of the board is a critical corporate governance issue and a subject of intense negotiation during venture funding rounds. The outcome of these discussions is driven by the power dynamics among the management team, the VCs, and other shareholders. How those negotiations play out has profound implications for the company, as the board controls approval of the company's operating plan, which governs spending, compensation, hiring, and firing. In addition, everyone in the company serves at the pleasure of the board. The board can remove any company executive, including the founders. That is an enormous amount of power.

The board of directors may have a few subcommittees with specific oversight responsibilities. The most common subcommittees are the Audit Committee and the Compensation Committee. The Audit Committee oversees the company's finances, ensuring that the books and records are kept clean, and sometimes has responsibility for risk management. The Compensation Committee has approval rights over pay scales in the company, bonus target setting and bonus payouts, policies around issuing incentive stock grants, and compensation for key and highly paid staff members, particularly senior executives.

Executives

The cadre of senior managers in a startup evolves from its inception. Initially, the founder is the CEO, with co-founders or friends of the founder occupying other senior management roles. This initial executive team is like a pick-up playground basketball team. Whoever is around when the game starts ends up on the court. As with any random selection of people, there is no guarantee that the early executive team in a startup has the experience or skills to build the company. They must step up, take little or no salary, bet on the dream, and roll up their sleeves.

I have been courtside in numerous companies when teams were picked. One of the more memorable moments I had at Fugue after moving from "acting" Chief Financial Officer to full-time CFO was on a board call when our principal investor from NEA asked our founder when he planned to hire a "real CFO." He had forgotten I was on the call!

I was a bit taken aback and then amused at the question, which resulted in a lot of hemming, hawing, and backpedaling by the board member after the meeting. It was instructive about how VCs view employees who happen to be present in the early days. Especially later when the VCs start exerting influence to bring in key executive hires with whom they have prior relationships.

As companies grow, the board or the founders may determine that the existing management team has limitations and may not have what it takes to take the company to the next level. They recruit departmental managers to report to the CEO and lead functional areas such as sales and marketing, product management, or customer success.

Change, however, is not limited to middle or senior managers. Sometimes new investors come into a company and insist on new senior leadership. It may be a precondition of their closing on the round. In those situations, the prior leadership may be re-cast into more minor roles that closely align with their skills. For example, a founding CEO may move into a technical position, such as Chief Technology Officer. It is also common for initial members of management to be ousted, especially if the company isn't making rapid progress.

The impact of these moves can be dramatic and long-lasting in an organization, especially if the board pressures the founder(s) to accept the arrival of seasoned executives. New executives arrive as outsiders who must assimilate into or transform the culture. Their jobs are made more challenging by dealing with founders who may resent being pushed aside but who retain loyalty from and influence with staff and customers. Failure by the board and new leadership to navigate these dynamics can permanently derail a company.

Leading Actors and Supporting Cast

The players' relative influence may vary slightly by company depending on who invests how much and who owns what percentage of the company's stock. Exhibit 2-2 depicts how the various players typically sit relative to each other on the startup stage. The actors are placed according to their invested capital as well as their power and influence.

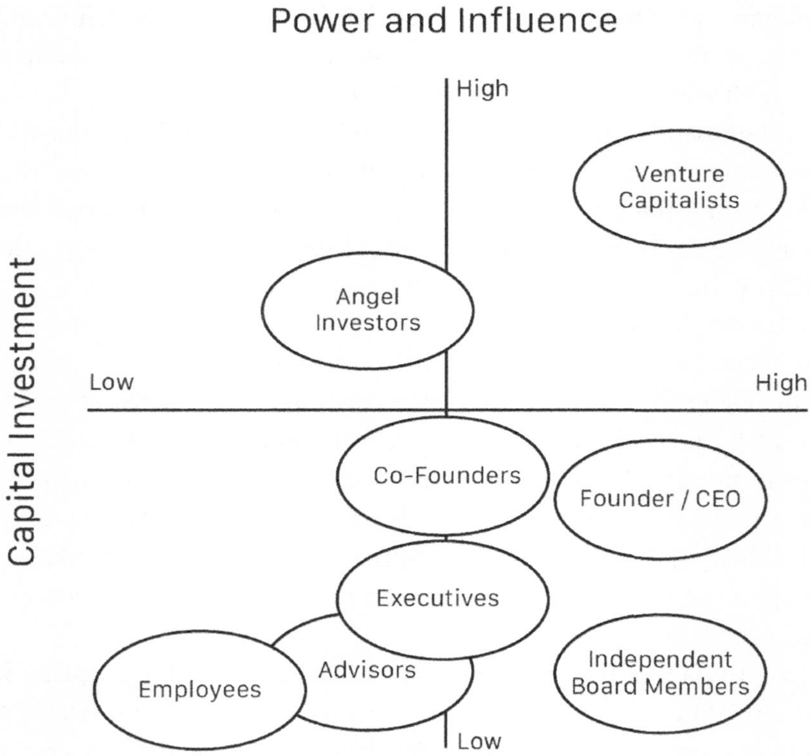

Power and Influence

Exhibit 2-2: The Investment/Power Matrix

The players' positioning relative to each other follows a consistent arc over time. Once venture capital investors enter the picture, they occupy the upper right quadrant with an outsized role in dictating the company's direction via the board of directors and their voting power on major decisions. The more they invest, the greater their percentage of company ownership and voting power, as well as their rights to determine the composition of the board.

Though likely to have invested relatively little capital to start the company, the principal founder maintains significant power while still in the CEO position. Founders can sustain their influence longer if they retain a high percentage of ownership through multiple funding rounds. The co-founders, angels, and advisors tend to be relegated to more minor roles over time, especially if they have not invested significant capital. With minimal ownership and occupying lower tiers in the hierarchy, most employees have few speaking parts and are barely mentioned in the playbill.

The Bottom Line

The actors in the roles and the dynamics described in this chapter have an enormous impact on the success of a startup. They have an outsized effect on company culture and performance. When the actors are all working in concert, company culture flourishes and motivation among staff is high. The sense of shared mission and objectives leads to increased achievement and success for both the company and those working there.

On the other hand, as an employee and investor, I have been part of startups when the breakdown of these relationships has been destructive to a company's prospects. Egotistical founders ignore market signals, refuse to accept limits on their power, and stubbornly turn down attractive funding offers or acquisition proposals, only to find they run out of money or are forced to sell the company for a low price later.

Resentful co-founders can undermine organizational cohesiveness by creating factions among the staff. Imperious boards may make unreasonable demands, setting the organization up for failure and affecting employee motivation and morale. Experienced executives new to the company may find that the organism rejects them culturally, derailing the company for months or even years.

There is no playbill to read before you join a company. The script for the play hasn't been written yet, and the actors come and go over time. Nonetheless, understanding who the founders are, who the investors are, who controls the board, and how decisions are made provides a foundation for evaluating their interplay.

Once you are inside a company, knowing who the players are and their motivations helps you understand what drives the company, its culture, priorities, and allocation of resources. Pay attention to who is aligned with whom and when those alliances may shift or become frayed. That enables you to anticipate whether the show you are part of ends up as a comedy, a drama, or a tragedy. You can then decide whether to stay until the final curtain or walk out at intermission.

CHAPTER 3

Prove It!

At the closing dinner for Fugue's **seed round**, one of our investors walked up to two of the company's four co-founders and asked them two simple questions. "Do you know what you're doing?" and "Is it going to work?"

At the time, his questions seemed flippant as we had already closed on the investment. Whatever the co-founders said wouldn't have affected the round. But embedded within those two questions are a whole lot of considerations. When evaluating a startup, you need to understand many aspects of the company, its markets, the competence of the team, and the competitive landscape to determine whether it is likely to be successful.

Most startups go through a series of phases before achieving a successful outcome. To traverse these stages, the team's management skills and composition must evolve. What a company requires when it first builds out its technology differs significantly from what it needs once it achieves product-market fit. Understanding where a startup is in its lifecycle helps you assess the risks and challenges it is likely to face and determine how well-positioned it is to meet those challenges.

The Proof Continuum

When I joined Fugue as a first-time CFO, I sought the advice of an old friend, Ron Kaiser, a veteran CFO who had led the finance function for numerous public and private companies. Ron laid out the stages of a startup's journey for me through a concept I have come to call the **Proof Continuum**. At each stage of a company's development, everyone on the team must understand where it stands and what it takes to move beyond the current phase. When to raise money, how much, whom to hire, and how to allocate resources are all decisions driven by a clear understanding of the company's progress. Companies that don't know where they stand on the Proof Continuum and plan accordingly can make costly errors.

The Proof Continuum for a startup consists of the following stages:

- Proof of technology
- Proof of product
- Proof of sale
- Proof of repeatability
- Proof of scale
- Proof of profitability
- Proof of positive cash flow

Venture capitalists hope to realize a return from each portfolio company within three to five, or at most, seven years. While each company is unique, that means companies must make steady progress through these proof stages. Exhibit 3-1 provides some general timeframes for the different stages. These timeframes can serve as a benchmark to understand how well a company is progressing. The longer a company stays in a stage while continuing to burn investor capital, the more likely that company is to move toward failure.

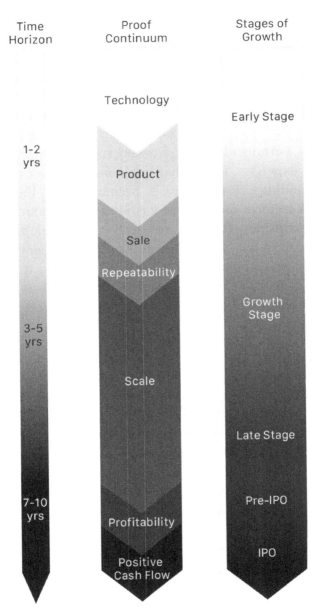

Exhibit 3-1: Timelines and The Proof Continuum

When evaluating a startup, considering where they are on the Proof Continuum and how long it has taken them to get there helps you determine the magnitude of risk you face if you join them. It also helps you determine how far the startup needs to go to achieve success. Let's explore each of these stages in more detail.

Proof of technology - The first stage is developing a technology that works and has the potential to apply to specific problems and industries. Turning ideas into working models requires significant work and expertise. Often that happens in a lab or garage with limited funding. However it is accomplished, the technology must work to form the basis of a commercial product. You would generally consider this the research and development (R&D) phase. The founders and technical team have a vision for valuable technology and maybe a vague idea of markets it could serve. But their focus is on building working prototypes as the basis for raising the earliest outside funding from angel investors to fuel the company's progress.

Proof of product - Many companies have developed ideas and even built pieces of technology. Then they search for a market only to find that the technology as built has deficiencies or limitations that hamper its marketability. Disciplined **product management** plays a critical role here as companies need to seek out market feedback to help mold their technology into a salable offering. Proof of product may involve launching an alpha version of the product and then giving away a beta version to trial users to gather feedback on its value and usability. The company launches the General Availability (GA) version once the product is refined to meet basic customer requirements. GA is prime time. At this point, the product (as well as any service and support requirements) must be ready to be sold to paying customers.

Proof of sale - Getting a customer to pay for your product is an enormous accomplishment and inflection point. Most VCs, even those specializing in early-stage firms, resist investing in pre-revenue startups. Showing that someone has paid for the product is huge! Those first sales happen at low prices, with many concessions to the customer and promises of new product features. They also often come from company friends willing to take a leap of faith and try the product even if no other customers are using it. Getting those first few sales lays the groundwork for learning, gaining customer references, focusing on future product development, and ultimately growing the customer base. The initial sales are often made by senior executives, even before the company hires a sales team.

Proof of repeatability - Moving beyond the first couple of sales and acquiring customers who were not previously familiar with the company is a sign of product maturity and the beginnings of market acceptance. At this point, the company begins to demonstrate the all-important product-market fit investors seek. Early customers can serve as references, and the company can start investing in customer success resources to optimize relations with current users. The focus turns to tracking customer satisfaction and positioning the company to reduce **churn** (i.e., loss of existing customers), secure renewals, expand purchases from existing customers, and attract new buyers.

Proof of scale - The transition to scale involves building the go-to-market team and developing repeatable and measurable sales processes. A marker for achieving scale is $3 to $5 million in top-line revenue metrics like **Annual Recurring Revenue (ARR)** or revenue measured under **Generally Accepted Accounting Principles (GAAP)**.

The assumption is that once a company reaches $3 million in ARR, it has achieved an understanding of its markets. It can confidently identify the target persona most likely to buy and invest in reaching those buyers through sales and marketing. The cost of customer acquisition becomes clearer, enabling a more predictable return on investment in customer acquisition efforts. Investment from growth-stage venture capital firms or even private equity firms becomes more likely at this stage.

Proof of profitability - Throughout the proof stages, companies should track gross margins to ensure they can deliver their product to customers without losing money on each sale. Ideally, companies show improving gross margins as they scale. This is especially true of software and software-as-a-service (SaaS) companies. Management should also be continually measuring, monitoring, and attempting to improve go-to-market efficiencies to lower the cost of lead generation and improve conversion rates at each stage of the sales and marketing funnel. Finally, keeping general and administrative costs (including such items as rent, legal and accounting fees, and employee benefits) under control is critical. Improving gross margins on product and service delivery coupled with optimized **customer acquisition cost (CAC)** and controlled administrative expenses leads to profitability at scale.

Proof of positive cash flow - Throughout the life of most startups, they continue to burn cash. An important metric investors look for is the company's **burn rate**—the amount of negative cash flow the company generates monthly. The final stage for a company is achieving sustainable positive cash flow, which means that it is no longer dependent on outside capital to fund itself. Many companies achieve profitability but keep burning cash as they continually invest in product development, staff growth, or additional overhead to grow. They may also invest heavily in sales and marketing to capture market share and drive rapid revenue growth. Companies with positive cash flow are generally mature and likely to have graduated from being startups. They are the companies that have already listed their shares on the public markets or are positioned to do so to achieve liquidity and attract additional capital to accelerate growth or develop new offerings.

Ideally, companies will move steadily through the stages of the proof continuum, showing good momentum as they go. But that is rarely the case. Progress doesn't often happen in a straight line. Many startup failures result from failing to make rapid enough progress through each phase to attract the capital needed to survive. The loss of momentum can result from a lack of market understanding, poor management, inadequate resources, strong competition, or even bad luck and timing from outside events such as the economy taking a downturn.

While Fugue was building out our forward-looking cloud security technology that few understood at the time and fewer chose to buy, competitors emerged providing simpler solutions. Though we deemed them inferior technologically, they addressed narrower problems customers recognized and gained much more rapid market traction resulting in lucrative exits for their investors. One of our investors sarcastically quipped at the time that using Fugue's offering required customers with brains the size of watermelons, while what we needed to offer were products that customers with smaller brains could wrap their heads around.

In the early days, we suffered from a failure in product management. We had yet to successfully connect our technology with what the market perceived as its pain points. We hadn't packaged our product in a way to make it easy for customers to adopt, but we mounted a full-scale effort to sell it anyway. This was a failure by management to accurately assess where we were on the Proof Continuum. While our technology was sound conceptually, we neglected to systematically seek and accept market feedback and refine our product accordingly.

After five long, difficult years, we finally settled on a product formulation and a market to target and began to develop product-market fit and repeatable sales. We spent years burning through tens of millions of dollars in venture funding along the way. It took bringing in senior leaders with product management experience to set the company on the course that eventually led to a meaningful exit.

Where Do You Fit?

The risk of startup failure is greatest at the idea phase and diminishes progressively as the company passes through the gates of each proof stage as depicted in Exhibit 3-2. Greater operational progress often coincides with a rise in valuation. Early-stage investors invest at low share prices and stand to reap the greatest rewards. But they also find their companies failing at much higher rates than investors whose portfolio companies have already achieved proof of sale or subsequent stages of the proof continuum.

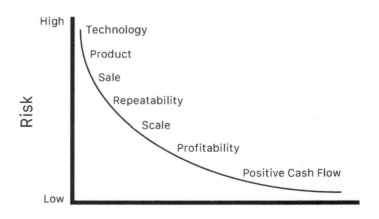

Proof Continuum

Exhibit 3-2: Relative Risk Along the Proof Continuum

Understanding where a startup stands on the proof continuum gives you an idea of how far it has to go to reach a successful **exit** and how much risk you would be taking on if you join it. It also helps you determine the skills the company needs to move forward. Assessing your risk tolerance, skill set, and passion determines where along the proof continuum you can find the greatest satisfaction, ability to add value to your employer, and success.

The best fit for me has always been at the earliest stages of a startup, right after the idea is hatched. I like to call it the creative chaos phase. It is when everything seems possible, and company building feels like molding a sculpture out of raw clay. There are countless strategic and tactical decisions requiring creativity, collaboration, intellectual curiosity, and rigor. It is the most fun in many ways, but also the most challenging phase, with the lowest probability of success.

While exhilarating, working at a company so early in its life cycle poses significant risks across numerous dimensions. The biggest challenge is securing enough **runway** (i.e., funding) to make mistakes, figure out where the market opportunity is, and establish a sustainable business model. Most of the companies I started or joined were at the earliest stage of the proof continuum and had yet to prove anything.

When we founded USLaw.com in the late 1990s, my co-founders and I saw a great need to democratize access to legal resources for consumers and small businesses. The Internet was just taking off, and many content websites were attracting significant numbers of visitors ("eyeballs"), the key metric of the Internet boom.

USLaw.com raised $14 million of venture capital and used the money to build innovative, web-based legal offerings. We blindly put them out on the website, hoping that people would come and buy. Hundreds of thousands came to the website, but few bought anything. The problem was the space was very new, and people had not yet learned to consume legal services online.

We never found a way to meaningfully monetize our offering and made the mistake of being on the bleeding edge instead of the leading edge. We reached proof of technology but never achieved proof of sale or proof of repeatability. Just before we sold the company for parts before running out of money, we laid off 91 employees, all of whom had nothing to show for a couple of years of effort. A few years later, LegalZoom created a successful business going after the same market with similar offerings. It turns out we were in the right place, just at the wrong time and without enough runway to last until we could get it right.

Joining a company at the proof of technology stage may be beyond most people's risk tolerance, and it probably should be. If you don't have the financial resources to survive a company failure, you are better off joining a later-stage company with a greater chance of staying in business or not joining a startup at all.

My wife Amena has historically found her greatest successes joining companies like OTG Software and VividCortex that had already achieved proof of sale and beyond. As an executive oriented toward helping companies scale their growth, that makes sense for her. When she joined companies earlier on the proof continuum, her skills were underutilized, and she spent years toiling away without realizing a meaningful payoff.

No two startups are the same. Companies at different stages of the proof continuum have varying characteristics. Your fit, comfort level, and ability to contribute to a company's success largely depend on your risk tolerance level and the skills and experience you bring. Gauging your risk tolerance relative to a company's progress is a personal choice. Determining whether what you bring to the table is appropriate is a business decision you and the company must make.

Joining when your strengths don't align with the company's needs can be fruitless and frustrating.

The Proof Continuum and Funding Rounds

It may not be obvious where a startup is on the proof continuum. But there are a few clues that help place them. You can glean whether they have a product or products launched by looking at their press releases and website. You can tell if they have attracted customers as they may list customer testimonials or have reviews on public websites like G2. Industry reports from companies like Gartner, Forrester, or others, if you can access them, can also give you an idea of how far along a startup is and how it is positioned in its sector. You can also look at their careers page to determine what kinds of employees they are seeking to hire. If they're hiring sales and marketing professionals, that's a sign they may be ready to start scaling top-line growth.

One way to get an idea of where a company is along its journey is to look at its funding history through press releases or sites like Crunchbase. This is not an exact science; significant exceptions exist when mapping progress to funding.

During exuberant times, such as in the early dotcom era, or in hot sectors, companies that have yet to develop proven technology or products might still find investors willing to throw millions of dollars at them. The reverse is also true. In many cases, investors want to see meaningful progress up to and including proof of sale before committing to a seed-stage investment, especially in challenging economic times.

Overall, however, venture funding rounds should track with company progress. Exhibit 3-3 correlates the parallel routes through the startup progression from the perspective of company progress and funding.

By examining the company's funding history, you can form a hypothesis regarding its progress. From there, test your hypothesis through outside research and in the interview process.

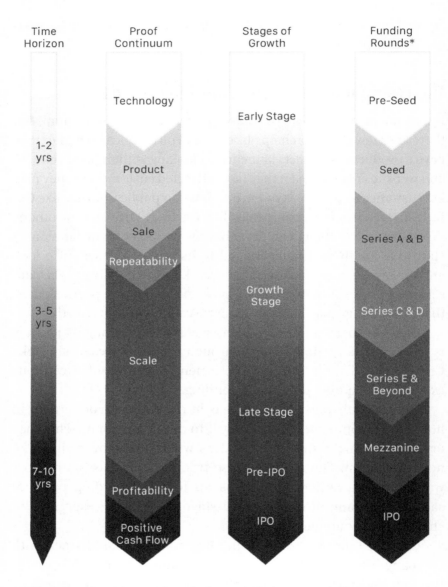

Time Horizon	Proof Continuum	Stages of Growth	Funding Rounds*
	Technology	Early Stage	Pre-Seed
1-2 yrs	Product		Seed
	Sale		Series A & B
	Repeatability		
3-5 yrs		Growth Stage	Series C & D
	Scale		Series E & Beyond
		Late Stage	Mezzanine
7-10 yrs	Profitability	Pre-IPO	
	Positive Cash Flow	IPO	IPO

*Company exit may happen via a sale at any point in the company's lifecycle.

Exhibit 3-3: Correlating the Proof Continuum with Funding Rounds

If a company is further along the proof continuum than its funding rounds would suggest, that could be a great sign. That means they are capital efficient, have good operating discipline and strong management, and likely have a product with strong market traction.

On the other hand, if a company has raised rounds ahead of its progress on the proof continuum, that should raise a red flag. Companies may face trouble when they get out "over their skis" and raise capital without matching operational advancement. They can have difficulty catching up with investor expectations, which often leads to tension between management and the board. They might encounter difficulty raising additional capital, leading to painful corrective actions such as layoffs or reductions in company valuation in future financing rounds that undermine the value of the **stock option** grants you receive to participate in the company's success.

The Bottom Line

The proof continuum is a simple framework for determining the company's stage and assessing whether it has the resources and capabilities to make meaningful progress. Whether you are considering joining a startup or already working in one, assess where a company stands along the proof continuum. To determine a company's chances of success and how risky it may be, you must figure out how far they still have to go.

The next step is to consider our early VC investor's questions. "Do they know what they're doing?" and "Is it going to work?" Company management (and the board) must clearly understand where the company stands, how the company intends to progress through the subsequent stages, and what resources are required. This will drive its operating plan and its fundraising strategy. If the company cannot articulate its roadmap for moving from one stage to the next to complete the journey, it may take some (or many) detours and be delayed in reaching a successful exit if it ever reaches it at all.

PART II

~

SHOULD YOU WORK AT A STARTUP?

CHAPTER 4

Is a Startup Right for You?

Get good grades. Go to a good college and graduate school. Get a good job with an established company. Build your resume. Pay your dues and work your way up the ladder.

For decades, young professionals heard these mantras. Few ambitious parents encouraged their children to work in small, unknown companies. They didn't offer job security. They couldn't afford to pay. Where would the opportunity be for advancement? Who would hire you without impressive brand names on your resume?

The premises that form the basis of these opinions are no longer universally true. The implicit contract between large employers and employees has eroded, so even larger companies don't offer the predictable career paths of the past. There are no guarantees of a sustainable, comfortable middle-class existence. You are not assured meaningful wealth creation throughout your career. And even if you set your sights on working for a larger, well-known company, there are no guarantees you will get hired by your employer of choice.

Fueled by online recruiting, the number of applicants for positions at well-known companies far exceeds the number of openings. For example, after my millennial daughter left

43

her public relations consulting job to work for a large tech
company, she learned there had been approximately 500
applicants for that one position.

With little guarantee of a predictable career path, stability, or
opportunity for wealth creation, even working in a larger company
bears some risk. The decision about where you go to work mainly
comes down to fit. What career path to follow is a personal choice.
The opinions of others, including parents, siblings, significant
others, and mentors, shouldn't drive your decision about where to
work. It's your life.

I remember the times I caddied for my son in junior golf
tournaments. Though I cared deeply about his success, I sometimes
gave him bad advice. When he followed my suggestions and found
himself in challenging situations, he became resentful of my
"forcing" him into making mistakes. He eventually understood that
I was the caddy (and an imperfect one), and he was the player. I was
there to help, but the ultimate responsibility for his choices was his,
not mine.

Your life caddies are there to provide you with their best advice.
Of course, they care deeply about you and only want what, in their
opinion, is best for you. But, in the end, your career choices and
their consequences remain yours.

Startups are "Cool"

Over the past thirty years, working for a startup has gained more
cachet than working in a stodgy old-line company. Venture capital
investment in new technologies is in the tens or hundreds of
billions annually. The valuations of upstarts can be absurdly out
of proportion to that of established companies. The headlines are
flooded with stories of overnight millionaires who went from the
garage to IPO or unicorn valuations in a few years, sometimes

faster. Joining a startup has acquired a "cool" factor that makes many people starry-eyed.

Not only has joining a startup become as acceptable as working for a big company, but it is now preferable for many. Bright, ambitious people want to be where the action is. The allure of getting in on the ground floor of the next Apple, Amazon, or Google can be irresistible. Approximately twenty-five percent of Harvard Business School MBA candidates consider careers in startups after graduation. That percentage would have been unheard of thirty years ago.

Should You Work for A Startup?

Determining whether startup life is right for you should involve careful self-reflection. There are many good reasons to work for startups. But doing so because you perceive it to be cool or you expect to get rich should be low on the list of reasons.

Startups Offer Great Experiences

One critical consideration is what you hope to get from the experience. Making money, building skills and experience, and advancing your career are core elements of any career decision. Each job is a stepping stone to the next.

Although the economics of startup careers are more uncertain, startups present many opportunities you won't often find working for larger companies. They can provide a greater sense of fulfillment, purpose, and community and broad-ranging responsibilities that are hard to gain outside the startup environment. Specifically, joining a startup can lead to the following:

- building something you are passionate about
- gaining responsibility for impactful projects
- working with equally passionate people on a small team

- working in an organizational culture that fits your values and work style
- building targeted sector experience, ideally in a fast-growing sector
- having greater and more consistent access to senior leadership
- enjoying greater flexibility in navigating work schedules and locations
- gaining a sense of ownership through both your impact and stock or options grants

But Startups are Risky

Many people dream about joining startups because they are frustrated working in larger companies with rigid work environments. They feel their work could be more impactful. Others join with the idea of riding the rocket ship of financial success by getting stock in a company that becomes a unicorn. While that can happen, it is the rare startup that ever gets there.

Unless your company has an innovative offering with a sustainable competitive advantage, you could spend years spinning your wheels with little to show for your efforts from a financial perspective. For every startup that becomes a media darling, raises hundreds of millions of dollars, and mints dozens or hundreds of new millionaires, hundreds more fail. You hear about the examples on the extremes, the runaway successes that dominate the NASDAQ, and the spectacular flameouts–like Pets. com from the dot-com era or, more recently, Theranos, the ill-fated biotech company whose founder, Elizabeth Holmes, was convicted of fraud. Behind those sensational stories are the tales of woe of thousands of companies that have quietly faded into oblivion after failing to find a market for their offerings, being outcompeted by better-funded industry rivals, or running out of money.

Building a successful startup isn't easy. First, you need an idea for a business. I have often joked with my family that there are no original thoughts. Nearly every idea I ever had for a startup product had already been thought of. Even companies with sound ideas face a steep uphill climb working their way through the stages of the proof continuum before they achieve success.

When I founded my first company in 1992, my way of solving the "idea" problem was to find one I liked and join forces with the entrepreneurs who had developed it. In my case, that meant buying a regional franchise of a rapidly expanding company. While buying a franchise doesn't meet my definition of a startup from Chapter 1, it provided a practical transition from being a management consultant with minimal operating experience to running my own business.

The benefit of joining a franchise system was that the franchisor had already achieved product-market fit. We hitched our wagon to a fast horse and were able to leverage their platform, eventually making it onto the *Inc. 500* list of the fastest-growing companies in America.[4]

New ventures that start from scratch don't benefit from the same head start I had as a franchisee. So much must go right for an early-stage venture to succeed. It needs an innovative offering with a sustainable competitive advantage, adequate funding, strong management, the resources to adapt to market conditions and excellent execution. A company that falters on any of those elements

---

[4] Potomac Dining LP, (d/b/a Transmedia), a franchisee of Transmedia Networks, was Number 410 on the 1998 *Inc. 500* list. The company is listed here as Transmedia: https://www.inc.com/magazine/19981015/1105.html

may struggle to achieve the success needed to win and reward you for your contributions.

As you consider the startup career path, recognize that the risks are significant. Few startups can guarantee job security, work/ life balance, a high probability of wealth creation, or rapid career advancement. It is admirable to let a mission drive your career choices. But a startup may not provide you with the stability and predictability you need. If you are looking for certainty or peace of mind, a startup may be the wrong place.

Is a Startup the Right Fit?

Joining a startup should be done with purpose, not on a whim. Apart from the risks, you must also be prepared for the intensity of startup life. With long work hours, tight deadlines, and limited resources to execute your job, working at a startup can take over your life. As you think about whether to jump into startup life in general or a given startup, make sure you have a good idea of what you hope to get from the experience and can live with the all-consuming dynamics.[5]

Your jumping-off point should be an examination of personal fit. The mindset, skills, and orientation required to thrive in large and small companies differ. Large companies move slowly. They can be rife with bureaucracy and internal politics. They are hierarchical. You can be pigeonholed into narrow jobs with a limited scope of responsibility. Access to senior management is rare. Moving up the ladder into middle- to senior management can take years, sometimes decades.

---

[5] Jeffrey Bussgang of Harvard Business School and Flybridge Capital has written extensively on startup life. I recommend his article: Jeffrey Bussgang, "Are You Suited for a Startup?", hbr.org, *Harvard Business Review*, https://hbr.org/2017/11/are-you-suited-for-a-start-up. (November-December, 2017).

If you are oriented toward a more dynamic, less hierarchical organization, that large-company environment is deadly. I started my career in management consulting at a global firm helping advise multi-billion-dollar corporations. It was excellent training for someone just out of college. But I was a small cog in a large machine full of wheels. I rarely interacted with the senior members of our consulting firm, let alone our clients' executives. And I was not very good at playing politics.

Though I learned a lot, I didn't enjoy being on the outside looking in. I detested the internal and external politics typical of most professional services firms. It didn't matter how much I got paid or how prestigious my firm was. It wasn't a good fit. I had a feeling that starting a company would address my dissatisfaction. But in the early 1990s, the startup craze among young professionals had not yet taken hold, especially on the East Coast.

At that time, the path out of management consulting generally led to finance jobs (venture capital or private equity) or senior management positions with the firm's clients. Neither alternative appealed to me at the time. I wanted a more direct role in building something, so I left consulting and started my first company.

Startups involve rapid change and uncertainty, especially in fast-moving sectors. So much happens week to week or even day to day. Work includes administrative tasks, customer deadlines, strategy sessions, product planning meetings, information demands from the board, weekly sprints, daily standups, and many unexpected crises to attend to. You wake up every morning and may have only a vague notion of what you will face or need to focus on that day.

Working in a startup is not for the faint of heart. Most startups walk a tightrope with no safety net. They're trying to solve big problems with limited resources on tight schedules. They are chronically underfunded and understaffed. The pressure to perform is intense, and the startup's existence as a going entity depends on it.

Despite all the high expectations and stress, you will likely get paid less than at larger companies, have less generous benefits, and often face more limited opportunities for advancement. Your only choice to achieve upward mobility may be to leave your startup for another one.

Assess if you will thrive in the chaotic, unstructured, volatile world of early-stage ventures. Determine whether you have the right mindset to handle uncertainty, jump into the fray without being asked, regularly take on responsibilities out of your comfort zone, and bounce back from frequent failure. Working in a startup takes passion, commitment, confidence, and resilience. Not everyone possesses all those qualities.

When interviewing candidates in my prior companies, I found that the most challenging part was figuring out if they would thrive, especially when they came from larger companies. Most people talk a good game about how they can put their ego aside, do whatever it takes, and operate in an environment where the rules are fluid and resources are limited. Those who can't walk the walk won't survive in a startup environment.

Questions to Ask Yourself

You should ask yourself several questions to determine if you have what it takes to succeed in a startup.

Are you OK working for a company nobody has heard of?

Your identity is often closely intertwined with what you do for a living and where you do it. Brand name companies elicit approving nods from others, instant acceptance, and clear status. Working at them requires no explanation or justification. Once you have a certain amount of status, getting caught up in the brand recognition game is easy.

I started my first company when I was 29. After traveling all over the world to exotic places for my lucrative consulting job, I found myself toiling away in the storage room of a local hotel, our first office. It wasn't the garage startup of Silicon Valley lore. There was, however, a vent to the hotel garage, and we could smell the car fumes when the hotel valets parked visitors' cars. The space was free, so we were willing to put up with a lot.

Soon after launching the company, I attended my fifth-year Harvard Business School reunion and found myself explaining my career choice to my masters-of-the-universe classmates. Some of them viewed my endeavor with envy, but most with bemusement. I soon realized I had to stop caring what other people thought about my career path and focus on making the business work.

Having attended a prestigious school for college and business school and worked for a top management consulting firm, I was used to the brand recognition conveyed when describing my job or background. My little company didn't do that for me, at least not at first. But even in the early days, it gave me a sense of accomplishment and fulfillment that nothing I had done professionally before ever had.

It takes emotional maturity to put aside the expectations and judgments of others and find a path that is truly yours. It took me years to get there. Some of us can't overcome the subtle, or at times not so subtle, pressure we feel to conform to the expectations of others or society. Working at a no-name startup might not suit you if you can't.

Can you handle uncertainty?

A common joke in startups is that as soon as you close on a funding round, you must start fundraising again. Most startups, at least those tackling substantial market opportunities, chronically need more cash. They must rely on multiple rounds of outside capital to sustain them while they build their offerings. It takes time to find product-market fit and gain sales traction. All the while, the company is growing its team, spending its capital, and racing against the clock. It may take years for a startup to achieve cash flow breakeven or reach a successful sale, and many, even ones deemed to be very successful, never get there.

This dynamic weighs most heavily on the founders and senior leadership, who are primarily responsible for putting enough gas in the tank for the company to keep going. Most startups fail because they run out of money before they find the product-market fit that attracts new investors or acquirers.

Employees are not immune to this dynamic. At Fugue, we tracked the company's "dry hole" date every month to know how long we had before we ran out of money. This all-important metric drove major decisions, including hiring, compensation changes and promotions, and research and development (R&D) investment in the product. Most painful of all, at a couple of tough points, we resorted to layoffs to extend the company's runway. You must prepare for these uncertainties and the prospect of suddenly finding yourself unemployed.

Unlike larger companies with more ready access to capital markets, including bank debt, startups rely on the strength of their progress to continue attracting more investment capital. They usually can't access bank debt because most lenders want to see profits and cash flow from which the company can repay the debt with interest over time.

Fundraising may not be the only form of uncertainty in a startup, but it is where everything comes to a head. Many factors and events can affect a startup's success. They can include competitive dynamics, the economy, industry shifts, dysfunctional management or board/investor dynamics, and the loss of key personnel. All these factors get stirred up as investors consider whether to back (or keep backing) a company. If backing doesn't come through, the only options may be a quick sale before the money runs out or as orderly a shutdown as possible.

As a startup employee, you rarely see the behind-the-scenes dynamics that affect your future. While employees may ask for more openness, and many management teams try to provide transparency, there's a tradeoff. Startup execs understand that the quickest way to destroy value in a company is to have significant attrition when employees get spooked about the company's financial stability.

Leadership has no problem sharing good news when everything is going great. When things start to go sideways, management spins and shares only enough information to keep staff anxiety to a minimum. Most startups face challenges along their journeys that appear to be existential threats. In those situations, your ability to tolerate or even embrace this uncertainty is critical to your professional and emotional survival.

How big is your ego?

In large corporations, your power and compensation can be determined by how big your fiefdom is. They are measured in the budget, scope of control, how many people work for you, or even by how big your office is and where it is located. Getting the corner office with a great window view signifies status. Having minions to handle the little things is a great ego boost. If you aspire to that, working in a startup is probably not right for you.

A good friend who left management consulting to go into a senior position at a major bank described that the overriding motivation among senior leaders in the company was to amass more and more direct and indirect reports into their departments. Why? Because that's how their power and influence were measured, which drove compensation and advancement. Her efforts to drive efficiency and consider using outside contractors and services rather than internal staff or homegrown inferior products were met with resistance. Those initiatives ran counter to the empire-building culture. She left after a year.

While I was working as a summer intern at Price Waterhouse, a senior consultant was promoted to manager and moved from a shared office into a private office. I happened to be in the partner's office when another manager marched in and filed a complaint. Although she had been a manager for a couple of years and had seniority, the newly minted manager had received a larger office.

The partner got up (and told me to tag along as a witness). He went into both offices and measured their dimensions by counting ceiling tiles. The more senior manager's office was 9-½ tiles across, and the new manager's office was 10 tiles across. I don't remember who got which office in the end. I do remember thinking that if this was what people in the company worried about, it was not a place I wanted to work.

Thriving in a startup requires you to park your ego at the door. You need to earn the respect of your teammates by stepping up and delivering, not demanding it by virtue of your position. There's little room for prima donnas. If you walk in with an attitude of entitlement or superiority, chances are the organism will reject you like a poorly matched organ transplant.

I have seen many talented individuals over the years fail, not because they didn't have the job skills but because they didn't mesh well with the startup culture. They demanded resources that didn't exist. They couldn't play well with others in a culture that was more collaborative than hierarchical. They tried to play politics with senior management, which doesn't work well in a small company where everyone works closely together, and secrets are hard to keep.

Even more than in large companies, the success of a startup rests on effective cross-functional collaboration. You have to get your job done with limited resources and support under intense time pressure. Being a team player means jumping in to help your colleagues, even when it's not strictly in your job description. You rely on them to do the same for you. Being territorial doesn't cut it.

You may find yourself assembling your office furniture, crawling under desks to plug in wires, taking your laptop to the Apple store because there's no IT department, or running out to pick up coffee and snacks for a meeting. You probably won't be working in Class A office space with a gym, game room, plush carpets, and a corporate cafeteria unless your startup is way overfunded, which can lead to its own set of problems.

I launched my first company with $50,000 of my own money and $500,000 of outside capital from angel investors. Five of us crammed into a 250-square feet office that required ducking our heads to enter because of the ductwork partially blocking the doorway into the room. It wasn't glamorous, but it was functional, inexpensive, and well-located.[6]

In a matter of a couple of months, I had gone from flying business class to Bangkok and Hong Kong and staying in five-star hotels to camping in a dusty basement with dirty carpets and rubbing elbows with my teammates as we worked cheek by jowl. I loved it!

When hiring people at my previous startups, one of the key questions was always whether the person would fit culturally. This was especially important when the candidate's career consisted of working for mainly larger companies. Startups can't afford the luxury of hiring the wrong people. It is a drain on management to deal with the dynamics, determine whether to keep the people on, and ultimately replace them and train their successors. When

---

[6] Coincidentally, when Fugue set up its first Washington, DC office, it was in a WeWork and the square footage per employee was also 50. It was anything but free. The rent was about $150 per square foot.

there's a bad fit, the discomfort is just as significant for the employee as for their colleagues. Think about what kind of person you are and the relationship you want to have with your employer and your colleagues before you dive in.

Are you an athlete or a position player?

Apart from keeping your ego in check and taking on menial tasks you wouldn't have to do in a big company, startups require a different kind of flexibility. You never know what new challenges you will face or what opportunities may arise. The skills necessary to tackle day-to-day variability differ from what you need in a mature company. In larger companies, jobs are more specialized and highly defined. In startups, management seeks out existing people to fill gaps and take on new responsibilities. Hiring is hard and takes time. Work needs to get done now. People often do the equivalent of two or three jobs, including jobs they didn't expect or sign up for.

In the early days of Fugue, we talked about hiring "athletes" rather than position players. We hoped to find those rare individuals who are multi-talented and adaptable. We needed a team of brilliant, flexible people whom we could rely on to take on varied tasks and get the job done. The athlete might not be the optimal resource to tackle any given task. But having people willing to step up and work effectively on multiple projects was more valuable than having position players with highly developed but narrow skills.

We went into the organization-building process with the mindset that flexibility and the raw horsepower of intelligence, drive, commitment, and experience were more important than specialization. Even among the engineers, we needed multi-talented developers who could tackle varied challenges, although there were exceptions to this rule as we were building a highly technical product.

If you are a Jack or Jill of many trades and can work outside your comfort zone, you can gain broad experience and quickly become a go-to person in a startup. You'll also gain more exposure to senior leadership, which has many benefits from a networking and career standpoint.

I have always been more of an athlete than a skilled position player, which is part of the reason I enjoy the seed and early-stage phases of company building. In a newly minted company, each day brings new challenges that draw on the full breadth of your skills and experiences. You overcome uncertainty and make things up as you go along to keep progressing quickly. While unpredictable at times, startup days are rarely dull. Highly stressful? Absolutely! Boring? Not in the least!

Are you comfortable working in an unstructured environment?

I was fortunate to start my career at a management consulting firm that hired legions of freshly minted college graduates. We were smart, eager, and pedigreed. But to be honest, most of us knew nothing about anything when it came to business. Through intensive training, close supervision, and tight performance management, the firm molded us into productive contributors to its strategic advisory practice. We had regular feedback sessions and semi-annual formal reviews.

Early in my tenure, expectations for our evolution as young analysts reflected a simple progression–Listen, Execute, and Add. First, our job was to keep our mouths shut, watch, and learn. Second, we were expected to deliver assignments on time to our supervisors for review and quality control. After six months, we might be allowed to attend client meetings and speak when spoken to, responding to questions about the analysis we had performed. Only after a year-long apprenticeship at the heels of more senior consultants were we deemed to have acquired sufficient experience and insight to offer opinions about the work.

This environment is 180 degrees opposite to the experience of working in most startups. You're expected to dive in headfirst and be productive right away. The exception to this may be the sales team, who have a ramp-up period of four to six months before they are expected to start delivering results. Training is on-the-job, supervision is highly variable, and performance management is haphazard, if it exists at all.

Many startups have neither the resources nor the internal processes to provide formal training. At best, new employees are referred to the company's website, sales and marketing artifacts, technical documents, and DropBox or Google Drive to review company materials. A quick round-robin set of discussions with senior leadership and your departmental colleagues to get the lay of the land, and off you go.

Lack of formal training may affect your job performance and have longer-term implications. Getting proper training in job-related skills such as financial modeling or project management early in your career is an accelerator that can position you for greater success and career advancement. Those skills have intrinsic value and are fully portable as you move positions. I often reflect on how well the formal training I received in my first consulting job has served me throughout my career. If I had started my career in a new venture, I would have had to learn all of those skills on my own.

Likewise, the level and quality of supervision in a startup can be highly variable and idiosyncratic to the supervisor. The supervisor's personality and style often dictate how much guidance they provide and how clear the expectations are. Thriving in the startup environment requires significant initiative in seeking out tasks and understanding your teammates and bosses' work styles and expectations.

There's no paint-by-numbers process. It's up to you to ask for the guidance you need to understand the expectations for your performance. You may need to seek out relationships with people outside of your team who can help you figure out how to manage your day-to-day work and interactions with colleagues. This isn't easy but is vital to your success.

Finally, performance management systems can be highly variable and even capricious in a startup. To be fair, startup founders don't always have broad general management experience. Given the pace at which startups operate, spending time on building human resources processes is not always a priority, especially in the early days when there are few employees.

How do you know if you're doing a good job? Without formal performance management systems, developing an open relationship with the people who evaluate you and seeking regular feedback is critical. Most people aren't comfortable seeking out feedback from their bosses. Likewise, many bosses resist regular performance check-ins because they feel like a tax on getting real work done. This is especially true if they must deliver difficult messages when performance falters.

If you don't proactively seek feedback, you may go for months without a clear indication of how you are doing. I believe that by the time you get to an annual performance review with an employee, there should be no surprises. Managers and their reports should communicate regularly and address any issues as they arise, but that rarely happens in a young company. Early on, the human resources function is focused primarily on managing payroll and benefits; the more strategic aspects of culture and performance management show up later. Without structured ways to measure and monitor performance, you can get blindsided or miss opportunities for increased responsibility, compensation, or advancement.

The anti-bureaucracy bias in startups can work to the employee's disadvantage without transparent performance management systems. Inertia sets in when people are working hard, focused on delivering results, and not complaining about their advancement or compensation. Management assumes everything is ok and people are happy, which means they may not work proactively to reward great work. Though easier said than done, you must take the initiative to advance.

I'm not saying you can't survive in a startup if you're not the kind of person who takes the initiative to dive in, start delivering value, and carve your advancement path. However, if you don't do those things, you may not reach a level of productivity high enough to advance as quickly as you might like. That could leave you unsure of what it takes to succeed, experiencing a lot of performance pressure, and feeling resentful and underappreciated.

Not diving right in and delivering value from the start can also lead to uncomfortable conversations with management and a parting of ways for reasons that should have been avoided. Employees leaving because they are underperforming or not advancing as they hoped is a lose-lose situation for both the employee and the company.

Can you live and breathe the mission?

Winning in a startup takes missionary zeal that exceeds the typical commitment required to succeed in a corporate environment. The pace of innovation in technology is rapid. Resources are limited. Your company may have a great idea and a head start. That doesn't ensure success. The competition is always coming for you. It is a fight to the death, as failing to achieve results could mean the spigot of funding gets shut off.

The founder and the team must overcome enormous resistance and inertia to mobilize resources and personnel to fight the battle. A win-at-all-costs ethos must permeate the entire organization for a startup to succeed. Victory in a startup is a sustained guerrilla action where everyone trusts that they can rely on their teammates to put in 150 percent daily. There's no room for slackers.

Practically speaking, you need to do whatever it takes whenever required. In our companies, we talked about having a sense of urgency. The company must meet product development milestones to secure the next funding round. Marquee customer deals often come to a head when you are on vacation, especially since the year-end is December 31[7]. You can't control the timing, and the concept of punching a clock just doesn't exist.

On the spectrum between working to live and living to work, startup life is much closer to the living-to-work end. The job and your commitment to the company's mission should intrinsically provide a sense of fulfillment. You shouldn't be there if it doesn't because the organization expects you to be all in. If you aren't, you become resentful, demotivated, and unproductive as the pressure mounts. Your colleagues start treating you differently, and your day-to-day job becomes far tenser and far less enjoyable.

Of course, we all want to achieve work-life balance, but the demands of the startup war rarely recognize personal boundaries. I always thought about this in terms of work-life integration rather than balance. Balance suggests a level of equilibrium or equal time. You shouldn't expect that in a startup.

When I first joined Fugue as Interim CFO, I agreed to work half-time. Hah! Within a short period, I was working 40 hours per week but still only getting paid as a half-time employee. Eventually, I started to resent the arrangement, recognizing that there was too much to do for me to be part-time and that I was being underpaid. For the relationship to work, the company and I had to be fully committed. I realized that in any meaningful role in a startup, there's no such thing as half-time. Half-time expands into full-time. And when I went full-time, it quickly became all the time.

When working in startups, I couldn't help but live and breathe the company's mission all day, every day (and even at night). Even in

---

[7] Company reporting to investors is based on quarterly and annual performance. It is critical to sign as many customer contracts by year-end as possible, so the winter holidays and even New Year's Eve are a time when many deals are finalized.

companies where the CEO respects people's personal lives, priorities must be triaged to ensure the needs of the business are met. Nights, weekends, and vacations don't mean much when deadlines approach.

In a startup, it is hard to unplug for extended periods. You can't let things slide for a week or two. Everyone's role is unique, and it's difficult for others to step into your shoes if you're gone. Organizational dependencies in small companies run deep. You must keep things moving so your colleagues can as well, even if it means taking calls while on vacation or answering emails late at night or early in the morning.

As CFO at Fugue, I was involved in every significant transaction. It became a running joke that whenever I was on vacation, we'd be in the middle of closing a funding round or negotiating a large customer contract. This became such a regular "coincidence" that whenever we needed a big deal to happen, our founder would tell me I needed to go on vacation. If you're looking for a 9-5 or 8-6, five-day-a-week job, a startup is probably not right for you.

When is the Right Time to Join a Startup?

Life's major decisions rarely happen in a vacuum. Determining that you are the kind of person who would thrive in a startup environment is just the first step. Your life situation also influences the decision to pursue a career in an entrepreneurial venture. In other words, timing matters.

Joining a startup is like buying a lottery ticket or playing the slots. When you ante up and place a bet, there is a chance that it could pay off handsomely. That excitement captures the imagination and sometimes keeps people from unemotionally considering whether the decision makes sense or if the time is right. It's good to recognize that the odds of a big payout from working at an early-stage venture are low.

Common sense dictates that you shouldn't bet with money you can't afford to lose. The gambling industry is about providing entertainment. The odds favor the house, and the entertainment comes from the chance of winning and the excitement of being in the arena and playing the game. People get into trouble when they take risks beyond acceptable limits, ultimately digging a hole they can't escape.

The stakes can be even higher when you're betting with your time, the one commodity you can't replace. Careers don't always progress in a straight line or a hockey stick, up and to the right. When you choose to take a job, you are closing off other available options. There is an opportunity cost[8] related to the road not taken. Every decision has risks and winning or losing is determined by luck and timing as much as by your hard work.

When I started my first company, it was a reasonably good time to take a risk. While I had recently gotten married, we didn't have any kids, and I didn't have a lot of financial responsibilities. I had just paid off my student loans, and my wife's career was starting to take off. Even though we had just bought a house, we could pay the bills on her salary alone.

Pouring our meager savings into a new business was undoubtedly a scary decision. I had months of sleepless nights before committing, pondering whether it was the right thing to do. It seemed like a now-or-never moment I would regret if I didn't seize it. I reasoned that I had an MBA from a well-known school and a lot of experience as a management consultant, and I had just gotten out of debt. We were as unburdened as we were ever going to be. It would haunt me for many years if I didn't grab the chance.

---

[8] *Opportunity cost* is the potential lost or missed benefit associated with other options that are not chosen. Choosing one job means foregoing the potential associated with other jobs you might have taken but decided not to.

Early in my startup journey, I was fortunate to be in a position to take risks. Not everyone is. When considering difficult decisions or advising my kids in challenging situations, I often ask myself, "What's the worst thing that can happen?" It's a simple yet powerful question. If the worst thing that can happen is something that you can live with, anything that isn't as bad as that should be tolerable too.

When starting my first company, I figured the worst thing that could happen was that I would have to retreat to a career in management consulting. While I didn't love consulting, I knew that at least I would be able to pay the bills if I went back. Fortunately, the worst thing didn't happen.

I did have to go for a couple of years without a salary so the company could preserve cash and invest in growth, but we turned the corner. Had my wife not supported me while I was getting the business off the ground, I might have had to abandon the effort and get a job. As with most startups, the key was hanging in there long enough to get through the early challenges until the business found its footing.

The success of that first venture set me on a path to continue my involvement in early-stage ventures. Not everyone is as fortunate. Fugue's founder, Josh Stella, is a brilliant technologist I first met in my second startup, USLaw.com. Josh is one of those rare individuals who could excel in a corporate environment but is also well-suited for and excited by startup life. He readily shares why he chose to abandon startup life after the failure of USLaw.com in 2001.

With a wife and young son at home, Josh couldn't afford to spend another few years rolling the dice on another startup. He chose instead to work for a larger organization that provided greater financial stability. He and I spoke periodically about startup ideas he wanted to pursue, but either the idea wasn't right, or the timing wasn't, until eleven years later. At that point, he finally felt that he could once again depart from the safety of corporate life, pursue his vision, and start a company.

Today's decision may not be tomorrow's decision. When to take the plunge into startup life is just as important as whether to do so. My story and Josh's speak to the nature of risk and the unpredictability of outcomes. If my first company hadn't been successful, I would most likely have gone back to a traditional job. If USLaw.com had been successful, Josh might never have returned to working for a big company.

You need to consider your upside if you're successful and your downside if not. Assess your risk tolerance. People who gravitate toward startups tend to have a higher baseline risk tolerance. Even considering that, risk tolerance is not a constant throughout your life or career. There are times when you can afford to take more risks. There are other times when it makes more sense to pull in your horns and take a defensive posture.

The U-Curve of Risk Tolerance

Over the years, I have observed behavior related to risk tolerance and startups that roughly translates into a U-curve based on where you are in terms of resources and responsibilities. When younger and unencumbered, you have few resources but a relatively high ability to tolerate risk. After all, you have little to lose and lots of time to make up for failures. Roughly speaking, that translates to your 20s, though that varies by individual.

As family and personal responsibilities mount, most people become more risk averse. They are trying to progress in their careers, working toward promotions, keeping their heads down, and working hard. A steady paycheck takes on the utmost importance. Taking a flier on a speculative venture, whether as an investor or employee, seems foolhardy. A failure that puts the family at risk of a lifestyle reset is too big a price to pay. If the risks taken in your twenties didn't pay off, voluntary risk-taking in your thirties and forties might become a non-starter.

By their fifties, many people have built more of a nest egg. Children may be nearing the end of college. Mortgages are getting closer to being paid off. Now, you may have more flexibility to take selective risks. That may come from getting more aggressive with your investments. It also may be a time to consider a second career in an area that is more fun, dynamic, and aligned with your interests and values.

Of course, the reverse may be true as well. If by the time someone has reached the second half of their working life, they have not achieved some measure of material security, that may drive them to stay conservative—for individuals in that situation, working at a startup may represent a risk that is too high to contemplate at any age.

When you have nothing to lose, you may be willing to risk everything. When you have something to lose and losing it would damage home and hearth, the prudent path is to be more conservative and risk little or nothing. If you reach the point where you have more than enough, you can think differently about risk and opportunity and take a flier.

Exhibit 4-1 represents a conceptual framework to capture the evolving risk tolerance of individuals in the workplace. The determinants of how much risk someone will comfortably take on are loosely correlated to age and are more tightly associated with that individual's relative resources and responsibilities. Age is a proxy for risk tolerance, but people can clearly be more or less risk tolerant depending on their circumstances.

As a family, we have moved through the U-curve and made decisions about our careers in the context of our resources and responsibilities. When our kids were young, my wife was recruited to lead marketing at a nascent cybersecurity company. The company had an open-source intrusion detection offering running like wildfire through the tech community. They had yet to generate a significant amount of revenue, and the concept of open-source software was just gaining acceptance. At the time, she worked for a well-funded public technology company earning a good salary and had a generous options package.

Despite being courted heavily by one of the most successful VCs in our region, the thought of leaving her stable, well-paying job to

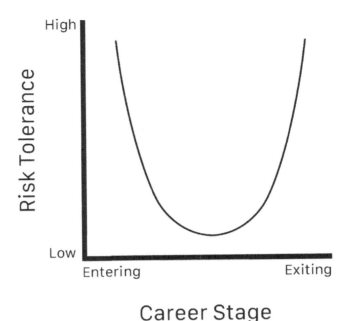

Exhibit 4-1: The U-Curve of Risk Tolerance

join a nascent startup with only $1 million in revenue seemed too risky. She declined, only to watch the company grow in subsequent years to hundreds of millions of revenue and ultimately get bought for over $2.5 billion.

Her decision not to join was heavily informed by the fact that we had two young kids at home, and I was already involved in a startup. The risk of jumping ship from her stable position was too great, and the timing for us was wrong. The decision cost us millions in foregone upside, but we couldn't have known that, and it was the right decision for us at the time.

Startup Risk Evolves Over Time

The factors that should influence your decision are not limited to where you are in your career journey but also include where the startup is along its path through the proof continuum we discussed in Chapter 3 (Prove It!). The risk associated with a given company evolves. The company may gain great market traction and secure substantial funding. Or progress may be slow, and the company might burn through its cash faster than expected. As companies progress through the growth stage, operational risk declines, which also usually drives financing risk down if the company executes and meets its goals.

Exhibit 4-2 portrays the interplay between personal risk tolerance and the intrinsic risk associated with startups at various stages along the proof continuum. You would consider a situation where your risk tolerance is greater than the intrinsic risk associated with the company a "go-zone," a situation that you might consider. The reverse is equally true. If intrinsic risk falls below your risk tolerance, that situation is a "no-go." Of course, risk is difficult to quantify. But conceptually, when you are in a position where your life responsibilities significantly exceed your resources, taking a flier on a startup early on the proof continuum may not be prudent.

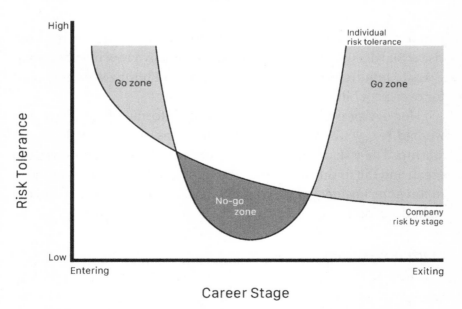

Exhibit 4-2: U-Curve Risk Tolerance vs. Proof Continuum Risk

I recall the decision of a single mother to leave Fugue at a time when she felt the company had become too risky. We weren't hitting our goals consistently (i.e., making progress through the proof continuum stages fast enough), and she feared the company could run out of money before securing a new funding round. She loved working at the company and didn't want to leave. But she could not afford to bet her family's well-being on a company in such a precarious financial position. She went to work for a large, established tech company that could provide the stability she needed at the time.

By contrast, a couple of us who joined Fugue early on were on the far-right part of the U-curve, where we could afford to take significant career risks. We were in our 50s and 60s with ample resources. Even though Fugue was at the concept stage, we saw an opportunity with significant potential to revolutionize cloud security and reap substantial financial rewards.

I took significant financial and career risks, working strictly for stock for the first year. In addition, my wife and I were also the first outside investors. That's an extreme version of risk-taking. I'm not suggesting that you should work for a startup for no cash compensation or even invest in the company. It's just illustrative of how much more flexibility you might have at the right tail of the U-curve.

Weighing Startup Risks and Rewards

Today, with the average tenure in most jobs about four years, you may switch jobs numerous times over your roughly 40-year career. Having a framework for making the right decision for you is important.

When considering a new job, most people tend to consider the opportunity from the outside in. Recruiters can be persuasive, and anything new is exciting. After all, it's nice to be wanted. Apart from the compensation and title, you might focus on a series of external questions including:

- Is it in a city I want to be in?
- What would my commute be?
- Is it in an industry I'm excited about?
- Do I like the people I have met?

While those external considerations are important, you need to give equal or greater weight to reviewing the opportunity from your inside out. The company evaluates whether they think you are right for them. You need to think about whether the company is right for you, especially if you are pursuing other opportunities at the same time.

Some key questions you should consider include:

- Are you at a stage of your career/life when this opportunity is a good fit?
- What is the opportunity cost of taking this job now versus staying in your current job or considering other options?
- What are the hours like, and how does that fit with your priorities and home life?
- What experience can you gain by working there, and how does that serve your long-term career goals?
- How risky is the company, and are you comfortable with that risk?
- Do you have a life partner, and what is their risk tolerance and ability to help mitigate risk from the opportunity?
- How much of a financial cushion do you have to absorb volatility in the company's fortunes?
- What is your fallback plan if the company fails?

The Bottom Line

Just like investing, choosing whether and when to work for a startup can be rewarding but involves a high degree of uncertainty and risk. There is no definitive way to know the correct answer in advance. Investors will tell you that they were wrong no matter how much money they invest in a company or a deal. They would have invested more if they had known the company would be successful. If the company fails, they'll wish they hadn't invested at all.

Despite your best efforts to do your due diligence, you may make mistakes throughout your career. You might choose to work for a startup and see it fail as my company USLaw.com did. Or you might pass up the opportunity to work for that hot startup that could have brought you life-changing wealth, as my wife did at that cybersecurity company. Either way, you want to look back with no regrets, knowing you gave the decision full consideration.

Deciding to join or not join a startup should involve a clear-eyed assessment of your risk tolerance, your evaluation of the company's chances for success, and how the opportunity fits you personally in terms of job content, values, culture, lifestyle, and timing. Be courageous, thoughtful, and thorough about asking the right questions. Consider the potential upside and downside for you and your loved ones. Hopefully, being diligent will lead you to the best possible decisions.

CHAPTER 5

The Hunt

Let's assume you have concluded that you want to work in a startup, and it's a good time to take the plunge. How do you go about finding the right opportunities?

Many people conduct their careers haphazardly, bouncing from one company to another opportunistically. They chase a few more bucks or the latest tech fad or simply respond to recruiters who reach out. They hang out in a place until something better comes along and then jump at it. The cycle continues, and they realize, in retrospect, that there wasn't much rhyme or reason to how they moved through their careers.

This approach can work but probably doesn't optimize your career progression. The most successful people I know have achieved success by being focused and purposeful and, of course, working hard. Many would readily admit they are not the smartest or most talented people. But they were targeted about their careers, adopting a hunter's mindset.

The hunter has a specific prey in mind. They position themselves for a successful hunt and seize opportunities to strike when they present themselves. The perfect job might come along when you least expect it. Or you might need to be patient and stay in a job you don't love for a while as you build up resources and plan your next move. Knowing what you are looking for is important, so you are prepared to grab it.

In early 1991, I concluded that I wanted to make a career switch out of management consulting. Over that summer, a business opportunity arose that I found attractive—I was open to it because I had already decided I wanted to leave my firm. I studied it carefully and planned my exit over four months, during which I researched the market and wrote the business plan. There was significant risk in leaving my job to start my first company. But I had laid enough groundwork to make a move with a reasonable prospect of success.

While biding time and paying the bills, consider what actions you can take to position yourself for a move. Being proactive doesn't eliminate uncertainty or randomness from the equation. However, maintaining focus and building your skills and experience helps you lay the groundwork to pounce when the time is right.

What is Your Career Thesis?

The first step in your career progression is developing a clear idea of what you are hunting for. You must understand where you are most likely to succeed and find fulfillment, not only in your next position but over the longer term.

You would do well to think like an investor. Successful long-term investors don't just throw money at any investment that comes along. They look at hundreds of potential deals and narrow their focus to just a few. They look at the fundamentals of each opportunity and consider many short and long-term factors before committing resources. They approach investments with hypotheses about what will make them work and how long they intend to hold them.

Most professional investors have an "investment thesis," a stated focus that defines the kinds of companies they invest in. That may include the sector, the stage of the business (seed, early, growth, or public), and the nature of the business (software, equipment, biotech, etc.). It includes the size of their typical investment, whether they seek minority or majority positions, and how much control they want in the companies they invest in.

By establishing an investment thesis, an investor creates a clear framework that helps focus their efforts. Limited partners who invest in selected venture capital or private equity funds know what the general partners plan to invest in. Companies seeking funding can assess their fit with the fund's objectives. The fund itself has a clear filter for evaluating which companies to invest in and, sometimes more importantly, which companies not to invest in or spend time evaluating.

Like investors with a particular approach, it is helpful to focus your job hunting by establishing a career thesis. This allows you to zero in on what you are good at and passionate about. The increased focus leads to you developing greater expertise, fueling your career advancement. It also allows you to seek targeted career development opportunities to enhance your qualifications or credentials and better position yourself to pursue your desired path. You can articulate your career thesis on your resume, LinkedIn profile, and in interviews to let prospective employers know what you are focused on and make the job "dating" process more efficient.

Your career thesis should consist of goals and criteria that represent your priorities and beliefs about where you might succeed. As you seek out and consider different opportunities, your career thesis is the lens through which you can see your options more clearly.

Identifying factors you consider deal-killers that automatically disqualify opportunities is valuable. These include inadequate compensation, mismatches between your skills and job responsibilities, founders with bad reputations, companies running out of cash, undesirable geography, or industries you may find morally objectionable.

My venture capitalist friend Jonathan Silver once told me there are 100 reasons VCs may say no to a deal, and it only takes one. The same applies to jobs—if something important is wrong, just say no.

Emotions can sometimes drive career choices, such as attending grad school or taking a cool-sounding startup position. Having a career thesis and a concrete framework for evaluating opportunities enables you to be analytical rather than emotional as you consider critical life decisions. Systematically and consistently evaluating your choices through your framework will help you address the hard questions and support your decision-making.

The Career Decision Matrix

I believe in the power of using structured frameworks to make decisions. When my daughter was looking at colleges, many of the informational sessions sounded the same, the tours were similar, and it became hard to distinguish one school from the others. After many circular discussions that didn't lead her any closer to a prioritized list, I suggested we build a decision matrix with weighted criteria to capture her preferences on college characteristics. She rated over twenty schools using established criteria, generating a score for each school on a scale from 0 to 100. The result was a rank-ordered list of schools that helped her decide where to apply. You can do the same for your job search.

Once you have laid out your criteria for your ideal job, do your homework to understand how different opportunities fit them. Eliminate the misfits to avoid jumping at options based on availability or gut feeling. In my daughter's case, the numerical framework became a powerful catalyst for articulating her key priorities, facilitating productive conversations, evaluating options, and settling on a decision.

High-level criteria for your career thesis may not differ all that much from a funder's investment thesis. These should include among other factors:

- Geography (although in a world of remote and hybrid work, that may matter less)
- Sector/Industry
- Size of Company
- Public vs. Private
- If private, stage of company (seed, early stage, growth, pre-IPO)

In Exhibit 5-1, you can see a sample set of criteria and an evaluation of three hypothetical job offers. You should develop customized criteria for yourself, but this list provides a good start. The criteria weights add to 100. Each offer is rated on a scale of 1 to 10, yielding a weighted-average score for each opportunity. The numerical score indicates how each opportunity stacks up (highest to lowest total score), absolutely and relative to other options. Use the numbers as a guide, but also use judgment and common sense before making your decision.

Criteria	Weight	Offer A	Offer B	Offer C
Industry sector	5	9	5	7
Company funding / stability	10	8	6	4
Size of market	5	6	9	5
Strength of management	15	8	7	6
Fit with career goals	10	8	10	7
Advancement opportunities	10	6	8	5
Learning opportunities	10	9	8	4
Geographic location	10	8	10	6
Cultural fit	10	9	6	9
Compensation / Upside potential	15	7	9	7
Weighted Total Score	**100**	**79**	**76**	**63**

Exhibit 5-1: Startup Offer Evaluation Criteria

No job is perfect; there are pros and cons to every opportunity you come across. Systematically considering your priorities and looking at options through a decision framework that weighs your priorities helps you target prospects that are a better fit.

Don't waste time considering opportunities that don't make sense. That time is better spent targeting companies and positions that fit your career thesis, evaluating them, and preparing to engage with them.

Hunting Season

How you find that (near) perfect position depends to some extent on whether you are the hunted or the hunter. If you have the right skills and experience, companies and recruiters interested in hiring you may reach out. Being courted is flattering, but just because someone likes you doesn't mean you must like them back. Just because a company reaches out to you doesn't mean the opportunity they present is worthy. It does put you in the position of being the buyer and should give you the ability to be more discriminating as you consider whether to engage.

The likelihood you are recruited increases substantially as you progress in your career, particularly if you have had success working for higher-profile companies. Being recruited is especially likely if you have established yourself in a leadership position. In high-flying sectors, there is a constant talent war going on, with technical, sales, and management talent in particularly high demand.

If a recruiter targets you, you have a decision to make. Leaving your current position is a difficult choice and not one to take lightly. You can't (or shouldn't) work full-time for both companies simultaneously.[9] The choice is binary– stay or go.

---

[9] With the rise of remote work during the pandemic that began in 2020, reports emerged of employees taking advantage of their employers by working two full-time jobs without either employer's knowledge. Jack Kelly, "The Remote Trend of Working Two Jobs at the Same Time Without Both Companies Knowing," *Forbes*, August 15, 2021, https://bit.ly/3PHJ7dS

To complicate matters, if being approached with an opportunity makes you consider leaving your current position, you may owe it to yourself to explore the possibilities more broadly and expand your options. Your current company and the company recruiting you are not the only companies in the market. If a recruiter values you enough to try to woo you away from your current employer, surely other companies would as well.

Where you work is like owning an investment portfolio consisting of one stock. If you could only invest in one stock, would you sell it to buy another one somebody is pitching you out of the blue? Would you hold onto it? Or would you look around to see if there are other stocks out there that might perform better?

If you are happy with your stock, don't sell it. Simply selling it because a broker contacted you and offered you a different stock seems rash and irresponsible. But often, when employees are recruited for a new job, they jump without investigating other options. Opportunities seem more exciting when they are new and different, especially if they offer more pay. The effort to beat the bushes to create more options seems too difficult. People tend to focus mainly on what is right in front of them.

A former colleague left Fugue for a larger company when she was offered more money and an opportunity to broaden her professional experience. After a month, she realized she hadn't done enough homework about her new employer. Our company was a better fit culturally for her. She also realized that she had underestimated the opportunity to continue gaining valuable experience at Fugue. She returned after a month, and we gladly took her back, which was fortunate for both of us as that usually doesn't happen.

On the other hand, if you want to leave your firm, your approach to job hunting should be different. Consider how urgently you need to find a new position, recognizing many factors may affect that. Once you answer that question, you can start looking around and targeting companies you are interested in. This is a more proactive process than reacting to a recruiter trying to pluck you from your current position.

Job hunting is challenging enough when you're looking at larger companies. Finding a great job in a startup is often more elusive. The specific skills companies hire for are influenced by where the company is on the proof continuum. There won't likely be a continuous recruiting effort across many departments as in larger companies.

Small companies don't tend to hire many people at a given time. There are a few exceptions, such as software development jobs that are hard to fill and may remain open for extended periods. Otherwise, hiring happens relatively quickly for most positions, and the application window is short. In addition, most startups don't have large recruiting budgets to broadcast their job openings on multiple platforms.

Finding startups that fit your criteria requires continuous digging to ensure you unearth what is out there and can apply quickly when new jobs are posted. You must be in the right place at the right time, which requires diligence. You can also help yourself by establishing a pre-existing relationship with the company, letting them know you are interested, even if there is no current opening. Recruiting managers often keep applicants' resumes on file for the day when they need to fill a specific position quickly. It is always a plus if a prospective employer knows you are interested in them in advance.

When my daughter Sonya was just a couple of years out of college working in a public relations agency, she decided she wanted to switch from client services and go in-house into a marketing position at a company. She identified a group within a target company that seemed the perfect fit. She networked with the woman who had the exact job she wanted and stayed in touch with her for more than a year. When that contact decided to leave the company to join a startup, she let Sonya know that the company was about to post the opening for the position. Sonya was prepared to strike when the position was posted, secured an interview, and got the job.

The exception to the modest scale of hiring in startups is right after they have closed a significant funding round. In the past, startup funding might have been used on inventory or capital expenditures, like servers. But given the dominance of software companies in the startup ranks and the advent of cloud computing which has reduced capital investment on computer hardware and data centers, most startup funding is now used to hire staff to build out products or invest in sales and marketing.

There are many ways to identify companies and career opportunities, and lots of information about job hunting is available online, so I won't spend much time on those here. A few suggestions for making your job hunt more efficient include:

- Utilize push notifications from recruiting sites: Take a targeted approach and leverage recruiting services offered by companies such as LinkedIn and Indeed that deliver notifications on job opportunities at companies that meet your criteria. If they look attractive, apply right away!

- Track funding news: Track news on companies that meet your career thesis and sectors of interest. Companies that have received venture funding often go on a hiring spree, so try to get on their radar. One site that tracks job openings at recently funded companies is fundedandhiring.com.

- <u>Target VCs and private equity firms</u>: Recruiting talent is one of the value-adds many investors bring to their portfolio companies. Research the investors in the companies you would like to work for. Larger VC funds and private equity firms often have recruiters on staff. Connecting with them might land you an introduction to one of their companies. You can also check out listings on ventureloop.com, a site dedicated to listing jobs at venture-backed companies.

- <u>Network, network, network</u>: Identify people you can connect with in your desired companies and sectors. Work your contact network for introductions. Reach out on LinkedIn. Tap your college or graduate school career office or former professors. The best way to get a job is to be referred by someone who knows you. You have instant credibility, and your resume jumps to the top of the pile.

- <u>Raise your profile</u>: Being visible to your target audiences helps build credibility and maximizes your chances of being noticed. For technical talent, contributing to high-profile open-source projects and building your presence on GitHub can serve as a powerful calling card showcasing your talents. For non-technical folks, consider establishing an online voice as an expert in your field or industry and make sure your online profile (e.g. LinkedIn) clearly articulates your career goals, targeted sectors, and your unique skills and experiences that an employer would value.

The Bottom Line

When it comes to job hunting, you can choose to take the jobs that come along during your career. If they don't work out, you'll move on and keep moving until you find the right one, a bit like casual dating until you find "the one."

I'm reminded of the saying, "You always find what you're looking for in the last place you look." Most people take the phrase to represent the frustration of not finding what you're looking for immediately. There is another fundamental truth in that statement—once you find what you're looking for, you can stop looking. But the question is, do you know what you're looking for?

It is better to seek out opportunities where you see yourself potentially settling in for the longer term, open to the possibilities that you and the company can grow and flourish together. In other words, be a hunter. To maximize your chances of finding what you're looking for, you need to be clear on what you are hunting for and be proactive in setting yourself up for success:

- Stay focused on your goals and build your skills.
- Develop your career thesis so you can evaluate opportunities through an established decision framework.
- Make your career interests and skills known through your LinkedIn profile, resume, and social media or on a GitHub profile if you are a technical professional.
- Put yourself in a position where you become recognized as a go-to person in a particular sector or discipline or with valuable, transferable skills.
- Keep building out your professional network on an ongoing basis.

Eventually, someone will take notice, or you reach the point where your skills and qualifications are too good for your targeted employer to pass up.

Success breeds success, particularly in the startup world. Companies want to hire proven performers. Investors want to invest in executives and teams with established track records. Position yourself over time as an asset to your company, not only in your day-to-day performance, but as a team member who enhances your employer's credibility with funders, customers, and the press. Once you do, you'll be in a great position to chart a path that leads you to your goals.

CHAPTER 6

Understanding the Offer

Getting an offer letter and deciding you want to work for a company is a bit of a chicken and egg process. Reaching the offer stage pre-supposes that you have sufficient interest to engage with and impress the company with your knowledge, talent, and enthusiasm. The company should meet many of the criteria contained in your career thesis. Once you reach the offer stage, the primary focus turns to the nuts and bolts. What is the company offering, and how attractive is it? Is it competitive with the market and with other options you may be considering?

You may have fallen in love with the company, its mission, the people you have met, and your prospective role. But all of that is irrelevant if the offer isn't right. Be analytical and detached. Don't let your excitement about the company cause you to jump too quickly without fully considering the ramifications and negotiating the best package for yourself.

Compensation

The irony of startup compensation is significant. Despite the high risk associated with working in an early-stage company and its uncertain **equity** value, many startups offer lower salaries than larger companies. According to the tech recruiting site startupsearch.com, an entry-level engineer can earn on average fifteen to thirty percent more in salary and bonus at a big tech company than at a startup.[10] At Fugue, we regularly found ourselves being outbid for employees by Amazon and Google by 20 to 30 percent on salary alone.

The lower salary in a startup is offset by higher incentive-based compensation in the form of stock options. The rationale provided to candidates is that they are getting in on the ground floor of a company with significant upside. With the potential for stock appreciation, startups argue cash compensation should be lower. But given the high percentage of startups that fail to reach successful exits, this upside can be a mirage.

Paying lower wages and granting equity is a backdoor way companies finance their operations. Lower cash compensation makes sense from the company's perspective. Especially in the early stages, the most precious commodity in a startup is cash. Anything the company can do to preserve cash has high value. So, startups ask employees to invest their time while forgoing market-level salaries, and in return, they receive a small amount of equity. In essence, by exchanging cash for equity, employees are investing in the company's stock.

Most startups are cash-constrained and can't always afford to pay market salaries. But even if they have adequate cash, the management team is responsible for carefully shepherding investor cash, especially if the company is still unprofitable. The most extreme example of this is the pre-funding startup. Unless the founders are self-financing the company, they might not be able to afford to pay cash compensation at all. In the beginning, many founders, early advisors, and contractors work for "sweat equity" (i.e., only stock, no cash).

---

[10] The differences in compensation between startups and big tech varies depending on the startup funding environment. When startup funding is abundant, startups may be in a better position to close the gap. "Startups vs. Big Tech: What Entry-Level Employees Are Really Paid.", startupsearch.com, https://startupsearch.com/early-startup-big-tech-entry-compensation#heading-1 (accessed April 18, 2023)

When I started my first company in 1992, I worked for nearly two years without taking a salary. More than thirty years later, when I joined Fugue in 2013 as an early employee, I did the same thing. The company had yet to raise its seed round and could not afford to pay me. The founder and I agreed to accrue my compensation until we closed the Series A round. Once the round closed, the company could have chosen to pay my accrued compensation but wanted to preserve funds to build the company. I agreed to take payment for my accrued salary in stock in the round. The catch was that not only didn't I get paid in cash, but when I received the shares, I owed taxes on their value. While I had the shares, working at Fugue part-time for the first year cost me about $25,000 out of pocket.

When you evaluate an offer, you need to consider its four compensation elements: salary; cash-based incentive compensation (i.e., bonus, profit sharing, or commission); equity-based compensation (such as stock options); and other non-cash benefits (such as health insurance, among others). Other parts of the offer letter that outline your job responsibilities and legal issues are also critical, but for now, let's focus on the elements of compensation.

Salary

For most people, the cash component of the offer, especially salary, should be primary.[11] When negotiating cash-based compensation,

---

[11] If you're joining as a senior executive, other elements of the offer may be just as important as salary, as the potential value of equity may be much higher than the cash compensation. An incoming CEO hired into a Series A or Series B startup will receive an equity grant of between five and eight percent of the ownership of the company. While the CEO's salary may exceed $250,000 per year, in the case of a successful exit, their equity payout may be in the millions or even tens of millions of dollars.

research market comparables. Glassdoor and Salary.com, among other sources, have a wealth of information about salaries for various positions and company sizes. LinkedIn Premium also provides salary data on specific jobs. Using these resources helps you gauge how your offer compares to the market. From there, assess how much you may be sacrificing to chase the elusive golden ring of that downstream equity payout.

If you are interviewing with multiple companies and are fielding more than one offer, you are in a better position to negotiate a package that gets you closer to what larger companies pay. Once there's competition for your services, the offers converge around market levels, and uncompetitive bidders fall out of the running.

Another aspect of salary you should explore is the company's policies on raises and promotions. A company may provide an attractive salary out of the gate. But if there is no regular process of performance reviews coupled with salary adjustments, you may fall behind the market a year or two into your job. Early-stage companies are notoriously bad at managing organizational processes like performance management. You would benefit from exploring the frequency of performance reviews and how salary increases work. You can even consider negotiating in a guaranteed raise after six months or a year, especially if you are taking a lower-than-market salary out of the gate.

Bonuses

The second component of compensation is cash-based incentive compensation. This takes the form of bonuses and profit-sharing for most employees. It can also include commissions for go-to-market professionals like salespeople, sales engineers, and sales management. Incentive compensation is a way to create added motivation that aligns the employee's goals with that of the company. Almost every company uses some form of bonus program, but how heavily compensation is weighted toward bonuses can vary widely.

Your offer letter might indicate the absolute amount of your target bonus or may express the bonus as a percentage of your salary. However, the offer letter will be short on details regarding how the bonus program works. Regardless of how big or small the bonus target is, it is a good idea to have a pointed conversation about exactly how the bonuses are calculated and when they are paid out. Don't leave that to chance, or you may be disappointed.

Bonus payouts are usually annual. Some companies pay quarterly and, in the case of sales commissions, even monthly. The payout amounts can either be formulaic (especially in the case of commissions) or fully discretionary at the whim of managers or the board. They may be based on your individual performance, company performance or profits, or a combination of the two.

Senior executives are tied more closely to overall company performance, while more junior staff receive bonuses closely aligned with their individual performance. With all this variability, it helps to dig into the details of the bonus program to understand how it works and your likelihood of receiving your bonus.

You should understand not only the structure of bonuses and commissions and the drivers of payout but also what the history of payout has been. Ask what percentage of target bonuses were paid in the prior year or the past few years. What is the expectation for payout in the current year? What determines whether bonuses get paid? Is the company on track to meet the goals that drive bonus achievement?

You can ask the human resources person or the hiring manager at the company, who may try to spin the program to reassure you that getting paid your bonus is a no-brainer. If you have a chance to ask your prospective peers, you may receive more meaningful answers and greater insight into what to expect.

Apart from using incentive compensation as a motivator, startups, especially companies paying below-market salaries, use incentive compensation to give the appearance of higher overall compensation. A greater percentage of the package tied to bonuses preserves a high level of total compensation (sometimes referred to as **on-target earnings** or **OTE**) while shifting more risk from the company to the employee. That comes in handy when the company does not meet its performance goals, or external pressures constrain cash flow.

When companies underperform relative to targets, bonuses are often paid at reduced rates or not at all. This is one of the dirty secrets of employee compensation. Management and the board consider bonuses discretionary, while employees consider them an intrinsic and expected part of their compensation. Even in a small startup, bonuses may add up to hundreds of thousands of dollars per year, so there is a strong incentive when times are tight not to pay them. Management may have some explaining to do, but by the time employees realize bonuses won't be paid, it will be too late as they will have worked the entire year.

When Fugue first established our compensation practices, we created programs with bonuses targeted at fifteen to twenty percent of salary. Doing this allowed the company to preserve cash by paying lower fixed salaries and tying variable compensation to high-level performance. One of the main justifications for this structure was the recognition that salaries tend to move up two to four percent each year. That exponential growth saddles a company with a rapidly increasing fixed salary base, especially after adding promotion-based raises. The company created a structural limit on fixed cost escalation over the longer term by keeping salaries lower and allocating more compensation to bonuses. We also deliberately improved our cash flow since bonuses were paid annually in arrears.

Most people received full bonuses for the first few years of the company. Over time, as the company started to miss critical milestones, full bonus payouts became rare, especially in the senior ranks. When the pandemic hit in 2020, we suspended bonuses, froze salaries, and eliminated promotion-related raises. The structural allocation of cash compensation to bonuses, coupled with salary freezes, allowed the company to reduce its compensation obligations by nearly $1 million overnight without having to take the politically explosive actions of laying off staff or asking people to take salary reductions.[12]

There's nothing wrong per se with accepting an offer with a significant incentive compensation component. The key is understanding what determines how that incentive-based compensation is paid and when. Gather as much information as possible to evaluate the offer with your eyes open. Forgoing a significant amount of guaranteed salary for incentive compensation is a tradeoff that could cost you. It may not be worth it relative to other job opportunities.

Recognize that the size and structure of the target bonus are often negotiable. Without changing the on-target earnings number, you should ask the employer to put more of your compensation into salary or guarantee most, if not all, of the bonus for the first year. If they want you badly enough, they can easily raise the salary and reduce the target bonus, lowering your risk.

In addition to incentive-based bonuses, you may also be able to negotiate some additional compensation and reimbursement payments. These include a signing bonus and a moving allowance. Bring these up in your negotiations if they are relevant to your situation.

Asking for a signing bonus may make sense if you are walking away from a bonus at your old company. A compensation package at your new company that is competitive going forward may not take into account lost incentive compensation from your old company.

---

[12] The company also took advantage of the federal Payroll Protection Program loan to supplement cash reserves and cover compensation.

This is often a timing issue. If your new employer needs you to start immediately, tell them that walking away from your old job will cost you, and you expect them to make that up to you. If they want you urgently, they should make you whole. Similarly, if your new job requires moving, the company should provide a moving allowance. This can be a set amount or an offer to reimburse your moving expenses.

Regardless of the special terms you negotiate with the employer, you should expect that the *quid pro quo* is that you agree to stay for a given period. If a company provides a signing bonus, they may expect you to commit to a year. If you leave the company voluntarily before the year ends, you are obligated to repay the company a proportionate part of the bonus you received. On the other hand, if the company decides to terminate you, they will likely waive the repayment, though that is not guaranteed.

Stock-Based Compensation

Stock-based (or equity-based) incentives are the most glamorous and fraught part of startup compensation. Owning company stock or options, with their upside potential, can be exhilarating, especially when things are going well. On the other hand, investors want to preserve as much ownership as possible for themselves. While cash is a precious commodity in startups, investors also try to limit equity issuance, doling out the minimum possible to attract and retain staff.

After Fugue closed its Series A round with nearly $4 million, our Founder/CEO told me that the board was concerned that I was being paid in equity and preferred to compensate me in cash. I thought I had been doing the company a favor by accepting stock instead of cash, yet that apparently ruffled feathers among the investors. Not unusual when equity is involved.

Company management and investors have orders of magnitude more information about the value of equity than the typical job applicant. Whenever there is asymmetrical access to information, the person with less information is disadvantaged. So when assessing the value of an equity-based grant, you need to take into account several factors:

- What percentage of the company does the grant represent?
- How will my ownership be affected through **dilution** (the reduction in your ownership percentage) over time?
- How big is the market opportunity for the company?
- How likely is the company to realize its potential opportunity?

Ownership Percentage

Start by considering the proposed amount of equity in your offer in terms of ownership. A common practice among startups is to throw out an equity grant expressed as a number of shares. This is a trick. To most employees, the notion of getting an option to purchase thousands of shares sounds impressive and attractive. Don't be fooled. What's important is not the number of shares but the percentage of ownership the shares represent. Knowing the number of shares you are being offered–the numerator–is meaningless without knowing how many shares are outstanding–the denominator.

When you receive an equity offer, your first question should always be what percentage of the company's **fully diluted** shares the offer represents. Fully diluted shares are the total number of shares that have been issued to shareholders and option holders and remain outstanding *plus* any shares in reserve for future equity issuances to employees, board members, and advisors. Knowing the fully diluted ownership percentage is vital. The company will continue to issue equity grants to future employees, and those grants will dilute your ownership percentage.

Once you understand the percentage ownership of your equity offer, you can do the same benchmarking exercise you did for the salary. Information about equity grants by position and stage of a startup is a little harder to come by than salary information. A combination of online research and reaching out to friends or others in your network should give you an idea of whether the proposed grant is fair and reasonable for the position you are assuming. If you have access to a human resources professional, they can also provide you with some benchmarking data through compensation databases they subscribe to.

Dilution Over Time

You should also attempt to gauge if the grant has the potential to yield meaningful returns to you. The equity component of an offer bears a significant risk of dilution and diminished value over time, especially if the company has to raise significant funding to keep growing.

If the initial grant is not a meaningful percentage of the company's ownership, it likely won't be worth much down the road. When the company completes numerous follow-on rounds of financing and issues incentive stock grants to dozens or maybe hundreds of future employees, your ownership percentage will be significantly reduced.

Company's Market Opportunity

Even if your ownership stake is meaningful and you don't get significantly diluted, the only way to realize a significant payout is through a liquidity event, such as a successful sale or IPO. Those rare events can lead to life-changing wealth creation for dozens or hundreds of a company's employees.

For your company to realize such a positive outcome, it must play in a sizable market. Companies operating in limited-size markets will not achieve the scale to go public and will have a harder time attracting buyers who see enough possibilities for large-scale growth to pay an attractive acquisition price.

Company Positioning

None of the above matters if your company is not positioned to build a leadership stake in its market. Stock in a company that doesn't succeed is worth nothing. You need to view the opportunity to gain equity from your work as any investor would, evaluating the company's competitive strengths and weaknesses, technology, management team, and competition. If the company is not positioned to win, neither are you.

An equity grant in a startup is a lottery ticket. Having one is exciting as long as the company stays in business. There's certainly a possibility that it pays off, and sometimes pays off big. But like any lottery ticket, the odds of winning are low. If the lottery game you are playing doesn't have a big pot for the company and investors, there is no way for you to win big.

If you choose to work for a company that isn't going after a significant market space or staking out a leadership position, even if all goes right, the ultimate value of your equity will be modest or even zero. With that in mind, the cash offer is where you will likely make most of your money. Any value derived from your equity is gravy. Don't assume the equity will compensate you for a subpar cash package.

One more word of caution. If a company is not in a position to be competitive on cash, consider if it has the resources to compete in the market and become a market leader, assuming it can even survive long enough to get there. When VCs fund a company, they expect a significant portion of their invested capital to go toward building the team. To do so, the company needs to pay competitively. An uncompetitive offer should sound alarm bells. You don't want to board a rickety dinghy and be underpaid while being taken for a ride to the bottom of the sea.

Benefits

Benefits are a significant part of what you get from a company and can impact your quality of life and well-being. If you expect a startup to provide market-leading benefits, you will likely be disappointed.

Most startups are sensitive to cash expenditures, and after salaries, benefits are one of the largest line items on a startup's profit and loss statement. Even though startups may perceive they are investing significantly in benefits, their offerings pale compared to larger companies. It's just a function of scale and negotiating leverage with the vendors that provide those offerings.

Healthcare and Retirement Plans

Most programs like health insurance or retirement plan offerings benefit from the scale of a larger employee base over which to spread risk or amortize plan administration expenses. Larger employers can negotiate lower rates or self-insure (reducing administrative costs) and provide a wide variety of generous benefits offerings. Many benefits larger employers offer are voluntary and have relatively low utilization rates. However, they can be valuable and should be factored into your employment calculus when considering the value of working for a small versus large employer.

A startup must offer basic benefits if it wants to be competitive. At a bare minimum, a reasonable major medical healthcare plan must be available, or most credible candidates won't join. It is worth asking for plan summaries[13] for the company's benefits before signing your offer letter. Examine the plan coverages and what proportion of the premium the employee is expected to cover. Your employee contribution to healthcare premiums, co-pays and deductibles can cost several thousand dollars per year out of pocket, so it's worth digging into the details.

Whether a company's offering is competitive gets murkier when it comes to additional benefits such as dental, vision, and disability

---

[13] A plan summary is a document issued by an insurance company or a retirement plan provider that details the specifics of the plan's offerings. It is usually a dense document, but worth reviewing.

plans. The value of these plans can be significant, but the coverage offered by startups varies widely. Some startups offer none of these additional coverages or may opt for less expensive coverage that limits choice and shifts significant cost burden to the employee. If you don't review the plan details, you won't know if you are able to go to your providers of choice or if you may end up saddled with high out-of-pocket expenses from cut-rate insurance plans.

Most startups after the seed stage should offer a basic 401(k) plan. A basic 401(k) plan is standard, but ask if the company offers a Roth 401(k), which can provide considerable tax advantages for earners in low tax brackets in the long run. See if the company offers a 401(k) match—usually 3 to 6 percent of your salary—and what the requirements are to get the match. Most startups can't afford to provide a company match or choose not to as they don't view it as a high-value way of spending investor money. But if they do, that benefit is worth taking advantage of.

Benefits are complicated, and most people hate digging into the tedious details. Failing to do so can be costly. While the value of different benefits across companies can be hard to compare, you should be able to tell whether the employer's benefits package is generous or basic. The main question is how much money the benefits the company offers put *in* your pocket or take *out* of your pocket.

Paid Time-Off (PTO)

Although startup life can be intense, one of the clear advantages a startup may have over larger companies is flexibility with paid time off (PTO). The days of two-week use-it-or-lose-it vacations are in the past for many early-stage companies. It is common for startups to offer unlimited PTO, which can be beneficial if you take advantage of it and don't abuse it.

Understanding the culture of paid time off at your prospective employer is essential. Especially when the company has a policy of unlimited PTO, you might find internal resistance when you want to take a vacation. With limited resources and too much to accomplish, some startups exert subtle or not-so-subtle pressure on employees who wish to take time off. Managers can view PTO requests as impositions, leading to uncomfortable, guilt-inducing responses. It's worth asking in the interview process how the company views employee paid leave.

Unlimited PTO was our policy at Fugue. First, we wanted to treat our staff as adults and trust them to do their jobs while recognizing that they had lives outside of the office. We cared about results, not time-clock punching. Second, as CFO, I understood that not tracking vacations would simplify our accounting.[14]

In practice, offering unlimited PTO resulted in staff taking less vacation than with use-it-or-lose-it policies. This may seem like a cynical approach to getting workers to work more. That was not the intention. After tracking the under-utilization of vacation for several quarters, we instituted "Fugue Fridays," closing the office one Friday each month to ensure employees unplugged. The policy proved so successful we kept it for several years until the sale of the company.

Similarly, you should explore the company's policies and practices around sick and maternity/paternity leave. This is not only a matter of the culture and philosophy of the company but also relates to

---

[14] Companies that track vacation hours must accrue earned hours each pay period and track the balance against PTO used. That is a burden on the finance team. For small companies trying to do more with less, unnecessary tasks that can be eliminated should be. By not accruing vacation hours, when employees leave the company, there are also no accrued vacation days that have to be paid out in cash, which cash-constrained startups find attractive.

whether the company maintains disability policies that cover a portion of your salary if you need to take extended leave. Many companies provide two weeks of paid leave and then offer unpaid leave afterward. A good disability policy goes a long way toward covering the earnings lost during extended leave.

Some other benefits, such as life insurance, wellness programs or legal plans, are usually only offered by larger employers but can substantially impact the value of your employment package. Most people don't focus on the totality of benefits offerings when considering competing offers. Don't ignore what may appear to be peripheral offerings. When you add them all up, they can be quite valuable.

Finally, if you are working remotely, your company may offer you reimbursement for certain expenses such as home internet, cell phone, and computer equipment. Ask about those policies during your negotiations and get a commitment on what costs they will cover.

Other Employment Terms

Apart from the compensation elements, offer letters are filled with legal language and references to which you should pay attention. Your offer letter represents the main legal agreement between you and your company unless you are a senior executive, in which case you may also have an employment agreement laying out the terms of your relationship.

For the moment, let's focus on the offer letter. Apart from the compensation details, there are a few key components to the offer.

Term of employment

The term of employment is the indication of how long the employer agrees to keep you employed. The most common and standard term in startups is **at-will employment**.[15] This means the company can terminate your employment anytime or for any reason without explanation. While some states may have varying regulations regarding at-will employment, in most cases, you serve at the pleasure of management and may find yourself out of a job at any time.

Working at a startup is the Wild West. There are few established rules, and every company has its own culture and codes. Decisions can be whimsical or impulsive, driven by the personality of the CEO or pressure from the board. So you have no guarantee of long-term employment or, frankly, any length of employment and no union to join to represent your interests.

You may feel like part of the family when you join the company. But you can be written out of the will at any time, especially if things go south for the business. Given this risk, you must try to discern how well-funded the company is and how much runway they have to keep operating. Your livelihood may depend on it.

In rare instances, for senior executives, a company may enter into an employment agreement with a committed time frame. In the absence of an employment agreement, companies address the risk of **termination** through **severance** agreements that compensate employees for a fixed period if they are terminated under certain circumstances.

Hours and Location

The job description for the position may specify whether the position is remote, in-office, or hybrid and if it requires travel. Employers are adopting different policies concerning where their employees work in the post-pandemic world. Given the difficulty many employers have attracting talent, especially tech talent, they

---

[15] At-will employment is not unique to startups. It is also a standard term of employment for large companies.

are reaching far afield geographically to find suitable hires. All of this creates the possibility for confusion and misunderstanding.

Establish an explicit agreement with your prospective employer regarding their expectations of where you work, particularly if you will work mostly remotely. If you are in a different time zone, you should also discuss expectations around work hours.

It may seem like overkill to put all these details into your offer letter. However, corporate policies may change over time. Or you may not always be working for the same manager who hired you. If you don't feel comfortable shoehorning these details into the letter, at the very least, you should document the expectations in an email. Confirm the terms of the offer and the expectations and retain that information in your records. That documentation will prove that you are fulfilling the agreed-upon terms and helps avoid misunderstandings.

Background Checks

Most companies reserve the right to conduct a background check on you. They will likely check your employment references and history but may go further. This is especially true if they are in a sensitive sector like healthcare or cybersecurity, where misuse of customer data can have significant repercussions.

Fugue was a cybersecurity company with products designed to protect sensitive technology. The clean backgrounds of our staff members were critical to actually maintaining security but also the perception of security. Many of our customers required us to conduct and keep background checks up-to-date while they reserved the right to audit our records to ensure compliance.

Hopefully, you don't have anything to worry about. If something may raise a red flag, consider bringing it up once you receive the offer. Many employers are willing to live with blemishes in an employee's past if they perceive the person to be a valuable hire. However, failing to disclose an issue that is later discovered undermines the employer's trust in you and sours the relationship. Your offer may be rescinded, and if something negative is discovered after you start, your employment may be terminated.

Identity verification

Employers are required by statute to verify the identity and employment eligibility of all staff that they hire. This ensures the company is not hiring undocumented or ineligible workers. Again, like the background check, usually nothing to worry about unless you are applying for a job under a false identity!

Non-disclosure Agreement and Proprietary Information and Innovations Agreement (PIIA)

If you are going to a startup, particularly a tech startup, you will undoubtedly be subject to confidentiality requirements. The offer letter may refer to a separate **non-disclosure agreement (NDA)**. Or the confidentiality and non-disclosure restrictions you are subject to may be incorporated into a broader document called a **Proprietary Information and Inventions Agreement (PIIA)** or something similar.

Apart from the non-disclosure provisions, the PIIA has provisions related to non-competition[16], non-solicitation of employees, and how you are restricted in using the company's **intellectual**

---

[16] Non-compete clauses across the US have been under scrutiny and may be watered down or eliminated. It is worth understanding how non-compete clauses are viewed or enforced where your prospective employer is located and where you plan to work.

property. The agreement also preserves the company's right to any intellectual property you develop while working there. You should be aware that these documents contain provisions that restrict your behavior and communications during and after your employment with the company.

Carefully review any documents you receive such as an NDA or PIIA. Most of us have become so used to just clicking through terms and conditions that we make the incorrect and sometimes dangerous assumption that there's nothing in those terms that can harm us. Even C-suite executives abhor reading legal documents and often avoid doing so. Not putting in the work and reviewing these agreements is a mistake. Violations of any of the provisions of those agreements may be grounds for disciplinary action up to and including termination or lawsuits after you leave the company.

If you are a technologist, signing a PIIA requires you to assign rights to the company for any intellectual property you develop or work on while employed. Your innovations are considered work for hire, and whatever you create or invent belongs to the company. Many companies add individual technology inventors to patent applications as an incentive and sign of recognition and may even pay invention bonuses. It's great recognition for your contribution, but don't be fooled. Even if your name is on a patent, you don't own it. If you developed it while working for the company, it belongs to the company.

The PIIA specifies that you agree to assign all rights to intellectual property to the company. Even if you don't, the company can use the PIIA to prove that you were under obligation to do so and prevent its IP from being clouded by subsequent employee claims. This right is critical to companies when investors or acquirers complete their due diligence to know that the company actually owns what it is trying to sell.

Finally, if you happen to own any intellectual property or have prior patents in your name, it is particularly important to pay attention to the exceptions and disclosures sections of the PIIA.

There should be a schedule where you can list previous patents and open-source projects you have created or collaborated on. Disclose everything that you can legitimately claim ownership over. If you don't, you run the risk that the company could later claim your work as its own, particularly if you use any of it while developing intellectual property for the company. This scenario may seem far-fetched, but better safe than sorry.

The founder of Fugue developed the idea for the company's technology before going to work for a major technology company known for being particularly aggressive regarding intellectual property. He and his co-founders filed provisional patents before he started working at the larger company and disclosed the patent filings before beginning work. Securing their intellectual property ownership was crucial when the founder left his employer to start Fugue. It turned out to be a core part of the due diligence conducted by our VCs to ensure the company owned its intellectual property outright.

Severance

Severance is the continuation of compensation in some form after an employee is terminated. While at-will employment is the standard term, most companies provide some severance for terminated employees. For the average employee, this is usually two to four weeks, depending on their length of service.

Pre-negotiated severance is a form of pre-nuptial agreement between you and the company and is not usually included as a term in the offer letter. It's an awkward topic to bring up. You and the company are in the throes of falling in love, and then you throw a bucket of cold water on the discussion by bringing up what happens if you get divorced.

Unless you are a senior executive, bringing up severance in the offer discussions is probably unproductive. As you rise through the ranks, you may reach the point where negotiating severance in advance makes sense. Companies wooing senior executives agree to severance arrangements to entice them to join. Severance mitigates the risk to the employee of walking away from their current employer, joining a new company, and then suddenly finding themselves out of a job for reasons out of their control.

For executives, severance is negotiable and usually provides from three to twelve months of salary continuation in the event of termination. Severance is paid when the executive is terminated **without cause**. **Termination for cause** (or **with cause**) means that the employee exhibited behavior that violates corporate policies or was illegal, they were grossly negligent in their duties, or they otherwise failed in a material way to fulfill their responsibilities or secure the interest of the company.

Suppose your offer letter includes a reference to a severance package. In that case, it specifies that the payment is contingent on your signing an agreement (typically a Separation and Release Agreement) acceptable to the company. Anytime a company offers severance, it is with the requirement that the employee releases the company from any liability related to their time of employment and the termination. This precludes the employee from filing a wrongful termination lawsuit or complaint with the government. It also ensures that the employee returns all company property, and that the employee does not disparage the company or its officers or directors.[17]

---

[17] If your offer happens to include a severance clause, ask for a copy of the Company's standard severance agreement, and try to pre-negotiate the language in the agreement at the time of the offer. If you wait until you are terminated, you will lose a lot of your leverage in negotiating the agreement. You really don't want to negotiate those terms when you are already at odds with the company.

There are two other considerations when thinking about severance: bonus payout and continuation of benefits.

<u>Bonus payout.</u> You might be terminated before bonuses are paid. Negotiate a *pro-rata* bonus payment as of the time of your departure. For example, bonuses are paid based on annual performance. If you are terminated after nine months and had negotiated the *pro-rata* bonus clause in advance, you might receive your bonus for the period you remained with the company. If the employer is unwilling to agree on this issue (maybe because future bonus payout levels are uncertain), this is an argument for extending salary continuation for an additional period.

<u>Continuation of benefits.</u> As part of the severance agreement, negotiate a paid continuation of benefits. It is one thing to have salary continuation, but for the average employee, especially one with a family, losing benefits can be scary and expensive, especially if you have any health issues in the family. If your company has at least twenty employees, you have access to benefits continuation through COBRA for at least 18 months[18], but you must pay the premiums out of pocket. It is reasonable to ask an employer to continue your benefits for at least the term of your severance to allow you to seek new employment without losing health insurance coverage.

Even if you don't have a severance agreement, you may have an opportunity to negotiate a severance package when you are terminated. Companies are sensitive about liability related to employment actions. A valuable bargaining chip is agreeing to sign a release waiving any claims against the company. This is particularly true of so-called protected class employees, which includes workers over forty, women, people of color, and employees with disabilities.

---

[18] U.S. Department of Labor, dol.gov, https://www.dol.gov/general/topic/health-plans/cobra (accessed July 8, 2023).

The Bottom Line

Accepting an offer to work for a new employer is a big step. Most people focus mainly on the salary and equity components of the offer, which is understandable. Those are the most salient and tangible parts of the package. The finer points of the offer can also be quite valuable and important, so don't overlook them.

There is a lot to consider, and some documents you encounter– NDA, PIIA, separation agreement, and even the offer letter –may be quite technical and complicated. Senior executives may hire an attorney to review the documents while drawing on their significant career experience to ensure they understand them and have negotiated the best terms possible.

Without qualified advice, you may have difficulty understanding the specifics of what you are signing up for. On the other hand, hiring a qualified employment attorney to review your documents could cost several thousand dollars or more, especially if you have them advise you on the negotiation.

The challenge for non-executive hires is that even if you are willing to spend the money on an attorney, you need time to engage one. An employer who makes an offer wants an answer quickly, usually within a week. There's pressure to say yes. Many employers resist giving an offer unless they are virtually certain of getting a positive response. Getting to a preliminary yes seldom allows you to fully tease out all the information about the terms of your employment discussed here. There just might not be enough time to consult with an attorney.

Beyond the offer, there is the bigger picture to consider–whether you will gain the experience you are looking for and whether the company is likely to be successful. Considering a new position is an emotional process. It is easy to get caught up in the moment and gloss over essential issues. Take a step back and follow a systematic approach. Go through all the documents closely and make a note of anything that you do not understand. Run concerns by a mentor or trusted friend. Document any questions or concerns and ask the company to explain before signing the offer letter.

Just like a VC evaluating a startup, you can choose to pass for whatever reason. Even if the employer gives you everything you are asking for. Even if the job seems like a good fit and the compensation and other elements are attractive, you can pass. Determine if the risk of going to work there is acceptable. If you're not sure, you are under no obligation to accept. Keep looking. It's a big world out there, with many possibilities.

If you decide the company is a great fit, has a strong chance of succeeding, and meets your criteria, negotiate the best offer possible. It's helpful to work from a checklist of terms to guide your discussions, such as the one in Exhibit 6-1. As you get more senior in your career, some of the items you might not be able to negotiate today may become possible. It is helpful to keep them in your back pocket for the future.[19]

To fully understand the economics of an offer you receive from a startup, put in the work. Do your research to understand the market rate on salary and total compensation. Evaluate whether the equity grant you receive has value, considering the percentage of ownership, the size of the company's opportunity, and its likelihood of winning in the market. Consider how much money the company has raised, its runway, and if it is likely to sell for a high enough price to pay out investors and have enough left over to reward common shareholders, including employees.

Put a sharp pencil to the value of the benefits. Consider whether any of the terms of employment are items you can't live with. Then put it all together and decide based on the totality of the package.

---

[19] Some of the items on the checklist will be explained in later chapters. Return to this checklist and review it after completing the book and use it each time you are entering into offer discussions.

	Yes	No
Salary and Position		
Competitive salary	☐	☐
Appropriate title and responsibility	☐	☐
Clear path to salary increases	☐	☐
Clear path to promotions over time	☐	☐
Bonuses		
Presence of bonus	☐	☐
Clarity on bonus determination and structure	☐	☐
Clarity on bonus pay-out	☐	☐
Clear documentation of bonus structure	☐	☐
First-year guaranteed full or partial bonus payout	☐	☐
Bonus opportunities for overperformance	☐	☐
Signing bonus	☐	☐
Commission Structure		
Sales commission	☐	☐
Recruitment commission	☐	☐
Allowances		
Moving allowance	☐	☐
Home office set-up	☐	☐
Equity Offer		
Competitive offer consisting of stock or restricted stock units	☐	☐
Reasonable vesting schedule	☐	☐
Early exercise provision	☐	☐
Extended period to exercise options past 90 days	☐	☐
Accelerated vesting on change of control of the company:		
Full or partial acceleration	☐	☐
single-trigger (no termination required)	☐	☐
double-trigger (change of control + termination with set period)	☐	☐
Benefits		
Full medical coverage	☐	☐
Dental coverage	☐	☐
Vision coverage	☐	☐
Disability	☐	☐
Retirement plan participation including company match	☐	☐
Paid time off:		
Holidays	☐	☐
Vacation	☐	☐
Sick leave	☐	☐
Maternity/Paternity leave	☐	☐
Severance		
Salary continuation	☐	☐
Accrued bonus payout (full or partial)	☐	☐
Benefits continuation period (COBRA)	☐	☐

Exhibit 6-1: Job Offer Checklist

---------- CHAPTER 7 ----------

Look the Horse in the Mouth

Very few things in life come without a cost, even if they seem like a gift. You may be excited about the offer you received to join that hot startup, but how do you know what you are getting yourself into? In the startup world, examining a company's potential and pitfalls is called **due diligence**. While investors do it for every deal, prospective employees rarely do.

On and off for years, I have attended events organized by a group called CONNECTPreneur, one of the world's largest communities of entrepreneurs and funders. At each event, between ten and twelve startups pitch their stories to hundreds of angel and venture investors. There is electricity in these events as the entrepreneurs lay out their visions to solve some of the world's most complex challenges.

I am inclined to see the glass as half full. I get excited about new business ideas and want to see the possibilities, not the obstacles. When I hear the visions shared by enthusiastic company founders, my initial gut reaction is usually positive. Then logic kicks in. I remind myself that, at best, ten to twenty percent of companies receive the outside funding they need. And maybe twenty to thirty percent of those that receive funding achieve meaningful success. Those are small odds.

The risk you take on is directly related to how early you join a startup. There is greater potential upside to joining an early-stage venture, but young startups have many more obstacles to overcome before achieving success. Determining the longevity and future success of a business is an inexact science. Even with perfect knowledge of the current market, many unknowns affect the outcome. Sometimes the best you can do is determine if a company has the resources to survive long enough to reach its next funding round and eventually figure out a market opportunity that leads to a successful exit.

Ignorance Is Not Bliss

Part of the challenge of engaging with a startup is the lack of information. As an investor, I have learned that what you don't know can hurt you. Even some of the savviest executives I know have gone into senior-level positions in startups only to find many buried bodies no one told them about when they were interviewing. There is a reason they are called private companies.

Publicly traded companies must file quarterly and annual reports and are subject to disclosure requirements by the Securities and Exchange Commission. Institutional mechanisms and regulations require that a wealth of information is publicly reported. However, even with public companies, it is nearly impossible for the average person to know everything important before investing.

Startups are far less transparent than their public company counterparts. They don't have investor relations professionals responsible for producing information for third parties. Even if they did, they probably wouldn't share sensitive information. Most startups are underfunded, resource-constrained, and burn copious amounts of cash. Even in the best cases, well-funded startups may have just enough money to last a couple of years after their last financing round. There is little value for a private company to disclose information about its operations, especially its financial condition, that could make prospective investors, employees, or customers uncomfortable about its stability.

Outsiders often judge a startup's success by the amount of capital it has raised, as that is one piece of data available in the public sphere through the press or sources such as *Crunchbase* or *Pitchbook*. For this reason, most startups make a big deal out of announcing their funding rounds. Being able to point to big-name funders and the influx of cash provides credibility they can trade on for recruiting, customer acquisition, and, ultimately, follow-on funding. But raising significant capital does not equate to a successful business. The funding is just the means to the end. It can take years for a startup to reach positive cash flow, if it ever does.

A company may not have impressive metrics on the customer or revenue side even if it has raised substantial capital. Remember, venture capitalists bet on the future success of their portfolio, so they recognize the companies they fund may continue to burn cash for months or years after they invest. However, prospective customers might be reluctant to do business with a company with a high burn rate. They may fear the company will go out of business and their products or services could vanish. To prevent fueling these concerns, startup executives do everything possible to avoid disclosing just how little market traction they have achieved.

You Are the Buyer, Not Just the Seller

When a company courts investors, customers, or employees, it wants to put its best foot forward. But the dynamics of how companies interact with these three groups differ. Investors and customers are not obligated to do business with a given company. They have plenty of choices about where to deploy their capital or spend their money, which puts them in the driver's seat. The Golden Rule of venture capital states "Those who have the gold rule."

Investors and prospective customers can force a company to be transparent about the state of its business. Before writing a check, they subject the company's claims to intense scrutiny in the form of due diligence. Any claims that can't be backed up by concrete information could be enough to kill the deal.

Due diligence by customers and investors can involve hundreds of questions and take weeks or even months to complete. Though the process is arduous, if the company wants the funding or sale, it has no choice but to play ball. The company also runs the risk that if it withholds material information, it could face potential lawsuits for misrepresentation or fraud.

For job applicants, the shoe is on the other foot. There are likely dozens, if not hundreds, of applicants for any given position. You probably won't have much leverage to demand information. By the time you have worked through several rounds of interviews and managed to get an offer, the process dynamics are stacked against your ability to do comprehensive due diligence.

Once an offer has been made, that moment of mutual excitement between you and your new prospective bosses has a short half-life. Your primary focus needs to be understanding and considering the offer in light of your current position and other opportunities. If you choose to negotiate for a better offer, you immediately place yourself in an adversarial position with your prospective new employer.

Imagine the reaction if, after you receive and negotiate an offer, you hand the company a list of 125 questions they need to answer before you accept. Looking out for yourself without alienating the people you will be working with is a delicate dance. After all, they control your job satisfaction, integration into your new company, and future progression and compensation.

The obstacles to getting the information you need to make an informed decision are formidable. Private companies don't disclose much willingly. The power is not in your hands, and time is not on your side. Employers may resist answering questions unless pressed, which most people are not inclined to do. Where does that leave you?

When interviewing for a new position, we are in sell mode. We are trying to impress our prospective employer. But the employer/employee relationship is more complicated than the idea that an employer is purchasing an employee's services. Hard as it is, resist the urge to see yourself only as the seller. You are also choosing to "buy" the opportunity for professional advancement and financial opportunity that the company is selling.

When selling the company on hiring you, can you also put on the buyer's hat and evaluate the company? Anyone considering working for a startup (or any company for that matter) should be skeptical. In fact, given the odds of startup failure, a healthy dose of paranoia is warranted.

Venture capitalists have teams of analysts, industry veterans, and advisors to rely on when making investment decisions. And even then, they get it wrong most of the time. It's conventional wisdom in venture capital investing that 20 to 30 percent of their investments will generate outsized returns that make the funds successful. VCs know that most startups they fund fail or at least fail to deliver meaningful returns. They are counting on the winners to far more than compensate for the losers.

The difference between you and a VC is that your portfolio of companies consists of only one investment. When you choose to work for a company, you make a venture capital bet with your time. Every day you get up and go to work for that company, you are making an investment and hopefully earning a return and positioning yourself for additional future returns. You can't rely on other companies to bail you out if your one portfolio company, your employer, fails. It's an all-or-nothing gamble.

With that in mind, you should assess the company the way an investor would by probing the key elements that determine a startup's likelihood of success. As with evaluating the offer itself, evaluating the factors contributing to a company's success or failure requires effort. The sources of information to assess a company should include interviews with members of the company and independent research so you can formulate an unbiased view. Remember, once a company decides they want to hire you, they should be selling you on joining. Your job is to determine if you should buy.

As you go through the process, you may interview with one or more C-suite executives, including the CEO/founder and possibly the CFO. At the end of those interviews, they may ask, "Do you have any questions?" Target your questions to the right people in the organization, and you may be surprised by how much you can learn and how impressed they are with your preparation. Asking the same questions of multiple interviewers may also provide insight into organizational challenges or divisions, especially if the answers are not consistent.

It is disappointing that in many cases when I have interviewed potential hires, they have few substantive questions. Failing to ask intelligent questions when you have the chance is a squandered opportunity to learn about and impress the company. When candidates came prepared with substantive questions, I knew they were serious and not just going through the motions of interviewing. The best questions usually came from those with significant work experience who had seen how companies can get derailed, and employees fail to be fully rewarded.

I always appreciated being challenged and engaging in deep conversations about the merits of our business, technology, or market approach. Once someone had done their homework and was satisfied with the answers, they would often become even more impressed with the company and committed to its mission and success.

Though you may need more time or resources to conduct full due diligence the way a VC would, try your best to probe the company's health, sustainability, and potential for success. Use the proof continuum from Chapter 3 (Prove It!) as a framework to gauge how far along the company is and focus on the following topics:

- The company's vision and product offerings
- The market opportunity

- The competition and competitive dynamics
- The company's go-to-market strategy
- The founders, company management, and management practices
- The company's **capitalization**, liquidity, and financial performance

Some of the information you are asking for is sensitive and confidential, so you should offer to sign a nondisclosure agreement (NDA). With an NDA in place, you can ask for documents such as the company's investor pitch deck, analyst reports on its market positioning, financial statements, and **capitalization table** listing the ownership. Even with an NDA in place, a company may be reluctant to provide all the answers or documents, so you'll have to decide if you can live with imperfect information.

The Employee's Due Diligence Checklist

Once you have the green light to fire your questions at the company, you need to develop a specific set of questions. While every company is unique in its vision, market positioning, and resources, you want to dive into detail on the topics outlined above. Use this checklist of questions as a starting point and customize it to develop your lines of inquiry.

Questions about the company's vision and product

- What significant problem is the company out to solve?
- Why hasn't this problem already been solved?
- How is the company's approach different from approaches tried in the market previously?
- What products or services does the company offer or plan to offer?

- Where is the company situated on the Proof Continuum (you may need to explain this)?
- How long will it take for the company to have an alpha, beta, or generally available (GA) product in the market?

Questions about the market opportunity

- What is the size of the market the company is going after?
- Is it local, national, or global?
- How fast is it expected to grow?
- What is the total addressable market in dollars and potential customers?
- Who is the buyer for the product or services? Companies? Consumers? Government agencies? Other?
- Does the company provide a sector-specific solution or a horizontal solution that can benefit many industries and buyers?
- Is the company a niche player, or does the technology have the ability to span a wide number of markets or applications?
- Does the company's product offer a broad solution or a point solution that must be combined with products or services from other vendors?
- How does that affect the customer's willingness to buy the product?

Questions about the competitive environment

- Who are its main competitors?
- Are they large or small companies? Public or private?
- How much funding do they have relative to the company, and how can the company compete with that?

- How does the company differentiate its products or services from the competition?
- Does the company have any datasheets it can provide comparing its offerings to competitors' offerings?
- What proportion of the time is the company competing with other vendors when engaging with prospects?
- How often is the company trying to unseat incumbent vendors versus selling to companies seeking a solution for the first time?
- Does the company have any patents pending or granted that would protect its market position?
- Does the company have any third-party, independent validation (such as from Gartner, G2, or other analysts) that you can provide?

Questions about go-to-market strategy

- What is the average price or contract size per customer?
- How does the company reach its customers? Direct sales? Channel sales? Direct Marketing?
- What is the typical sales cycle for landing a customer?
- What is the company's churn rate on customers?
- Are there "**land and expand**" opportunities with existing customers?
- What is the company's **net revenue retention (NRR) rate on customer revenue,** also referred to as **net dollar retention (NDR)**?
- What does the company's go-to-market organization look like? Marketing? Sales team? Customer success?
- How does the company approach product management? Is it technology-led or customer-led?

- What process does it use to capture customer feedback and incorporate it into product development?
- What is the customer journey from initial lead generation through renewal and expansion?

Questions about the founder, the management team, and management practices

- Review the company's Team page on their website and scour LinkedIn to learn about the backgrounds of the management, board, and key employees. Use your primary and secondary contacts, if possible, to make discreet inquiries.
- Can you tell me about the founder(s) and what drove them to start the company?
- Who else is on the management team? What are their backgrounds? What is their track record in building companies?
- How is the company managed? Top-down from the CEO? What is the degree of collaboration across departments? How are short and long-term planning done?
- What is the company's mission statement? What are the company's values? How does management reinforce and uphold them?
- How often does management meet to set company goals? To assess progress against goals? Is progress against goals regularly and fully shared with the whole company?
- How active is the company's board of directors in day-to-day management of the company?

Questions about liquidity and financial performance

- What is the company's revenue or annual recurring revenue (ARR)? How has that grown over the past three years?

- What growth is the company projecting over the next two to three years?
- How much money has the company raised since inception?
- When was the last round of financing completed? How much was raised?
- Who were the investors, including the lead investor?
- What was the valuation of the last round of financing? Previous rounds?
- How long is the company's funding expected to last given your burn and growth plans?
- What are the plans for raising the next round of financing?
- What does the company need to accomplish to get that round done?
- What is the company's most likely exit? Acquisition? IPO? When is that exit likely to occur?
- Has the company had interest from potential acquirers?
- Is the company currently profitable or cash flow positive? If not, when do you expect to achieve cash flow breakeven and profitability?
- How much money must the company raise to get there?

The Employee's Due Diligence Checklist is not an exhaustive list by any means. Many more questions may arise in your conversations. Getting answers to those questions takes you a long way toward developing critical insights into how attractive the opportunity you are evaluating is.

The Bottom Line

You can never know everything there is to know about a company you are considering joining. You seek sufficient evidence that the company is on a successful path. You want to understand where the company is today, where it is trying to go, and what resources, human and capital, it currently has and will need in the future to fuel its journey.

There is a cadence to how fast venture-backed startups move through the proof continuum. Some companies move at lightning speed. Some spend years without making material progress. The laggards burn through cash while they cast about looking for product-market fit and additional funding, hoping the clock doesn't run out. For companies you are engaging with, it's important to figure out which end of the spectrum they fall on.

The earlier you join a company in its journey, the greater the potential rewards may appear—a sense of getting in on the ground floor of something promising. With that potential also comes much more risk across many dimensions. The due diligence process discussed in this chapter will help you assess if the company has the right stuff to succeed. Knowing where the company is on its journey tells you how much risk remains before it reaches the promised land of a successful exit and can help you decide if you are comfortable taking on that risk yourself.

PART III

HOW STOCK
AND OPTIONS WORK

CHAPTER 8

Taking Stock

Cash may be king in employee compensation, but the allure of joining a startup often rests in owning equity that could rise significantly in value. The success stories in startup careers rarely involve a company building a highly profitable business that throws off a lot of cash in the form of dividends. That's more how real estate investors get rich. Startup employees realize equity value when a sale or a public offering converts their options and stock holdings to cash.

Growing a startup's value (as reflected by its share price) is the underlying focus of the management team, the board, and the investors. The means to that end is creating great products that meet market needs. With luck, timing, and persistence, the employees benefit from the rise in the company's value. However, the major owners of the enterprise (i.e., investors and to a lesser extent senior management) reap the greatest rewards when the company succeeds.

Life is good as long as the incentives of the shareholders and the staff are aligned. As the company grows and its value rises, everyone wins. But specific characteristics of equity ownership in startups can drive a wedge between investors and management and even between management and employees. This occurs because of the different classes of shares within a company's ownership structure. These classes of shares have varying economic, voting, and governance rights that drive how important decisions are made. The shareholders' incentives are also driven by whether the company has taken on debt or other obligations.

Gaining familiarity with the different types of securities in a startup and their characteristics illuminates where various stakeholders' interests lie and their biases in decision-making. This is crucial to assessing the potential value of your equity and your likelihood of realizing that value over time.

The terminology around ownership varies depending on the type of corporate form used to establish a business. The main types of entities available are corporations, partnerships, limited partnerships, and limited liability companies (LLCs). Corporations have shareholders who own shares. Partnerships have partners who own partnership interests. LLCs have members who hold membership interests.

The purpose of these entities is to insulate the shareholders, partners, and members from personal liability from creditors, but each has unique characteristics and is used for different purposes. There is a wealth of information available about the pros and cons of each type of corporate organization, so I will not elaborate on that topic here.

Most venture-backed startups are organized in a corporate form called a C Corporation (C Corp), the corporate form of most publicly traded companies. Switching an entity's corporate form is a complex and messy administrative process, so any startup aspiring to go public or to be acquired by a public company starts out as a C Corp or, early on, becomes a C Corp before raising too much outside capital. As a rule, most venture capital investors only fund C corporations. For these reasons, I will concentrate the discussion on C corporations, their classes of stock, and their various sources of capitalization and ownership.

The Waterfall

When considering the potential payout from your stock grants, it helps to have a protocol laying out the priorities of claims on proceeds from a transaction, otherwise known as a liquidity event. As a reminder, this protocol is called the waterfall. Debt holders get paid before stockholders, and preferred shares have preference over common shares and options when the company is sold or goes public.

The waterfall reflects the distribution of funds each party receives from a liquidity event (i.e., sale) as spelled out in the company's articles of incorporation or charter as well as in the investment documents created for each round of funding.[20]

Generally, after accrued salaries to employees are paid, payments go out in the following order:

- First to pay obligations to creditors (i.e., debt)

- Second to preferred shareholders (outside investors, including venture capitalists and angel investors) until certain returns or thresholds are met

- Finally, to common shareholders and option holders (including the founders, employees, independent board members, and advisors and maybe some early investors if they bought common stock).

As an employee in a startup, if the company is sold, you will receive any salary you are owed. But when it comes to getting paid out on your equity grants, you are sitting in the back of the bus. As you endure the

---

[20] The Articles of Incorporation and the Charter are two foundational documents that specify the core provisions around the issuance of C corporation stock, including economic rights and governance provisions. Additional documents issued during funding transactions include the Stock Purchase Agreement, Investor Rights Agreement, Voting Rights Agreement, and Disclosure Schedule.

long and bumpy ride to startup success, after the investors take their share of the goodies, hopefully, something is left over to have made your ride worthwhile. That isn't always the case.

The Capitalization Hierarchy

The waterfall directly reflects the priority of the different securities a company has issued during its lifecycle. When you look at the balance sheet of a startup, the right side of the balance sheet lists the company's liabilities (debt and other obligations) and equity (stock). These basic accounting items tell you how the company has financed the items on the left side of the balance sheet—its assets (such as cash and equipment). Collectively, these sources of financing are called the company's capitalization, and the equity components appear on a schedule called the capitalization table that breaks out ownership in the company by category of stock.

The main types of security with claims on the company are debt and equity. But within each category, there are sub-categories of securities that vary in their economic and governance rights. In this chapter, I will go over the different kinds of debt and equity securities to provide the context for you to understand your equity holdings as an employee.

Debt Securities

Startups are rarely profitable, so banks typically do not lend to them. But it is not unusual for startups to have some form of debt on their balance sheet. When the company is sold, the debt holders are repaid before equity holders (i.e., preferred or common shareholders) receive any proceeds.

The main types of debt, which I will explain briefly, include:

- Conventional debt
- Trade debt, lease obligations, and accounts payable

- Venture debt
- Convertible debt
- Revenue-based debt

Conventional Debt is a loan bearing an interest rate with an established repayment period. This type of debt is typically issued by banks to profitable companies with positive cash flow that can repay the debt. Since most startups are neither profitable nor cash flow positive, they usually do not have access to conventional debt issued by a bank or similar institution.

Trade Debt, Lease Obligations, and Accounts Payable are obligations the company owes to vendors or contractors for work performed or products purchased and can be significant items on a company's balance sheet. In the case of an acquisition, the buyer adjusts the purchase price to account for these liabilities. The largest of these liabilities is often office lease obligations, which reflect multi-year obligations and can run into hundreds of thousands of dollars even for a small startup.

Venture Debt is similar to conventional debt in that it is a loan bearing an interest rate and repayment period but also includes equity participation in the company for the lender. Traditionally, venture debt has been issued by technology sector-oriented banks, such as Silicon Valley Bank or Bridge Bank, which specialize in working with startups. Increasingly, those tech-focused banks have been purchased by larger banks interested in participating in the innovation economy. Private non-bank firms have been playing a greater role providing venture debt as well.

Venture debt is often offered to startups that have closed on a significant funding round led by a credible VC. The funder typically opens a line of credit for thirty to forty percent of the equity raised during the funding round. The company can draw on the line of credit to fund its operations, with the short-term obligation limited to just paying interest on the amount borrowed. After eighteen to twenty-four months, the borrower must start repaying the loan in monthly installments, usually over two or three years. If a liquidity event happens, the entire principal amount of the debt plus any outstanding interest due must be repaid before proceeds are distributed to shareholders.

Venture debt is available mainly to startups that well-established VCs have funded, as the lender relies on the financial strength and reputation of the investor to sustain the company as it continues to grow. With backing from the VC, lenders have confidence that the company is more likely to repay the loan.

VCs often have many portfolio companies that do business with the bank, and the VC itself may keep its own funds in the bank. This broad and deep relationship fuels the bank's willingness to take a leap of faith and trust that the VC will back the company long enough for it to be acquired or secure another funding round and pay back or refinance the loan.[21]

To compensate the bank for the risk of lending to companies that are not profitable, the company typically issues a form of equity called a **warrant**, which is a right to buy shares of company stock at a very low price. Possession of the warrant, referred to as an equity kicker, allows the bank to participate in the upside as the company stock value rises and is a critical part of venture lenders' business model. On the capitalization table, the debt component of venture debt has priority over equity payouts, but the warrant is lower on the priority stack and is paid out when common shareholders are paid.

Convertible Debt is a form of obligation to investors that, upon certain conditions, converts into company stock. **Convertible**

---

[21] Venture banks such as Silicon Valley Bank concentrated on their broad relationships with venture capital and private equity firms to fuel their growth during boom times in the innovation economy. Ironically, it was this over-concentration on the sector that led to the collapse and subsequent takeover of Silicon Valley Bank when the tech markets stagnated and venture funding for risky startups dried up.

debt is issued during a funding round and specifies how much an investor invests but leaves the valuation of the investment until a later date. It is typically a way of getting funding from angel investors who want to let professional venture capitalists price the company's stock in a subsequent round. This instrument simplifies the negotiation process for both the investor and the company.

The convertible debtholder can convert the debt into preferred shares or demand repayment when the subsequent priced round is closed. In a conversion, the principal amount of the debt (plus any accrued interest) is divided by the price per share of the stock sold in the round (the **conversion price**). The conversion price is usually discounted to allow the debt holder to receive a greater number of preferred shares upon conversion.[22] If the debtholder chooses not to convert, the company must repay the debt with interest as part of the closing (the completion of a sale or funding transaction).

Convertible debt can also be issued in a **bridge** round (often funded by current investors through an **insider round)** when a company needs a short-term infusion of cash to tide it over until the next financing round or an impending sale.

Revenue-Based Debt[23] is an emerging category of venture debt that involves financing against future revenue receivables, particularly annual recurring revenue (ARR) receivables. Given that ARR is a somewhat predictable stream of revenue, lenders can advance funds and base repayment on a percentage of future revenues made from the company's cash receipts.

---

[22] The discount to the conversion price associated with convertible debt is an incentive for investors to commit to funding the company in advance of a future funding round.

[23] Consult this article for a brief history of and explanation of revenue-based lending: "Revenue-Based Financing: A Powerful Lending Option", Saratoga Investment Corp., https://saratogainvestmentcorp.com/articles/revenue-based-financing/, June 30, 2020

Equity Securities (and Derivatives)

When you think about investing in the stock market, you usually think about buying common company shares. When you think about owning part of a startup, assuming that your ownership is also in common shares is natural. That's not always the case. It depends on who you are.

There are a variety of ownership types (i.e., equity and equity-related instruments) that can exist in a startup including:

- common stock
- preferred stock
- simplified agreement for future equity (SAFE)
- equity-based incentive grants (such as stock options)
- warrants

I will explain each form of equity, but first I would like to provide some context. Each of these instruments has different rights and serves different purposes. For example, founders start off owning common shares. Employees are usually issued a form of derivative security known as options that give them the right to purchase common shares at a set price per share.[24] Investors buy preferred shares with priority rights to cash distributions over common shares. Warrants are usually issued to banks or key customers or vendors (sometimes in lieu of cash) as an incentive for doing business with the company. Failing to understand the difference between common and preferred shares, among other equity instruments,

---

[24] A derivative is a security derived from its relationship with another security. For example, an option to purchase common shares is dependent on the underlying common shares for its existence. Without the common shares, there would be no option; the option has no value except in reference to the value of the common shares.

can be costly when considering the potential return on investment of working at a startup.

To assess the investment-related value of working at a startup, you must know how many shares (or options) you will receive and understand what percentage of the company they represent. But determining the percent ownership just scratches the surface. In addition, you must understand the priority claims that preferred shares may have on cash distributions. This is a complicated calculation, as even small startups can have multi-tiered capital structures.

The breakdown of ownership by different types of shares and share classes (e.g., common and preferred) is captured in the capitalization table or **cap table** for short. The cap table is a spreadsheet listing all shareholders, how many shares they own of each type of share, and the percentage ownership by class of shares and overall.

Equity ownership percentages are calculated in two ways:

1. **Issued and outstanding**: based on the number of shares and options issued and held by specific shareholders, or

2. **Fully diluted**: which includes all the issued and outstanding shares plus unissued options or incentive stock held in reserve in an option pool to compensate new employees or issue additional grants to existing employees, board members, etc. in the future.

A large unallocated incentive stock or option pool can have a significant impact on ownership percentages. So, when considering percent ownership, it is critical to distinguish whether the calculation is based only on issued and outstanding shares or fully diluted, including unissued shares in the option pool.

The more conservative approach when considering your equity ownership percentage is to calculate fully diluted ownership. If the company is sold, there is no payout for unissued options. They get wiped off the cap table. The company's sale price is divided by fewer shares, so each issued share is worth more, which creates upside for all shareholders.

Common Stock is the basic unit of ownership and the least common denominator when it comes to equity in a C-corporation. Other forms of equity, and even some forms of debt, usually have the right (or sometimes the obligation) to convert to common stock under defined circumstances. It is also the form of stock that underlies employee option grants.

Common stock is initially issued as founder's shares with the individuals who start the company starting out owning 100 percent of the equity. Each share equals one vote for ratifying major corporate decisions, so it is the most democratic of all forms of equity. Even before a company raises outside capital, it may issue common stock or options on common stock to advisors and employees. In the early funding rounds, angel investors may also purchase common stock, which puts the investors on the same footing or **pari passu** with the founders.

Preferred Stock is a form of equity with priority claims and rights above common stock. Most established or sophisticated investors demand that companies issue them shares that have preferential characteristics before they commit their investment dollars. The equity containing these special rights is known as preferred stock.

The most valuable benefit to preferred stock is that preferred shareholders are entitled to priority cash distributions from a liquidity event. Before common shareholders get paid from a company sale, preferred shareholders have the right to distributions equal to at least the original amount of capital invested and sometimes accrued dividends or other designated payouts.

This prioritized distribution right is how investors reduce risk and shift it back onto the company and the common shareholders. This risk-shifting arises because preferred shareholders have the right to convert into common shares. If a company sale is at a high price and results in the preferred shareholders getting paid more by converting into common shares, they will convert. If not, they keep their preferred shares and take their priority distribution.

The relationship between the preferred and common shareholders is a zero-sum game. The total sale price of the company doesn't change. Based on the conversion decision, what changes is how much the preferred shareholder gets paid and how much is left for the common shareholders (and, by extension, the option holders). In either case, the choice made by the preferred shareholders to maximize their payout has a direct, negative dollar-for-dollar impact on how much money the common shareholders receive.

How dividends on preferred shares are structured can also have an insidious effect on returns to common shareholders. If dividends are set up to be cumulative year after year but are not paid, preferred investors are entitled to get their capital back first plus the accrued dividends. Dividends that have accrued at six or eight percent interest per year for several years can take an additional substantial bite out of what remains for common shareholders.[25]

Preferred stock also comes with corporate governance rights, including appointing board members, approving spending above certain limits, and controlling or blocking critical decisions such as when to sell the company. Preferred shareholders have the right to vote on critical corporate issues collectively as a class of shares separate from the common. This effectively gives them veto power over the company making certain strategic moves and provides

---

[25] Typically, the dividend feature of preferred shares required dividends to be declared by the board. Additionally, undeclared dividends were non-cumulative from year to year, so if undeclared, presented no obligation for payout by the company. This is a relatively benign and common dividend construct, but not all venture deals are structured in such a company-friendly way.

significant leverage to negotiate deals that are beneficial to them. These governance rights can be detrimental to the interests of the common shareholders and employees.

Looking at the cap table of a company that has raised multiple financing rounds, you see the series preferred shares listed as Series A, Series B, Series C, and so on as we discussed in Chapter 2 (The Cast). These represent different funding rounds and sometimes different investor groups.

The rights and privileges of preferred stock can be extensive. Hammering out these rights begins with a **term sheet** from a lead investor laying out the broad terms of a deal. The investment documents codify the nitty-gritty details when the round is closed. When a company has raised three or four rounds of capital or more, the corporate governance protocols representing the rights of the various classes of shareholders can get complicated, usually requiring a law firm to determine how the company must follow voting and approval protocols.

There is a robust body of literature (books and online) examining how venture capital deals involving preferred shares are structured. The best book on this topic is Brad Feld's *Venture Deals*.[26] As his book thoroughly covers deal structure, I will not cover the topic in depth. The essential points to remember are that preferred shareholders have significant power over the company's operations. In addition, their priority claims on sale or liquidation proceeds diminish the payouts to common shareholders, especially if things don't go well for the company.

It is worth looking at a couple of different features of preferred stock, so you have an idea of how benign or punitive these preferential economic rights can be. The two most prevalent are non-participating preferred versus participating preferred.

---

[26] Feld, Brad and Mendelson, Jason, *Venture Deals*. 2nd Edition. Hoboken, New Jersey, John Wiley & Sons, 2013.

- *Non-Participating Preferred*

  The most benign form of preferred stock is **non-participating preferred**. Almost all preferred stock bears the right to a **liquidation preference**. Until and unless preferred stockholders convert to common stock, they have a priority right to receive their invested cash back from a company sale before payouts to the common shareholders. Non-participating preferred is the plain vanilla form of security issued to venture capitalists. New investors like to see prior investors have non-participating preferred in prior rounds, as it keeps the cap table relatively simple and clean when considering ownership breakdowns.[27]

  With non-participating preferred, there is a threshold sale price at which it makes more sense for preferred shareholders to convert their preferred shares into common shares. Simply, it's the price at which the percentage of common stock they would hold after converting would result in their payout being greater than just getting their money back through their liquidation preference as preferred shareholders.

- *Participating Preferred*

  In funding rounds when prospective investors have greater negotiating leverage over the company, they can drive a harder bargain and structure the preferred to be participating. While non-participating preferred is entitled to a preferential payment *or* conversion to common shares,

---

[27] The cap table is cleaner without participating preferred shares. Participating preferred complicates the flow of funds in a sale. New investors want a clean hierarchy of cash distributions represented in the waterfall without prior round investors having priority claims over the new investors' distributions, which participating preferred may have in certain situations.

participating preferred gets the preferential payment *and* the right to convert to common shares after receiving that priority distribution. So, preferred shareholders receive their investment capital back and then get to convert into common shares to participate proportionately in the proceeds to the common shareholders. That is having your cake and eating it too.

A Deeper Dive into Preferred Shares

Whether preferred shares are non-participating or participating can be the single greatest factor in how the proceeds of a sale are distributed. Because of the significance of this issue, it is worth taking a closer look at this important type of equity.

Let's take a simple example that compares four different scenarios of a preferred shareholder who buys 50 percent of a company for $10 million. The variables are: 1) whether the investor purchases non-participating or participating preferred shares, and 2) a company sale price of $15 million versus $30 million.

Scenario 1: Non-participating preferred with $15 million sale: If the company sells for $15 million, the preferred shareholder gets their $10 million of invested capital back, and $5 million would be left to distribute to the common shareholders. Although the investor owns 50 percent of the equity, they receive two-thirds of the sale proceeds. If the preferred were to convert to common, they would get only $7.5 million (or 50 percent of the proceeds). It would not make sense to convert as they would receive $2.5 million less if they did.

Scenario 2: Non-participating preferred with $30 million sale: If the company sells for $30 million, failing to convert would yield the preferred shareholders only $10 million (the return of their investment). If they convert, they would own 50 percent of the outstanding common shares and would be entitled to receive $15 million. Clearly, they would convert and pocket the extra $5 million. Here, the investor owns 50 percent of the company and receives 50 percent of the proceeds of the sale, an equitable outcome.

Scenario 3: Participating preferred with $15 million sale: With participating preferred at a one-time preference, in the event of a $15 million sale, the investor would get their $10 million back. Because they *also* have the right to convert into common shares, they also receive 50 percent of the remaining $5 million, for a total of $12.5 million. That leaves the common shareholders with only $2.5 million instead of the $5 million they would have received under the non-participating preferred scenario. The investor purchased 50 percent of the equity, but the participating preferred feature resulted in their receiving five-sixths (83.33 percent) of the proceeds.

Scenario 4: Participating preferred with $30 million sale: The participating preferred would get $10 million off the top *plus* 50 percent of the remaining $20 million—an extra $10 million—for a total of $20 million. That leaves only $10 million for the common shareholders. In this scenario, the investor takes two-thirds of the proceeds. Even though the investor bought shares totaling 50 percent of the ownership, they would receive 66.7 percent of the proceeds from the sale, leaving the common shareholders with only 33.3 percent.

When comparing the $15 million versus the $30 million scenarios, both preferred and common shareholders benefit from the higher company sale price. But how much each benefits varies by millions of dollars depending on whether the preferred shareholders own non-participating or participating preferred shares. These examples show why common shareholders hate participating preferred and negotiate hard to avoid the participation feature when raising funds.

	Non-Participating Preferred Scenarios ($ Millions)	Participating Preferred (1x) Scenarios ($ Millions)
Preferred share investment	10	10
Ownership purchased	50%	50%

$15 Million Sale Price Scenario

Preferential payout	10	10
Payout to preferred after conversion	0	2.5
Total payout to preferred	**10**	**12.5**
Total payout to common	**5**	**2.5**

$30 Million Sale Price Scenario

Preferential payout	0	10
Payout to preferred after conversion	15	10
Total payout to preferred	**15**	**20**
Total payout to common	**15**	**10**

Exhibit 8-1 Company Sale Outcomes - Participating versus Non-Participating Preferred Shares

At Fugue, we struggled to find investors in our last funding round before selling the company. The investors who did come in negotiated for participating preferred with a two times liquidation preference. In other words, upon sale of the company, they would receive payment equal to two times their invested capital and then have the right to convert to common stock and participate proportionately (or "*pro rata*") in the remaining proceeds. This feature turned out to be very expensive for the common shareholders when the company was sold.

That is a rare situation. Most venture capitalists would typically pass on the deal if a company is struggling so much that an investor can impose those terms. In our case, more than forty or fifty VCs did pass. But our lead investor was a private individual investing his own money, not a traditional VC fund, and he had a different approach. When a company has its back against the wall, management and the board must swallow hard and take what is offered, even if the taste is bitter.[28] In the end, however, the company would not have survived without that infusion of expensive funding and it was able to reach a successful exit within less than a year after closing the round.

Simplified Agreement for Future Equity (SAFE)

One other form of equity gaining popularity is the **Simplified Agreement for Future Equity**, or **SAFE**. This form of financing instrument was introduced in 2013 by Y Combinator, a Silicon Valley-based tech accelerator.[29] Since its introduction, most startups use the SAFE structure for their seed and even bridge funding, replacing the historically high use of convertible debt.

The SAFE is designed to allow companies to raise equity without having to negotiate a valuation on the shares. Investors agree to invest at a pre-negotiated discount to the valuation in the next financing round. Subsequently, when a lead investor sets the price of the next funding round. The SAFE holders must roll their investment into the next series preferred round. The number of

---

[28] A commonly used term for an investor who imposes onerous terms on distressed companies with the aim of extracting large gains when the company sells is a "vulture capitalist."

[29] Further explanation and sample SAFE documents can be found at: https://www.ycombinator.com/documents.

shares they receive in that priced round is calculated based on the price per share in the new round, less the pre-negotiated discount.

For example, suppose a SAFE holder invests $1 million with a 20 percent discount to the next round. If the next round is completed at $5 per share, the SAFE holder converts their investment at $4 per share ($5 minus the 20 percent discount) and receives 250,000 preferred shares. Without the discount, the SAFE holder would only receive 200,000 preferred shares. The extra 50,000 shares compensate the SAFE holder for investing earlier than the priced round and taking on additional risk.

Startups prefer SAFEs as an alternative to convertible debt to raise funds when there is no lead investor to set pricing for the round. The problem with convertible debt is that it is, as its name connotes, debt. Convertible debt sits on top of equity in the waterfall and must be repaid if it is not converted to equity. Unlike holders of convertible debt, investors in SAFEs do not have the option to call back their investments.

When we did our first round of funding at USLaw.com back in 1998, we sold convertible notes. SAFEs didn't exist then, or we certainly would have used that form. When it came time to close our Series A round and ask the convertible note holders to roll into the Series A, most did. Two investors chose to redeem their notes rather than convert them into equity. It was an unusual move that siphoned off much-needed cash from the company to repay them. Given that most of our convertible debt holders lost their investment after converting to the Series A, the two who redeemed turned out to have made the right call.

There is one additional twist to SAFEs. Many SAFE offerings have a valuation cap on conversion into the next round. The cap allows SAFE investors to put money in with some uncertainty about valuation but without the risk of a rapid runup in valuation in the next round. Without a valuation cap, early investors may find that the number of preferred shares they receive upon conversion of the SAFE is disproportionately low relative to the risk they took investing in the earlier round.

Expanding on the example above, suppose the SAFE had a valuation cap of $5 per share. Assume instead of completing the round at $5 per share, the company completed a priced round at $10 per share. Without the valuation cap, the SAFE holder would convert their $1 million investment at $8 per share, resulting in holdings of 125,000 shares. With the valuation cap in place, the conversion results in the issuance of 200,000 shares ($1 million divided by $5 per share), a difference of more than 75,000 shares.

With a valuation cap in place, if the company's valuation takes off, the discount to the next round will be larger than the pre-negotiated discount. In the example above, the SAFE holder receives a 50 percent discount rather than the 20 percent discount built into the SAFE terms. The cap provides early investors with a significant valuation pop. The valuation cap also allows the company to calculate ownership percentages assuming the SAFE holders convert at the maximum valuation specified in the agreement.

Equity-Based Incentive Grants

In addition to the types of equity described in the preceding sections, companies also issue incentive-based equity grants to employees. The most common of these are stock options, but there are other forms of equity grants. I will discuss those in detail in the next chapter.

Warrants

A warrant is a right by the holder to purchase shares of the company's stock at a set price. They are similar to options but have three differences.

1. They are issued to non-employee entities.

2. They often are issued at an **exercise price** (also called a **strike price)** that is very low and unconnected to the underlying value of the stock. It is common for **penny warrants** to be issued, which colloquially refers to warrants where the exercise price to buy the underlying stock is 1 cent per share or lower.

3. Warrants have no expiration date, unlike stock options, which by law must expire after ten years.

Warrants can be used to sweeten the pot for investors and are commonly issued to funders who issue venture debt. They are also sometimes used as incentives for early marquee customers to use the company's products since an early big-name customer can put a startup on the map and help it get funding. Either way, warrants tend to be a relatively small part of the cap table and should have a marginal impact on the sale proceeds to you.

The Capitalization Table

With many shareholders and types of securities on a startup's balance sheet, companies need a summary document to keep track of the ownership structure.[30] That document is the capitalization table, or cap table for short. The cap table provides a breakdown of ownership by investor for each share class based on the company's funding and operational history. It also lists any outstanding options, warrants, and how many shares remain in the option pool to be issued as incentive grants.

With the cap table, you can determine aggregate ownership by shareholder (including all classes of shares) and voting power by

---

[30] The capitalization table only captures equity ownership and does not list debt obligations other than potentially convertible debt that can convert to equity.

share class and overall. What is missing in the numbers are any special features, priority claims, or rights the various share classes may have. For example, if any preferred shares have a participating preferred feature, that may not be evident from the numbers in the cap table; it may, however, be disclosed in footnotes to the cap table. To fully understand the details of a given share class, you need to review the legal documents associated with the issuance of those shares.

Exhibit 8-2 is an example of a simplified cap table for a company that has completed its Series B financing. The shareholders listed include the founder, three angel investors, and three venture capital firms. It shows how many shares were issued to each party at the outset and during each funding round through the Series B. While levels of ownership among the shareholders may vary across companies, this sample cap table is a reasonable representation of the post-funding ownership structure of a Series B company.

The cap table is a snapshot of ownership at a point in time. Each time new equity is issued, either in the form of options or through a funding round, the current cap table must be updated. Embedded within the cap table is a history of how ownership in the company has evolved. Each of the columns represents a different class of shares. Except for common shares, which can be issued at multiple points directly or through option **exercises**, other share classes such as series preferred correlate to specific funding rounds.

The two far-right columns detail ownership based on two calculations–issued and outstanding shares or fully-diluted shares (including all unissued options). Most of the time, ownership is expressed as a percentage of fully diluted shares. However, when a company is ultimately sold, the unallocated option pool will be dissolved, and the percent ownership used for the allocation of proceeds will be based on issued and outstanding shares at the time.

Examining how share ownership evolves after each funding round (going from Seed through Series B in the exhibit) provides an enlightening picture regarding dilution of ownership for the early shareholders such as founders and angels. In this example, at the formation of the company, the founder and co-founder were issued 1 million shares, with the ownership split 60/40 between them, respectively. After the Series B financing, the combined fully diluted ownership represented by the founder's and co-founders' shares dropped from 100 percent to just under 28 percent. This is due to the sale of shares to investors and the establishment of the option pool from which option grants were issued.

It is common that after several rounds of financing, investors would own a majority of the issued and outstanding shares. In this case, after the Series B, the investors own approximately 55 percent—10 percent in the hands of angels and 45 percent held by venture capitalists. By contrast, non-founder employees hold a small percentage, just over 5 percent. Finally, the unallocated shares in the option pool represent 8 percent available for future option grants, which may or may not ultimately be issued.

Funding Round	Common	Seed	Series A	Series B	Total Shares	Percent Owned	Percent Owned
Security issued	Common	Preferred	Preferred	Preferred		Issued & outs.	Fully diluted
Shareholders							
Founder	600,000				600,000	17.52	16.11
Co-Founder(s)	400,000				400,000	11.68	10.74
Angel investor 1		150,000	45,000		195,000	5.69	5.23
Angel investor 2		100,000	30,000		130,000	3.80	3.49
Angel investor 3		50,000			50,000	1.46	1.34
Venture capitalist 1			500,000	200,000	700,000	20.44	18.79
Venture capitalist 2			250,000	100,000	350,000	10.22	9.40
Venture capitalist 3				700,000	700,000	20.44	18.79
Employee options (issued)	200,000				200,000	5.84	5.37
Warrants (issued)	100,000				100,000	2.92	2.68
Option pool (unallocated)	300,000				300,000		8.05
Total by class (issued and outstanding)	1,300,000	300,000	825,000	1,000,000	3,425,000	100.00	
Percentage (issued and outstanding)	37.96	8.76	24.05	29.20	100.00		
Total by class (fully diluted)	1,600,000	300,000	825,000	1,000,000	3,725,000		100.00
Percentage (fully diluted)	42.65	8.05	22.15	26.85	100.00		

Exhibit 8-2: Sample Capitalization Table for a Series B Startup

The cap table is a critical document that company management and the board use to understand ownership structure and company governance (voting power) and to make key decisions about equity grants to employees and fundraising. Companies take great pains to ensure the cap table is accurate and up to date. During the fundraising or company sale process, investors and their lawyers will conduct extensive due diligence to ensure the pre-transaction cap table is accurate. The company must certify its accuracy as any mistakes on the cap table will affect the price per share in the funding round or sale and have real dollars and cents implications for shareholders.

Of particular relevance to employees is how the company will use the cap table to manage equity grants and the option pool. From the cap table, you will know what percentage of the company you own relative to two numbers–the total shares issued and outstanding and the fully diluted share total (including unissued shares in the option pool). As I discussed in Chapter 6 (Understanding the Offer), it is not enough to know how many options you have; you need to know what those options represent in terms of ownership.

The Bottom Line

As is evident from the variety of securities startups can issue, there is a lot of complexity in a company's capitalization table. Grasping the various elements of the cap table and their specific terms is critical to understanding the waterfall or proceeds distribution in a liquidity event. Beyond knowing the ownership percentage that your grants represent, you need to dig deeper to learn what the liquidation preferences are in the company and where the thresholds are at which common shareholders and employees start to realize returns on their equity holdings. This probably requires a conversation with the founder/CEO, CFO, or a finance team member.

Part of your decision to join or stay at a company may be determined by the likelihood your equity is worth something meaningful. A company with promising prospects that has not raised an enormous amount of capital may represent a strong opportunity for you to benefit financially from its exit. But if the liquidation preferences are substantial and the company's chances of realizing a sale price significantly exceeding them are low, you may be left with an empty plate after years of effort working there.

CHAPTER 9

What Are Your Options?

I was playing golf with a doctor friend. He mentioned that his daughter had taken a job with a small technology company. She called her father and told him that she had received something called "options." Then she asked him, "Is that a good thing?" Fortunately, my doctor friend sits on two public company boards and, with authority, assured her that it was.

Founders get equity by starting companies. Investors get equity by buying it. So, what about employees? Employees acquire ownership in their companies primarily through incentive grants at the time of hire and additional grants over time for promotions or retention incentives. Receiving an option or equity grant is undoubtedly a good thing. They are the main way startup employees can participate in the company's success and build significant wealth if the company achieves a lucrative exit.

In rare situations, as an employee, you might also be invited to invest alongside outside investors during funding rounds, especially early in a company's life. Buying stock in the company is separate from your incentive stock compensation and requires you to put your own capital at risk, which you may not be able to do. Those opportunities are limited and get more expensive over time as the company's value increases.

Chapter 6 (Understanding the Offer) discussed incentive stock grants as an important but sometimes inscrutable part of a startup employee's compensation. Companies put enormous time, effort, and money into constructing employee stock incentive plans. Issuing and tracking grants also requires significant resources. But they take on the burden because allowing employees to participate in the company's upside is a major recruiting and retention selling point. Even if companies issue these grants with the best intentions, as an employee, you are hard-pressed to evaluate what you are receiving or its value over time.

In this chapter, we discuss the different types of equity grants, how they work, and some critical considerations around managing them.

Setting a Price for Equity Grants

Before discussing the specific types of **incentive equity** grants you might receive as an employee, let's talk about how these incentives are priced upon issuance. The price of your incentive stock grants determines your upside and taxes when the company is sold.

Each year (or sometimes more frequently), a startup that plans to issue incentive stock grants must complete a process called a **409A valuation** conducted by an independent, third-party firm. That process places a value on the company's common stock and sets the stage for issuing grants to employees and others. The most recent 409A valuation of the common stock sets the minimum price for equity grants at that time. As long as equity grants are priced at or above the 409A valuation, the company and its board of directors have legal protection against claims of excessive compensation to senior managers.[31]

---

[31] An independent valuation of a company's common stock is required under Section 409A of the Internal Revenue Code to set the minimum price for option exercise prices. The purpose of the valuation is to ensure that company management and the board are offering incentive-based equity compensation at fair-market value. This is designed to protect shareholders from self-dealing on the part of company leadership.

Because of the priority treatment preferred shares receive and the fact that there is no public market for trading the common stock, shares of common stock usually are valued far lower than preferred shares held by investors—as much as 50 to 90 percent less. This discrepancy in value turns out to be a potential windfall for employees in the case of a liquidity event.

The company's board of directors uses the 409A valuation to establish the issue price of equity grants. While the board usually uses the exact price of the common stock valuation, it is within their purview to set a higher price. Once the board establishes the issue price, the company can propose issuing specific grants.

Employee Equity Grant Types

There are two main types of employee equity grants that startups issue: **options** and **restricted stock units (RSUs)**. Each has advantages and disadvantages for both employers and employees. The issuance of one or the other reflects the company's view of equity versus cash compensation as a motivator and how flush the company is with funds. Companies able to afford less cash often issue options, while companies with higher valuations that have raised a lot of money may favor restricted stock units.

In addition to options and RSUs, some companies also issue **restricted stock**. Restricted stock (distinct from RSUs) is usually given to senior executives and has certain more favorable tax features than RSUs associated with them.

Options

A stock option grant confers the right to buy a set number of shares of a company's common stock at a set price. Remember that common shares sit below all other forms of equity on the capitalization table.

Upon issuance, options are **unvested**, which means that the rights associated with the options are not yet active. The rights become active or **vest** as the option holder works for the company for a specific period (the **vesting schedule**). Once the option has vested, the right to buy the shares, called exercising the option, becomes active. At that point, the employee has the right to exercise the option by writing a check to the company to purchase the shares at the agreed-upon price listed on the option grant, called the **exercise price** or **strike price**.

Options have significant benefits for employees. First, the option strike price is determined by the board using the 409A valuation. Because the 409A values common stock at a substantial discount to preferred stock, the option's exercise price is much lower than what investors pay for their shares. In a successful sale, when investors convert their preferred shares into common shares, all shares receive the same payout per share. Because employees had the opportunity to acquire shares by paying the low exercise price, they stand to realize a windfall from the difference between that low exercise price and the higher price per share investors paid to buy their shares.

Second, an option holder can hold the option for up to ten years without exercising it. You can wait to see what happens with the company before you invest any of your hard-earned dollars into exercising your options. If the company is sold while you're still an employee, your vested options are automatically cashed out as part of the transaction.

Third, options have a **bargain element**, which means that the cash proceeds you receive represent the difference between the price per share the company is acquired for and the exercise price. If your company sells for $1 per share and your exercise price on the option is $0.25, you receive $0.75 per share times the number of options you hold (less applicable taxes). At the time the company is sold, you will receive that value for all of your vested options without having to worry about exercising them.

The main downside of options is that you don't own anything until you exercise them. So, if you leave the company and never exercise your options, after a short time, usually 90 days, they are forfeited. That would be as if you never held them in the first place.

Restricted Stock Units (RSUs)

As an alternative to stock options, some companies issue Restricted Stock Units or RSUs to employees as incentive compensation. RSUs are actual shares of stock rather than the right to buy shares of stock. At the time of issuance, an RSU is worth the actual price per share of the stock being issued as determined by the 409A valuation. This differs from options, which are not the actual shares, but rather the right to purchase shares at the exercise price.

For example, if a company's common stock is currently valued at $1 per share, an RSU is worth $1 at the time of issuance. By contrast, an option provides the right to buy the stock at the current price of $1. When the option is issued, there is no difference between the price of the stock and the strike or exercise price. Both are $1, so the bargain element of the option at that moment is $0.

Companies typically issue fewer RSUs than options, sometimes less than half in terms of the ownership percentage it represents. The rationale is that the RSU has an inherent value at the time of issuance while options have no inherent value until the stock price goes above the exercise price. Since an RSU is worth a lot more at the time of issuance than an option, the argument is that employees should get fewer RSUs. The benefit to investors is that when the company issues RSUs, they experience lower dilution of their ownership than when the company issues a higher number of options.

From an employee's perspective, RSUs have advantages and disadvantages. The advantages have mostly to do with the ownership characteristics of RSUs. The disadvantages relate to how companies view RSUs as a form of compensation relative to options, as well as how RSUs are treated for tax purposes.

Advantages of RSUs

1. When you receive and vest into an RSU, you now own the stock. Unless there are clawback provisions where the company can repurchase the stock at an agreed-upon price, once it vests, you can leave the company and still own the stock.

2. Since you own the stock, even after you leave, you realize the proceeds if the company goes public or is sold. You don't have to exercise RSUs as you do with options. You don't have to write the company a check or risk losing the shares when you leave. You simply own them.

Disadvantages of RSUs

1. You receive significantly fewer RSUs than options, so if the company does well, there is less upside. This is simply a numbers game. Suppose you have 100 RSUs compared to 200 options to purchase shares at $1. If the stock price rises from $1 to $10, your RSUs would be worth $1,000, whereas your options would be worth $1,800 because of the bargain element (200 shares at $10 per share minus the exercise cost of 200 shares times $1 per share). For every incremental dollar the stock price rises, the RSU grant would increase $100 while the option grant bargain element would increase by $200.

2. The value of RSUs is taxed as ordinary income when they vest. That is because you own the stock, which is considered compensation once your ownership is realized upon vesting. Options, by contrast, trigger a taxable event only once you exercise them or the company is acquired.

3. This taxation feature of RSUs poses a risk. You incur the tax liability and must pay the taxes at the time they vest, but you don't receive cash for the value of the stock until the stock is

sold. Subsequently, the value of the stock may decline; the company may even go out of business. But you have already made your tax payment. You may be able to claim a tax loss on the value of the stock, but recouping your full value is not guaranteed. That tax issue can't happen with an option unless you exercise it, the timing of which is wholly within your control.

Restricted Stock

RSUs and Restricted Stock have similarities and a couple of important differences. Both are actual shares of company stock representing the full value of the stock, unlike options as explained earlier. The main differences are that restricted stock, even prior to vesting, has voting power and offers more favorable tax treatment.[32] Neither options nor RSUs have voting power.

Employees come into possession of restricted stock in one of two ways. First, it can be issued directly by the company. Second, sometimes option grants come with early exercise provisions that allow the grantee to exercise the option before it is vested. When an employee exercises an option and buys shares of common stock through an early exercise provision (i.e., before the option vests), the shares purchased are considered restricted stock. The employee hasn't yet vested into their ownership. If they leave the company, the company has the right to repurchase the restricted stock at the price the employee paid.

Comparing Options, RSUs, and Restricted Stock

The main differences between the three types of equity grants we have described–options, RSUs, and restricted stock–comes down to three main issues–ownership, taxes, and voting rights.

---

[32] As restricted stock is usually issued only to senior executives, I will not spend a lot of time on it here.

	Options	Restricted Stock Units	Restricted Stock
Definition	The right to buy a company's common stock at a set price	Shares of actual stock issued to employee directly	Shares of stock acquired through early exercise before vesting
Vesting	Vest as employee works for company	Vest as employee works for company	Bought before vesting is complete
Taxes	Have to pay taxes on the value of the stock at the time of purcase	Taxed as income on the value of the stock	Has the option to pay taxes on the value of the stock when issued
Voting	No voting	No voting power until vested	Voting power

Exhibit 9-1: Comparison of Options, Restricted Stock, and RSUs

While voting rights and vesting schedules are important, the main issue that affects employees is taxes. Vesting will happen as dictated by the company's incentive stock plan and in accordance with the details of each grant. Employees generally hold a small percentage of company ownership, so whether they get to vote on important company issues probably will have little impact on the outcome. But the tax treatment of equity incentive grants will have a direct and material effect on the value derived from each grant.

When you exercise an option, you pay ordinary income tax rates on the bargain element at the time. When the company's stock valuation rises, the longer you wait to exercise, the more ordinary income tax you incur upon exercise. With RSUs, as described above, you incur taxes as the RSUs vest, and then capital gains on any additional appreciation in the company's stock when it is sold.

By contrast, restricted stock offers a potentially more favorable tax treatment than the other forms of equity incentive grants. The recipient of restricted stock (unlike RSUs) has the option to pay income taxes on the current value of the restricted stock when issued and benefit from capital gains treatment as the stock price appreciates in the future. This allows the grant holder to lock in the **basis** of their stock immediately without having to wait for the restricted stock to vest. This practice can amount to substantial tax savings in the long run if the company is successful.

How Are Equity Grants Issued?

If you receive an equity grant as part of your offer, the offer letter likely references it. Along with the number of shares in the grant, you typically see a phrase that reads "subject to approval by the Company's Board of Directors." This statement provides a small window into the messy sausage-making that results in employee stock grants being approved and issued.

All options must receive **board approval** in accordance with the company's **incentive stock plan**. Once approved, they are issued out of the **option pool**, a reservoir of unissued common shares held in reserve by the company. The following sections discuss these elements of the option approval and issuance process.

The Incentive Stock Plan

Before a company can issue incentive stock grants, it must establish an incentive stock plan. The plan is a lengthy legal document that ensures the company remains in compliance with all the tax laws and regulations associated with issuing incentive stock compensation to employees, directors, and advisors. The plan provides guidelines and guardrails to ensure these issuances are done correctly and do not abuse shareholders.

You should receive a copy of the company's incentive stock plan as part of any grant. The plan enables the company to issue the grant and governs your rights and restrictions as a grant holder, including establishing the standard vesting schedules. It also confers upon the company certain rights to repurchase or claw back (i.e., forcing you to return) your options or RSUs and under what circumstances. Finally, it establishes what happens to those grants if something happens to you, such as your death or disability.

Most incentive stock plans are boilerplate legal documents that outline the terms and mechanics by which the company can issue incentive stock compensation, as approved by the Board of Directors. A few key things to look for are whether the documents allow for the issuance of options with early exercise provisions and whether there is any **acceleration** of vesting upon a **change of control** (for example through the sale of a majority interest in the company).

Recognize that most incentive stock plans specify that options don't vest until a minimum of twelve months after the employee starts working at the company (known as **cliff vesting**). This is a critical feature. Suppose your company has a liquidity event or you leave or are terminated within the first year of your employment. None of your options vest, and you cannot exercise them or benefit from your underlying stock ownership.

The Option Pool

When investors look at funding a company, they confirm it has an acceptable incentive stock plan document. A key element of an investment term sheet provides for the establishment or replenishment of an amount of unissued stock available to be issued as incentive stock. This reservoir of shares is called the **option pool**.

In the beginning, all of a company's equity is in the hands of the founders. Then investors fund the company by buying additional shares authorized for issuance at the closing of the funding round. In addition to the shares they purchase, investors, along with company management, want to ensure that as the company grows and hires new staff, a block of unissued stock is authorized and available to be issued as incentives in the form of options and stock grants.

Determining the size of the option pool is a negotiation between the company and the investors that impacts how the round's valuation is calculated and the company's ability to operate after the funding round closes. If the option pool is too small, management may be constrained in hiring key talent. An option pool that is too large can have a dilutive effect on the prior owners of the company and the investors.[33]

Most startups start out with an option pool that represents between 10 and 20 percent of their outstanding stock. If the company already has a strong group of senior managers (including the founders) with experience building and scaling companies, they may be able to proceed with a smaller pool. They may not need to hire many senior executives going forward, and mid and lower-level hires don't tend to get large equity grants.

On the other hand, if the company needs to hire several C-suite or vice president-level executives, a larger pool may be necessary. Hiring a new CEO typically requires issuing a grant of five to eight percent of the fully diluted stock. Attracting other senior executives may demand grants in the 0.5 to 2 percent range. With a few executive hires, the numbers can add up quickly.

As more and more employees are hired, the option pool becomes depleted. New employees join the company. Current employees get promoted. As employees vest into their options or RSUs, management may refresh or **regreen** their options with

---

[33] Dilution occurs when options from the pool are actually issued. The existence of a large option pool does not intrinsically cause dilution since unissued options or incentive stock shares would not affect the distribution of proceeds at the time of a liquidity event.

new grants and vesting schedules to provide golden handcuffs for retention. So, a pool that started out at 10 or 20 percent of the company's shares may end up with just a few percentage points of unallocated shares left.

A company expects to refill the option pool each time it completes a funding round. Negotiating an increase in the option pool outside the funding process is anathema to most boards and management teams. Boards often dig in their heels and become stingy and critical of management for over-issuing stock grants, or they simply become adversarial in approving new grants, making the process more contentious. Consequently, investors and companies try to forecast the right size of the option pool to cover the company's needs between funding rounds.

Board Approval

With the incentive stock plan in place and the option pool established, the issuance of incentive grants seems like it should be straightforward. Guess again. It's one thing to establish the legal foundation for grants and deposit the shares in the bank of available options. But it's another thing to put forth grants to individual employees for board approval.

Understand it from the investors' perspective. There is a difference between shares that are issued and outstanding and shares that are authorized for issuance but not yet issued, like those in the option pool. When a company is sold, only issued and outstanding shares are entitled to a payout. Authorized but unissued shares get wiped off the cap table in a transaction and don't count in calculating the sale price per share.

Every time a new equity grant is issued, more shares are outstanding. When it comes time to sell, there are more mouths to feed when distributing the sale proceeds. The more shares outstanding, the more the price per share goes down. Investors want to maintain a high price per share and keep as much ownership for themselves as possible. As they ultimately reduce the investors' payout, every equity grant, especially large ones, comes under scrutiny.

Companies may manage this process by establishing target equity issuance bands (i.e. guidelines) for employees at various levels and having those bands pre-vetted through the compensation committee of the board or the board as a whole. The theory is that if new grants fall within pre-established bands, the board approval process should be a rubber stamp process. But not all startups are that organized, and even with pre-established bands, the board may still push back on individual grants.

After Fugue closed our last round of financing in a major recapitalization, we reconstituted the board to include two representatives of the new investors, and two prior investor board members left the board. Within days, we turned our attention to the equity grant proposals. The management team argued that after the employees' prior option grants had become worthless due to the **recapitalization**, employees should be made whole with grants equaling their pre-funding ownership stakes. The team had shown remarkable resilience and loyalty to the company, sticking it out through the pandemic and continuing to build value without raises, bonuses, or promotions for more than a year. The board was unconvinced. The contentious negotiations dragged on for more than two months. Two additional long-standing board members resigned during that time. Eventually, grants were issued to all the employees at approximately 80 percent of what management had proposed. The investor board members then used a significant portion of the shares left from reducing the employee grants to issue grants to themselves.

Most board approval processes for giving equity grants are not this challenging. But even under normal circumstances, garnering board approval for option grants can be fraught and time-consuming, especially for larger grants to senior hires. Either way, the board controls approvals. Management can propose, justify, rationalize, and cajole. But grants can only be issued once the board approves them.

Mechanically, the approval of grants takes place through a board resolution outlining the specific grants and their detailed terms. The board must vote on the resolution at a live board meeting or provide approval through unanimous written consent. Given that startup boards tend to meet every other month or once per quarter, don't be surprised if it takes two or three months for your options to be issued after you start employment.

The Bottom Line

Incentive equity grants are the mechanism through which you benefit from the success of your startup. Recognize there is significant pressure at the board and senior management level to keep equity grants for employees as modest as possible. Your best opportunity to influence the size of your equity grant is when negotiating your offer before you join.

After you join a company, the opportunities to increase your equity ownership are few. The important thing is to follow up and make sure your grant is actually issued and that the grant terms are correct—you would be surprised how often employee paperwork for option grants is delayed or has errors in it, especially in a startup with limited administrative resources. You might not receive the grant until a few months after you join, and it is easy for you and your company to lose track of the details. At the very least, by ensuring the paperwork is issued and that all the details of the grant are correct, you can get the full benefit of what was promised when you joined.

Regarding the attractiveness of the different types of equity grants, each has its advantages and disadvantages. Despite some of the potential tax implications, I would generally opt to receive restricted stock over RSUs, and RSUs over stock options, especially if the number of shares is equivalent or close. Having the actual shares associated with restricted stock or RSU grants rather than options leaves you owning your vested equity without having to exercise options, even if you leave the company. That can prove very valuable.

CHAPTER 10

Vested Interest

Equity grants—whether options or restricted stock units (RSUs)—are designed to motivate you to stay at the company for an extended period. Of course, you are paid a salary and bonus. But equity grants serve as golden handcuffs that employers use to make it harder for you to walk away.

The retention appeal of equity grants relies on two components—a rising stock price and the vesting schedule. Vesting is based on meeting pre-conditions such as time of service, after which your grants are yours to do with as you please. Once you fulfill those conditions, you are entitled to the rights and benefits associated with the vested RSUs or options you hold. Conversely, unvested grants are not yours until you meet the vesting requirement. If you leave your company and have not yet met the vesting requirement, you lose your unvested equity grants.

Even if you meet the vesting requirement, you have a set timeframe after you leave, usually ninety days, to exercise your vested options and purchase the common stock. That means shelling out cash to convert your options into shares. If you don't pay up, even the vested portion of your grant is forfeited upon your departure.

The most common vesting is based on time of service, but other types of vesting can occur. In this chapter, we explore the types of vesting you might experience depending on your job and the company's situation.

Recognize that the concept of vesting applies to more benefits than just equity grants. Some companies, particularly larger companies, may have vesting schedules associated with other benefits, such as 401(k) retirement plan contribution matching funds. Whatever the concept is applied to, its purpose is to avoid prematurely rewarding you too richly while you are new to the company and then, once you become a valued employee, to tie you to the company for as long as possible.

Time-Based Vesting

The most common form of vesting in startups is time-based. When companies establish their incentive stock plans, they create a standard vesting schedule that applies to all grantees by default. The time-based vesting schedule specifies that each grant transitions from unvested to vested in increments, provided the grantee remains in the continuous service of the employer.

The most common vesting time frame for regular employees is four years. A standard vesting schedule may contain a cliff vesting point at which a meaningful portion of the grant vests, say 25 percent after 12 months. That leaves the remaining 75 percent to vest in equal increments over the remaining 36 months of the vesting schedule. The grant is fully vested once the employee has worked the entire four years from the vesting start date.

You may wonder why the first 25 percent usually doesn't vest for a year. Wouldn't it make sense that you would start to vest immediately, and the equity would vest equally over the entire vesting period? The underlying rationale is that new employees are not very productive to their employers. It takes a lot of time, effort, and money to recruit new hires and get them up to speed.

The one-year cliff reflects a probationary period. Employees may leave if they are unhappy. The company may terminate them if they are not progressing quickly enough. The company doesn't want employees to own equity until they have been around long enough to prove themselves.

While the 12-month cliff followed by equal monthly vesting may be a standard schedule, incentive stock plans allow company management and the board to modify the vesting schedule as they see fit. It is rare to see vesting schedules for employees shorter than three years or longer than five years. Some companies backload the schedule so that a smaller proportion of the grant vests during the first couple of years and a larger proportion vests in the later years. This may feel punitive, but it preserves more equity for the investors and rewards employees who stick it out for the long term.

Other modifications may apply to non-employee grantees, such as board members or advisory board members. Board members may not serve the company for an extended period, and most startups pay no cash compensation to individuals in those roles—equity is their only payment. In those cases, the vesting period may be reduced from four years to three or even two years. By shortening the vesting schedule, a startup gives accomplished business leaders a greater incentive to join as board members or advisors because they know their grants will vest quickly.

Incentive grants also compensate interim executives or consultants who may only plan to be with the company temporarily to fill a gap. At Fugue, we hired an interim VP of sales to work for the company for less than a year. The size of his option grant reflected that tenure. Since vesting is based on continuous service, it would have been unfair to grant a short-timer options with a vesting period longer than he was contracted to stay with the company.

Milestone-Based Vesting

Beyond the time-based approach, equity grants can be set up to vest based on the company or individual reaching a goal. The goal can be revenue-oriented or operational. Achieving the goal results in designated equity grants converting to vested from unvested.

Milestone-based grants are relatively rare and can be a strong motivator for individuals or teams to focus on achieving critical company or individual objectives. You can think about them like commissions for salespeople. If the employee meets the goal, the grant vests, and the employee realizes the value of the grant. If not, they won't.

One variation on milestone-based vesting is that some grants may have a time-based component with a kicker. If a milestone objective is achieved, irrespective of the time-based vesting schedule, some or all the grants may vest on an accelerated time frame.

Milestone-based grants can also serve as an alternative to bonus payments if a company becomes cash-constrained. In the early days of Fugue, I agreed a couple of times to swap performance-based cash bonuses for options.

Milestone-based vesting can come in infinite forms and reflect the company's priorities and particular objectives for the individuals who receive them. You may never receive a milestone-based grant, but they are a potential sweetener as you negotiate your compensation package. Consider asking for this feature for special projects or committing to going above and beyond to move your company forward.

Accelerated Vesting

Most options vest on a time-based schedule. The phrase *accelerated vesting* refers to the vesting of all or a portion of an equity grant in conjunction with a liquidity event (i.e., sale, change of control, or IPO). These events are called **triggers**. Accelerated vesting is an enormously valuable feature of your grant if you can get it. It is typically reserved for senior executives, board members, and outside advisors, but you can try to negotiate for it.

The fundamental value of accelerated vesting is that it activates a designated proportion of unvested stock immediately upon the triggering event taking place. When the previously unvested grant accelerates, its value can be realized immediately. In the case of a company sale, the vested portion of a grant gets paid out of the sale proceeds, while unvested grants don't. If a portion of the grant flips from unvested to vested due to acceleration, it becomes eligible to participate in the payout. If you have accelerated vesting as part of your grant, it can mean many thousands of extra dollars to you.

What Happens When Your Grant Becomes Fully Vested?

Once you have been at your company for a few years, your equity grant becomes fully vested. Since vesting is designed to keep you tied to the company, shouldn't the company issue you a new grant? If they don't, what incentive do you have to stay? At this point, your company has a decision to make.

Assuming they want to keep you, the obvious answer is that when your options get close to being fully vested, your company should give you more equity and try to lock you in for another four years. This action is called *regreening*. Some companies have protocols that regreen employee stock grants and issue new grants when the prior grant has vested 50 to 75 percent. That is a sophisticated program and indicates a more mature company. For most startups, regreening is an afterthought. If they do it at all, the process is haphazard and subjective.

Whether or not your company chooses to regreen your equity grant varies based on several factors, including the type of equity grant. If the company issues RSUs, once your grant vests, you can walk away while still owning your RSUs. In that situation, your cost of leaving the company is relatively low, so the company may feel compelled to regreen your RSUs to keep you around. Some larger companies issue RSUs yearly so there is always a layered set of vesting schedules that never reach full maturity on all grants.

If your company issues options, the situation is not as clear-cut. Even if your option grant is fully vested, choosing to leave forces you to exercise your options unless you have an extended post-termination exercise period. Having to lay out cash creates a high cost for you to leave. Your company may be counting on the fact that you would like to keep your options but don't want to shell out a lot of cash to exercise them.

Combining the need to lay out cash with the tax consequences of buying shares that you can't sell because there is no market makes for an even tougher decision. Knowing that the decision to exercise options can be costly for employees, companies can afford to be less generous in refreshing option grants, even for fully vested employees. The fact that the employee holds unexercised options may be enough to keep them at the company, even if those options are fully vested.

Once your options have fully vested, you may feel that your company should regreen you. It seems fair and appropriate right? In theory, yes. The whole time you have been working, you have been earning cash compensation and vesting into more equity. Once you fully vest, you're not earning more equity unless you get a new grant, so it is as if you took a significant pay cut to keep working there.

In practice, however, given the dynamics at play and the general reluctance among startup boards to issue equity and further dilute shareholders, don't count on getting a new grant unless your company has an explicit regreening policy. Sophisticated company management recognizes the retention power of unexercised options as well as the upside potential still embedded in vested options.

If you feel getting a new grant is important, have a conversation and advocate for yourself. There is an implicit threat that if you don't get what you want, you might leave, so be diplomatic. If you get a new grant, it will likely be a fraction of the size of your initial grant, start vesting from zero, and bear a higher strike price with lower inherent upside than your prior grants (assuming the company's valuation has been steadily rising).

Unvesting

Sometimes, outright holders of stock are asked to subject their holdings to a vesting schedule. This is a rare but painful situation for those holding the stock. In Chapter 8 (Taking Stock), we discussed that company founders issue themselves stock when they start their company. Unless there are multiple founders and they are particularly forward-thinking, most founders do not apply a vesting schedule to their stock. When the company is founded, they own their shares outright.

It can be tricky when co-founders enter a partnership and issue their stock without applying a vesting schedule. Once a founder owns their shares outright, they can leave the company and retain all their shares. At that point, there is likely no good mechanism for clawing back equity without a painful and often unsuccessful negotiation. If the founders enter this situation, it can be highly disruptive to the company. So, co-founders should issue their initial shares with a vesting schedule that clarifies how long they are expected to stay at the company to own their founder's shares outright.

Having no vesting schedule on founder stock also creates an interesting dynamic when the company goes for outside funding. While founders want to hire employees and incentivize them to stay through equity grants that vest over time, those same golden handcuffs do not apply to founders whose stock is fully vested. Investors have a strong incentive to ensure that key employees, including the founders, stay at the company. So, they have to address this double standard.

As part of the terms for funding the company, investors may insist that the founders **unvest** their stock. In those situations, the founders must agree to earn back their founders' shares through continuous service to the company for an agreed-upon period. If they don't agree, the investors may not fund the deal. It may not be the full four years of a standard vesting schedule, but it will likely be at least two.

As part of Fugue's early funding, our VCs insisted that the four company founders agree to a thirty-month vesting schedule on two-thirds of their previously fully owned stock. The founders had no intention of leaving the company, so it turned out to be a non-issue.

While the founders may not intend to leave the company, having their stock unvested poses a risk. When new investors take significant roles on the board, they can restructure management. The board could terminate a founder or co-founder whose shares have been unvested, causing them to lose a substantial part of their ownership stake. So part of the negotiation also needs to address what happens if the founder or co-founder is terminated.

What Happens When Your Company is Acquired?

The ultimate hope among option holders is that someday, someone pays a good price for your company, and you realize the fruits of your labor. But what about your unvested options? Again here, the answer is it depends. For most employees, there is no immediate payout for unvested stock. After all, at the time of the company sale, unvested grants won't yet have accrued the rights and privileges associated with ownership.

In certain situations, unvested grants vest through acceleration for select team and board members, and they get paid out from the sale proceeds. For those holding unvested RSUs or options, it is a bit of a crap shoot. The acquiring company may choose to roll over your unvested grant and allow you to continue to vest into the new company's stock. This involves a conversion ratio of the options to represent the fact that your company's stock is valued differently from the acquiring company's stock. Alternatively, they may choose not to honor the existing unvested portion of your grant. In that case, the remainder of the unvested grant is terminated.

Assuming they want to keep you, the buyer would have to offer a new equity grant. It may or may not be as generous as what you had before. You also must start over from day one with a new vesting schedule on the new grant you receive. The boulder you pushed up the hill to vest your grants will have rolled partially or fully down the hill, which can be demoralizing.

There are other tradeoffs in receiving grants from the acquiring company. On one hand, the new grant will likely be at a relatively higher valuation than the grants you received in your company before it was acquired. On the other hand, the acquiring company will probably be farther along the proof continuum we discussed in Chapter 3 (Prove It!). You may have less of the "ground floor" potential of receiving a grant at an early-stage startup, but the fact that the acquirer is farther along in its journey may reduce your risk. They may be closer to an IPO or a sale of their own. Or they may already be public. You could be holding stock with less upside but a greater likelihood of realizing a payout when your new employer has its own liquidity event.

The best situation may be if a public company acquires your company. At that point, if you are issued new options as part of the conversion, you can vest into options that can be exercised for shares in the public company and sold immediately. Public company shares are readily tradable, so you can convert those shares into cash anytime you want.

Not long after my wife's company, OTG Software, went public in 2000, it was acquired by another public company, Legato Systems. A few years later, Legato was acquired by EMC Corporation, an even larger public company. After each acquisition, the acquirer rolled the employees' unvested options into their plan. The employees who remained with the company, including my wife, continued vesting into their grants and realized substantial value from their options, which they were able to cash out because EMC was public.

The Bottom Line

Equity grants are designed to keep you tethered to your company long-term. Over time or based on certain milestones or achievements, you vest into your equity grants and realize the rights and benefits of owning company stock. Owning stock does not guarantee a large payout, as there remains an underlying risk that the company may not succeed. But part of the allure of working for startups is equity ownership, and vesting is the mechanism through which most people realize that goal.

Equity is only one compensation component keeping you at your company, and it is the least certain. Cash compensation is more critical in the short term. If your cash compensation is not competitive with the market, the equity you earn may not ultimately compensate you for the opportunity cost of foregoing higher cash earnings elsewhere.

More importantly, the decision to stay at a company for the medium to long term should rest heavily on whether you see the company progressing toward success, whether your career is advancing, and whether the company remains a good fit for you personally and professionally. Don't let the gold-plated handcuffs of equity grants bind you to a situation that is not right for you.

---CHAPTER 11---

Equity and Inequity

We have been discussing the concept of equity as it pertains to ownership in a company. An equally important definition of "equity" sometimes gets lost in startups–fairness and impartiality.

Startups allow employees to participate in their companies' upside through issuing incentive-based equity compensation such as options. From the investors' perspective, giving equity to employees is required to motivate employees to stay committed and help build the dream. Without the employees who do the work, there would be no company.

Investors don't, as a rule, reward employees for no reason. Equity grants and other rewards are a *quid pro quo*. Investors grant them to achieve an outcome. When investors or senior managers demonstrate fairness or generosity toward employees, it is typically driven by the need to stay competitive with the marketplace. It should be no surprise that raises and promotions are often offered only when an employee has a competing job offer and is ready to leave.

Investors, who have a substantial degree of control over the affairs of most startups, are first and foremost looking out for their own interests. Their primary objective is to deliver high returns for themselves and their firms' limited partners. In fact, it is their duty.

Startups have an institutional bias in favor of investors. By design, company officers serve at the pleasure of the board of directors, many, if not most, of whom are representatives of the major investors. Those officers and board directors have a fiduciary responsibility to look out for the interests of the shareholders, who, in large measure, are the investors. So any decisions or rewards that favor employees are weighed against this responsibility.[34]

Given the governance structures that exist in most venture-backed startups, the economic deck is stacked against the average employee. We saw this clearly in Chapter 2 in Exhibit 2-2, with VCs in the upper right of the chart and employees in the lower left. As long as all the players' incentives remain tightly aligned, your interests should be well-served by investors' actions and decisions. There are times, however, when your interests diverge from those of your company's investors. In those situations, the power dynamic among investors, management, board, and employees often results in the investors winning and the employees losing.

"All animals are equal, but some are more equal than others"

In George Orwell's *Animal Farm,* a group of farm animals throws off the yoke of human oppression and attempts to establish a utopian society. Regardless of their initial rhetoric about egalitarian values and equality, societal stratification inevitably emerges, and a small group of animals led by Napoleon the Pig ends up on top of society.

Many startups try to portray an image of egalitarianism. They profess to be flat organizations with open-door policies. They promote the impression that all team members have equal value

---

[34] Real or even perceived failure on the part of company management and the board to fulfill their fiduciary responsibilities to investors can result in litigation pitting the investors against the company. This often happens at the time of a company exit when the distribution of proceeds becomes clear.

and that everyone can significantly influence the direction of the company. The layers of hierarchy in a startup may indeed be fewer than in a large corporation. But that doesn't change the fact that there are deciders and doers. Even among the doers, some animals are "more equal". On top of all the "animals" in a startup sit the equivalents of Napoleon the Pig–the board and investors.

Startups represent a pure form of capitalism. Those who invest capital and accumulate power walk away with the lion's share of the profits. Those who serve at their pleasure receive what's left. When we sold Fugue, one of our team members, after realizing how minimal his payout was relative to the outside investors, declared to me, "I need to figure out how to get on the investors' side of the table!"

You can't blame former startup veterans who choose to become investors in the next phase of their careers rather than continuing to slog it out working in the trenches. Investors have the upper hand with stock ownership in the company in a whole host of ways. Their relative privileges extend from the company's capital structure to control over policy-level governance, and even, in the case of very involved investors, how the company runs day to day.

Recognizing the myriad ways the deck is stacked in favor of investors may help you navigate some situations to your benefit. At the very least, you can understand some of the decisions your investors and senior leadership make and recognize that they are rarely made with your best interest as the primary consideration. So, let's explore exactly how investors are "more equal" than others in the typical startup.

Investors' shares are more equal than employees' shares

When it comes to the structure of ownership, there are several differences that benefit investors, including the following:

- Investors own preferred shares, while employees own common shares or, more frequently, options on common shares.

- Often, the vast majority of common shares are held by a small number of founders and senior executives who are beholden to the board and the investors for their positions.

- Non-founder employees typically hold less than 10 to 15 percent of outstanding common shares.

- Investors own their shares outright. Employee shares or options must vest, and unvested shares are subject to forfeiture if not exercised when employees leave.

- If there is a **down round** when the company raises money at a lower valuation than previous rounds, investors have **anti-dilution provisions** that result in them getting issued more shares. Common shareholders do not have anti-dilution provisions. That process causes the ownership of common shareholders to get additionally diluted, often substantially.

- With normal liquidity preferences for preferred shares, investors have the choice to either take their money off the top or convert to common shares to get higher payouts depending on the price of the company sale, whichever is better for them. The difference comes directly out of the pockets of common shareholders and option holders.

- With participating preferred stock, investors not only get their money (or a multiple of it) back, but they also get to convert their preferred stock to common stock and participate in distributions to common shareholders on a *pro-rata* basis.

- When investors grant themselves shares or options for serving on the board, they typically have shorter vesting schedules than employee shares, and they receive full accelerated vesting in a liquidity event, which most employees don't.

Investors' governance rights are more equal than employees' rights

Along with the beneficial economic provisions associated with investors' shareholdings, an equally important privilege investors have is the ability to control major decisions through governance provisions spelled out in the company charter and the investment documents. These privileges mean that investors have governance rights that employees do not have, as follows:

- Investors appoint directors and often serve as directors themselves, which gives them extraordinary power over the affairs of the company.

- Investors get to vote. Option holders, which most employees are, don't. Neither do RSU holders whose shares have yet to vest.

- Investors get to vote as a separate class of preferred shareholders, often giving them veto power over major decisions.

- Investors also have the right to vote with the common shareholders on an as-converted basis[35], giving them double influence to affect decisions.

Investors' operational control is more equal than employees' control

The investors' governance rights come along with operational-level controls that influence how the company is run. Employees do

---

[35] "On an as-converted basis" means that preferred shareholders receive the right to vote alongside common shareholders as part of the common share class based on the number of common shares their preferred shares would convert into, even if that conversion has not yet taken place.

not have the same degree of operational control. Some differences follow:

- Investors approve the operating plan, so they are the *de facto* appropriations committee dictating how and how much money gets spent.
- Investors show up for board meetings four to six times per year, expressing opinions that can be confusing or disruptive, sometimes causing company leadership to veer from established plans to respond to investor concerns.
- Investors can demand that the company control its burn, including the curtailment of essential product or marketing initiatives; suspension of bonuses; salary, promotion, and hiring freezes; and layoffs.
- Investors exert enormous influence on who the senior executives are and often control the hiring of new executives. They can install individuals they know are loyal to them and who may want to work for the investors' portfolio companies again.

Investors' downside risk protection is more equal than employees' risk protection

Investors have much less risk of suffering financial hardship if a startup fails than employees do. Startups are inherently high-risk ventures. The economic and governance privileges that investors have protect them from being wiped out if things go awry. If their startup fails, employees lose their jobs and any money they have invested to exercise options. Some of the differences include:

- Investors usually (although not always) invest other people's money. They may not have a lot of their own skin in the game. If the company fails, it's a minor blemish but doesn't put them out of work.

- If things get tough, investors can walk away and refuse to invest more to keep the company going. The fallout of a failed company may be political for partners in a VC firm. Continuing to invest if they expect the company will not succeed would be a bad decision and could put their standing and career advancement in their partnership at risk. Sometimes, they would rather let a company fail than commit to putting more time and capital into a deal.

- Even if they do walk away, investors still own their shares. If employees leave, they lose their unvested options and must exercise their vested options or lose them as well.

- If there is a distress sale, investors may provide incentives to key management personnel to stick out the transaction (known as a **management carve-out**) for whatever the company gets. In those situations, rank-and-file employees get nothing and may find themselves out of work.

Can You Level the Playing Field?

Investors have formidable structural advantages. You probably can't change their underlying incentives or the direction of the company. But you can do a few things to optimize your situation. It starts with information. From there, determine what power you may have to make changes that can benefit you.

- First, understand your company's situation. Is it growing or stagnant? Is it well-funded or running on fumes? Is it winning in the market or struggling to compete?

- Second, as discussed in Chapter 2 (The Cast), study each player and their motivations. Are the board, investors, and management aligned on the company's direction? Is the board supportive, indifferent, or just looking to salvage their investment and get out?

- Third, consider your stature in the company. Do you fill a critical role? Are you a key player? What is your relationship with senior management? How strong is your position to advocate for yourself? What levers can you pull to reduce your risk or improve your upside?

In the context of these questions, consider your most significant concerns and formulate a strategy to address them. You won't be able to affect the company's governance, but you can try to insulate yourself from downside risk or secure more upside.

If you are worried the company may not survive, focus on maximizing your cash compensation in the short term and develop an exit plan. If your company is on a path to success, determine if there are ways to lock in your upside, such as asking for accelerated vesting on change of control or an extended period to exercise your options if you leave.

One of my wife's companies had an unusually employee-friendly option exercise policy. Once an option grant was fully vested, the employee would have five years to exercise those options after leaving the company. The policy recognized that once employees had made significant contributions, they should reap the rewards without being forced to exercise their options within the standard 90-day post-departure window.

The ways you might advocate for minor or major modifications to your compensation or terms of employment are too many to list. But as with any negotiation, consider your leverage points relative to your company. Ask for changes that benefit you while costing the company relatively little, and you may succeed in lowering your risk and improving your odds of winning.

The Bottom Line

A successful outcome for a startup is by no means guaranteed. Most startups fail. On top of those long odds, the deck is heavily stacked in favor of the investors. Not only do they control most of the stock, but they make the rules and are heavily incentivized to create rules that favor themselves economically.

For employees to do well, the company must do extraordinarily well. Of course, success is relative. To an employee, a payout of a few hundred thousand dollars may be life changing. Investors, however, may consider the deal a bust if they don't clear tens or hundreds of millions.

In the end, you have little control over how the company does. You have even less control over the rules that investors make up to protect their interests. The dynamics of startup equity are intrinsically unfavorable for employees. When you factor in dilution from multiple funding rounds, liquidity preferences, vesting, the short time window to exercise options if you leave, and the lack of liquidity of private company stock ownership, the odds of employees realizing a meaningful payout can be extremely remote.

If it makes you feel any better, misery loves company. Similar dynamics often apply to the early angel investors who provide seed-stage funding. They provide the fuel to get the rocket launched. But once larger institutional investors come into the deal, angels are often cast aside and their interests are subordinated to larger, later-stage investors.

The irony is that the employees and early investors take the most risk but often end up just helping the richest get richer. The only way you can try to change that dynamic is through the power of information and careful consideration of what battles you can fight to capture a little more of the pie for yourself.

CHAPTER 12

The Life and Times of an Equity Grant

My journey with Fugue started on a cold winter day in the second week of February 2012. My old friend, Josh Stella, wanted advice on a business idea. I listened with interest, as I had done a few times before, but with the skepticism of an angel investor who had been burned a few times.

Josh and I met in 1998 at USLaw.com, a company I co-founded that ultimately ran into the implosion of the tech markets when the Internet bubble burst. Unable to raise our Series B, USLaw.com limped into oblivion, leaving 91 people out of work. Josh was the company's Chief Technology Officer (CTO), and despite USLaw's ill fate, we developed a strong friendship and lasting mutual professional respect.

In the years to come, he would call every so often, reminding me that he had a small group of fellow developers interested in starting their own company and exploring ideas. On previous occasions when Josh had called with startup ideas, I quickly dismissed them as not big or differentiated enough. This time was different.

Josh laid out a vision for a security approach for distributed computing systems that struck me as a big idea. He explained that with the advent of cloud computing, traditional security approaches

185

focused on protecting the perimeter of data-center computing systems would become obsolete. Not being a technologist myself nor knowledgeable about cybersecurity, the best I could offer was a general opinion that the idea sounded intriguing and the promise to introduce Josh to a friend.

Tim Webb had been making angel and venture investments in cybersecurity companies for more than twenty years. After I made the introduction, I didn't think about it until a couple of months later when Tim called to talk again. He wondered out loud what rock Josh had been hiding under. A technologist with Josh's vision and talent should not have gone unnoticed for so long. Josh had been building technology for the Coast Guard in West Virginia, not exactly a hotbed of venture investing. Hidden from the spotlight of the nation's hot tech markets, Josh and his prodigious capabilities had gone unnoticed. That was about to change.

Tim believed that Josh was onto something. He suggested we wrap our arms around Josh and his co-founders to help make their vision a reality. In November 2012, Josh asked Tim, my wife, Amena Ali, and me to join his advisory board. We readily agreed and began the quest to chart Fugue's path forward.

The Grant is Issued

Over the coming months, it became evident that the company needed someone to help organize the business side of the house. Josh and I agreed that I would join the company half-time as the Interim Chief Financial Officer. My goal was to install the business infrastructure to run the company and help Josh raise the company's seed round. All the founders were still working other jobs and needed funding to be able to focus full-time efforts on their startup. I anticipated a four to six-month effort. After that, I would make way for the company to hire a permanent financial executive to replace me.

Having raised no capital to date, the company could not compensate me in cash for my services, so we agreed on an equity grant of 10,000 shares of common stock. Tim and Amena also received grants for their advisory services. The notional price[36] of each share was set at $1, placing the overall company valuation at $1.2 million.

I provide this background to illustrate the dynamics of an early-stage venture and stock-based compensation. I received that initial stock grant in May 2013. Over the next 2-1/2 years, I progressed from half-time interim CFO to acting CFO to full-time CFO in April 2016. Despite intending to be at the company for only four to six months to help it get off the ground, I ended up staying until October 2021, nearly eight-and-a-half years.

While I received numerous additional grants for my services over those eight years, I want to focus on the evolution of what that initial grant represented in terms of ownership and nominal value. The ups and downs of this equity grant over its life cycle are somewhat extreme. But its evolution demonstrates how a meaningful equity grant may turn out to be different from what it appeared at the outset.

What Goes Up Might Come Down

The initial grant I received represented 0.833 percent of the shares of the company at the time of issuance. By the time the company completed its first four rounds of fundraising (through the Series D Preferred), the percentage ownership had been diluted by two-thirds. At that point, the shares represented less than 0.3 percent ownership. But with the dramatic rise in the company's valuation, the initial $10,000 worth of stock was now worth more than $400,000 on paper!

---

[36] I say "notional price" because valuing a startup is an inexact process, especially prior to any outside funding. The value of the shares was assigned without reference to any metrics or valuation methodology.

While raising money at increasing valuations is what you usually want in a startup, Fugue had raised outside funding at valuations far above the company's progress on the proof continuum. We developed great technology but failed to productize it to appeal broadly to commercial customers. So, while we managed to raise $75 million due to the exuberant support of our lead investor from NEA, the company's fundamentals hadn't kept up. It was a house of cards poised to collapse.

For a couple of years after closing the $40 million Series D, Fugue struggled to build market traction. In mid-2018, Josh and the investors brought in an accomplished CEO, Phillip Merrick, to help chart a new course. By late that year, Phillip decided to jettison the company's original product, focus product development on a new offering, and discontinue serving some early customers. To cut cash burn and extend the company's runway to pursue the new strategy, we laid off half the staff. It was a bet-the-company moment.

The new direction proved sound. However, by mid-2020, it became clear that the company would have to raise another round of capital to keep going. We had acquired a few dozen customers with our new approach, but revenue was far from enough to justify the lofty Series D valuation. To attract new investors, we were forced to swallow a painful pill and accept investment at a significantly lower valuation than the Series D—a phenomenon known as a down round or **recapitalization.**

After a long and challenging fundraising process, we accepted a term sheet for the Series A-1 round at a valuation more in line with a typical Series A startup valuation. Despite Fugue's significant progress, the market valued the company more than 90% lower than in the preceding financing round four years earlier. The down round triggered the anti-dilution provisions of the previously issued preferred shares, dramatically diluting the ownership of the common shareholders. That chain of events was catastrophic for my original 10,000 share grant.

In Exhibit 12-1, you can see the changes in the ownership percentage represented by that initial grant of stock and the corresponding value of the stock over time. By the time Fugue was acquired in February 2022, the ownership percentage of my initial stock grant had plummeted from 0.833 percent to 0.003 percent. After the 67 percent dilution from the initial grant through the Series D, the dilution from the last round caused the percentage ownership of those shares to drop by an additional 99 percent.

Factoring in all of the funding rounds, the ownership percentage represented by those original advisor shares dropped by a whopping 99.96 percent. Putting this in dollar terms, when the shares were issued, they had a nominal value of $10,000. At their peak, their worth rose to more than $400,000 on paper. But when the company sold for approximately $120 million in early 2022, I received proceeds of only $3,000 for those shares.[37]

	Preferred Round	Capital Raised ($ Millions)	Post-Money Valuation ($ Millions)	Post Funding Ownership (Percent)	Value of Shares ($ Thousands)
May 2013	Initial Grant	–	1.2	0.83	$10.0
Feb. 2014	Series A	3.8	13.3	0.71	$94.0
Aug. 2014	Series B	10.0	33.0	0.49	$162.0
Dec. 2015	Series C	20.0	90.0	0.38	$342.0
Dec. 2016	Series D	41.0	161.0	0.28	$451.0
Jul. 2021	Series A-1*	10.4	20.4	0.003	$0.6
Feb. 2022	Exit**	–	120.0	0.003	$3.0

*The Series A-1 round was part of a recapitalization of the company through which all prior preferred shares received anti-dilution treatment and then were forced to convert to common shares in a significant down round.

**The value of shares at exit were calculated after payments of the participating preferred shares held by investors.

Exhibit 12-1: Advisor Grant Value Over Time

[37] The shares were worth $10,000 when originally issued and $3,000 when sold, so I could claim a capital loss of $7,000 on my taxes, recouping a portion of my loss.

Even though the company sold for 100 times its value when my shares were first issued, by the time of the sale, the value of my shares dropped by 70 percent. To put that in perspective, had the shares still represented the initial ownership percentage at which they started (0.833 percent), they would have yielded $1 million in proceeds instead of $3,000.

Almost everyone who worked at Fugue saw the value of their equity grants issued before the Series A-1 drop dramatically because of the successive rounds of funding and the crushing recapitalization. Those who left the company before the Series A-1, including two co-founders, saw the value of their common shares decline to negligible amounts.

On the other hand, those still at the company after the round closed received new options at a much lower price and realized the opportunity for material upside when the company was sold. The new options were issued with an exercise price of $0.10 per share and yielded proceeds of $3.00 per share at the time of sale—a 2,900 percent rise in value.

The investors in the Series A-1 round in 2021 reaped significant rewards from the rapid turnaround and sale of the company the following year. Fortunately, a few colleagues and I also participated in that round, hoping to salvage some value from our years working at the company. With the low valuation and the company's progress in the market, we believed it would be the best time in the company's history to invest. We could have been wrong and lost our investment, but we had progressed far enough along the proof continuum that a lot of the risks had been addressed. We had a proven product, were attracting and retaining great customers who seemed to love our product and were operating in the hot cloud security space.

Not all employees had the funds or risk tolerance to put their cash on the line. Considering that the company had nearly run out of money and gone out of business before securing the Series A-1 funding, the risk of losing our investment was high. But in the end, I made more money by investing in that round and holding that investment for less than a year than I did from all the incentive equity grants I received while working at the company for more than eight years.

My experience wearing two hats—investor and employee—represented the broader outcome for everyone in the company. The investors in the Series A-1 round walked away with tens of millions in profits after less than a year. The employees who built the company over more than ten years, including the founders, reaped a much smaller fraction of the rewards. Those who left the company earlier and early investors who chose not to participate in the prior rounds failed to reap significant rewards from the sale.

The Bottom Line

Owning equity in your company is motivational. It gives you a warm and fuzzy feeling to know you stand to gain from the company's success. However, until those shares or options are converted to cash through a company sale, they may not be worth the paper they are printed on. I have accumulated many worthless share certificates from defunct companies over the years. Some are from investments I made that failed. Some are from equity grants in companies like USLaw.com that never realized their potential.

Funding rounds that whipsaw valuation around are not usually as dramatic as they were in Fugue's case. Every funding round has an impact, positive or negative, on the value of your equity grants. It is exciting to see the value go up when the company raises money at a high valuation. But as in the example, there is no guarantee your grants will be worth much in the end, even if you stick it out until the company exits.

Tracking and understanding milestone events such as funding rounds is critical to gauging the value and trajectory of your holdings. Armed with an understanding of your company's funding trajectory and status, you can better decide whether to stay or leave, exercise your options, or take advantage of the opportunity to invest if you have the chance.

CHAPTER 13

Optionality:
Two Types of Employee Stock Options

In this chapter, we briefly focus on two types of option grants that can result in different financial outcomes once you consider their tax treatment. As a startup employee, you may receive two types of options:

1. **Non-Qualified Stock Options**, also referred to as **Non-quals, NSOs,** or **NQSOs**

2. **Incentive Stock Options (ISOs)**.

The main difference between the two types is that ISOs offer significantly more favorable tax treatment if you follow specific guidelines about exercising them. These savings can add up to more than 20 percentage points. This favorable tax treatment comes from two sources:

- Capital gains tax treatment rather than ordinary income tax treatment, thus avoiding payroll taxes.

- Gains that qualify for long-term capital gains taxes rather than short-term capital gains taxes.

These two benefits occur because ordinary income is taxed at your marginal tax rate and is subject to payroll taxes like Social Security and Medicare. To qualify for capital gains treatment, you must exercise your options and hold the underlying stock. Once your gains in the stock qualify for capital gains treatment, you avoid payroll taxes when you sell the stock.[38] This is true regardless of how long you hold the stock and whether your capital gains are short or long term.

In addition, if you exercise your options and the underlying gains when the company is sold qualify for long-term capital gains taxes, you may save substantially on federal taxes depending on your income tax bracket.[39] To achieve optimal tax treatment, ISOs and NSOs require you to exercise the options *and* hold the underlying stock for at least a year. So, if you are going to exercise, the sooner you get the clock ticking on the holding period, the better.

On the other hand, if you never exercise your options, the tax treatment for both ISOs and NSOs is the same when your company is sold. By not exercising the options, regardless of the type of option you hold, you pay ordinary income taxes and applicable payroll taxes on the profits.

A word of caution. While there is a tax benefit to exercising and holding options, exercising your options means writing a check to the company and putting your capital at risk. The value of the stock may go down, or the company may fold before you cash out. Unless you are an investor, board member, or part of senior management, you have little or no control over if or when the company is sold. With this risk in mind, the decision to exercise your option grant should rest on whether you conclude exercising is a good investment, not solely on tax considerations.

---

[38] As of 2023, the employee's portion of payroll taxes could be as high as 7.65% on wage-related income.

[39] As of 2023, the savings in federal taxes from long-term capital gains treatment could be as high as 22%.

Non-Qualified Stock Options

NSOs are the most common form of options startups issue to employees. They can be issued to anyone for services rendered to the company. That can include employees, contractors, officers, directors, and advisors. They are called non-qualified because their characteristics do not qualify them for the favorable tax treatment that ISOs receive.

Like all options, NSOs are issued with an exercise price and follow a company-determined vesting schedule, which can include early exercise and vesting acceleration provisions. From a tax perspective, NSOs have the least favorable tax treatment among employee incentive equity grants. When an NSO is exercised, the difference between the exercise price and the then-current price or 409A common stock valuation is taxed as ordinary income on the employee's W-2.

For example, suppose you receive an NSO option grant for 1,000 shares with an exercise price of $1. After a year, 25 percent of the grant, or 250 shares, has vested. The company has completed a 409A valuation that established a new price of common shares at $2. If you exercise your vested options to buy 250 shares, you are taxed on the implicit gain of $250 (250 shares times the current 409A valuation of $2 minus the exercise price of $1). This gain is taxed as ordinary income and is deducted from payroll, just like any other wage-oriented tax withholding.

Once you exercise an NSO and pay the ordinary income tax from the transaction, the 409A valuation (in the example, $2) becomes your basis in the stock. Any additional appreciation in the stock price above the basis is subject to capital gains taxes when the stock is sold. So, if the company later sells for $5 per share, you will have capital gains of $3 per share ($5 per share sale price minus the $2 per share basis).

The tax rate on those capital gains depends on whether you hold the exercised stock for less than or more than a year. If the holding period is less than a year, your capital gains are considered short-term, and your rate is your marginal ordinary income tax rate. In this case, the main benefit you realize from exercising is that you avoid payroll taxes like Social Security and Medicare.

In the preceding example, if you chose not to exercise your shares and your company is sold for $5 per share, you would have a gain of $4 per share ($5 per share sale price less the $1 per share exercise price). Because you didn't exercise your options, you would not qualify for capital gains treatment, and the entire gain would be subject to ordinary income tax plus payroll taxes (Social Security and Medicare).

Incentive Stock Options

Since not all incentive stock grants are created equal in terms of their tax treatment, it is helpful to understand the differences between ISOs and NSOs. Let's start with the basics. Incentive Stock Options (ISOs) are issued exclusively to employees. Non-employees, including board and advisory board members and outside contractors, can only receive NSOs.

The purpose of ISOs is to provide valuable incentives to those actively building the company who are willing to exercise their options. That commitment of both their blood and treasure merits a powerful incentive. ISOs have a somewhat magical quality. If managed correctly, they can give you capital gains treatment on the difference between your exercise price and the share price when the company is sold. This represents a substantial financial benefit.

So, how do ISOs work? The company's incentive stock plan authorizes the issuance of either ISOs or NSOs, with board approval. The approved grant document designates the option as an ISO. The tax benefit of ISOs requires the option holder to exercise the option and hold the stock for at least one year from the exercise date or two years from the issuance of the option grant, whichever comes later. If these conditions are met, the stock purchased upon exercise gets long-term capital gains treatment *for the entire gain,* including the bargain element of the option at the time of exercise. Unlike NSOs, the tax is not due until the stock is eventually sold unless it is subject to the Alternative Minimum Tax.[40]

To illustrate the benefit of exercising ISOs, let's look at a simplified example of what happens in a liquidity event depending on whether you exercise. Suppose you receive a grant of 1,000 ISOs at an exercise price of $1 per share. You stay at the company long enough for the grant to become fully vested, and the company is sold more than a year after you fully vest.

Exhibit 13-1 shows the differences in tax liability on your proceeds from the sale depending on whether you exercised your options. Either way, your profit from the sale is $4,000. If you exercised, you would receive $5,000 for the stock that you previously paid $1,000 for when you exercised. If you didn't exercise, you would receive $4,000 ($5 per share minus the $1 exercise price netted from the automatic exercise at the time of the sale). The difference comes in when considering taxes.

If you didn't exercise, you would pay ordinary income tax rates. Ignoring state and local taxes and payroll taxes and assuming a 35 percent marginal Federal income tax rate, your tax liability would be $1,400 on the $4,000 profit. By contrast, if you did exercise, you would only owe the long-term capital gains tax rate of 15 percent or $600. So, in this example, by exercising you realized tax savings of $800 (a full 20 percentage points). That is a powerful incentive to exercise ISOs if you receive them, again, assuming you think the company stock is a good investment.

---

[40] Exercising ISOs may subject you to the Alternative Minimum Tax (AMT). If the bargain element is significant (i.e., you have a large built-in gain) when you exercise, the deferral of the taxes on the gain is considered phantom gains and potentially subject to AMT. Before exercising ISOs, consider the impact that action will have on your tax liability. ESO Fund provides a good explanation and gain calculator for ISO exercises. https://bit.ly/3XINRSL

Shares	1,000	1,000
Exercise price per share	$1	$1
Excercised?	Yes	No
Cost of Exercising	$1,000	$0
Sale price per share	$5	$5
Profit per share	$4	$4
Profit from sale	$4,000	$4,000
Tax treatment	Capital gains tax	Ordinary income tax
Tax rate paid	15%	35%
Taxes paid	$600	$1,400
Net	**$3,400**	**$2,600**

Exhibit 13-1: Comparison of ISO Tax Treatment in a Sale Scenario

In the example, we assumed you held the exercised shares for more than a year before the liquidity event. What happens if you don't meet the holding period? The ISO simply reverts to an NSO. Ordinary income taxes are due retroactively on the difference between the exercise price and the 409A valuation when you exercised. You owe capital gains taxes on further appreciation beyond that at the time of sale, just like with an NSO. You just need to keep good records to calculate the taxes correctly after the fact.

ISOs have one final complication. To avoid creating excess incentives for senior executives, ISO treatment is limited to $100,000 of vesting options yearly. Companies must multiply the exercise price per share by the shares that vest each calendar year. If the calculation exceeds $100,000, the excess reverts to being an NSO, usually automatically as a rollover provision in the incentive stock plan. This automatic provision prevents the company and employees from running afoul of the tax laws. Most employees do not vest enough options annually to trigger the $100,000 ceiling on

ISOs, but it requires vigilance, especially for senior executives who receive large grants.[41]

The Bottom Line

When I try to remember the distinction between ISOs and NSOs—and the tax treatment and protocols for realizing the benefits of ISOs—I have to consciously remind myself of what they are and sometimes even look them up again. It's not something you think about every day or necessarily remember in detail, and it is certainly not intuitive. Unless your company has a practice of issuing ISOs, it may not be something you need to worry about.

Exhibit 13-2 provides a reference table to help remind you of the differences. In brief, if you don't exercise the option, the financial characteristics of the two types of options are identical—your gains are taxed as ordinary income when the company is sold. The major difference is that ISOs provide an additional tax benefit over NSOs, but only if you exercise them in advance of a liquidity event and are able to hold them for the required period of at least a year after exercising.

Given the complexities of dealing with ISOs from the company's and employees' perspectives, many companies choose not to issue them. Tracking ISOs and ensuring the company treats them correctly takes resources. Besides, in most startups, only a small percentage of employees exercise their options. Shouldering the burden of dealing with ISOs for the benefit of just a small number

---

[41] An example of a large grant of ISOs: An executive receives a grant of 1 million shares that vest over 4 years at an exercise price of $1. Each year, 250,000 shares vest. Only 100,000 of those vested options would qualify as ISOs each year (100,000 options x $1 per share). Each year, the remaining 150,000 options would become NSOs. Over the life of the grant, 400,000 options would be ISOs and the remaining 600,000 would become NSOs. There is still a substantial potential tax benefit if the executive takes advantage of the ISOs and exercises them, and the company is ultimately sold for a substantial price.

	Non-Qualified Options	Incentive Stock Options
Eligible recipients	Employees, board members, and contractors	Employees only
Tax treatment upon exercise	Ordinary income plus payroll taxes on bargain element upon exercise New basis established at 409A price upon exercise	Tax on gain deferred until stock sold May be subject to alternative minimum
Tax treatment if unexercised	Short-term capital gains on difference between sale price and price of 409A at time of exercise	Ordinary income tax plus payroll taxes
Tax treatment if exercised and held less than 1 year	Short-term capital gains on difference between sale price and price of 409A at time of exercise	Short-term capital gains on difference between sale price and exercise price
Tax treatment if exercised and held more than 1 year	Long-term capital gain on difference between sale price and 409A price at time of exercise	Long-term capital gain on difference between sale price and exercise price

Exhibit 13-2: Comparison chart of ISOs and Non-Quals

of employees is a cost/benefit tradeoff many companies don't find worthwhile.

However, if your company issues ISOs, consider whether to exercise them to take advantage of the favorable tax treatment. Depending on the outcome of the sale of your company, the difference you pay in taxes could be worth many thousands of dollars.

----------CHAPTER 14----------

Weighing Your Options

Once you have received an incentive stock grant, how do you think about what it is worth today and in the future? The value of an option grant at a point in time seems simple. You take the current price of the company's common stock, subtract the option's exercise price, and multiply by the number of shares. But the value of an option grant is much more than that.

How Do I Value My Grant?

A privately-owned startup has no stock exchange where the company's securities trade. You can't look up a stock quote online to determine the current price. Information about a startup's stock is closely held and sometimes hard to come by. So how do you figure out the value of your incentive grant? Well, it depends.

When examining the value of your equity grant, what you choose to focus on is determined by what decision you're trying to make. You may be considering whether to exercise options, leave the company or both. Or you might simply be considering some financial planning that has nothing to do with your employment status. Each of those decisions puts a different spin on the calculation.

Start with the fact that your grant has both vested and unvested components. If you plan to leave your company, you may only care about the vested portion you can exercise upon departure. If you plan to stay through a liquidity event (i.e., sale or IPO), you would keep vesting until that happens, so valuing the full grant is more relevant.

Let's start by asking what the current value of your entire grant is at a given time. You can approach the valuation exercise from the top down or the bottom up. The top-down approach to valuation involves understanding your ownership percentage and the latest valuation of the company. The bottom-up method involves looking at how many shares you own and calculating the price per share applicable to your holdings. In a private company, both methods are somewhat imperfect but should lead you to similar answers.

For simplicity, both approaches assume there are no priority claims on cash distributions (such as debt or participating preferred shares) and that all investors convert their preferred shares into common shares. That is only true in the case of a liquidity event at a high price, so generally speaking, the following valuation methods represent the *maximum* value of your holdings. They could be worth much less depending on the priority claims from a liquidity event before common shareholders get paid.

The other issue to bear in mind is taxes. As you perform the valuation of your holdings, you will derive a gross valuation. But any transaction through which you realize the proceeds from your holdings will be subject to taxes and reduce your net payout accordingly.

Top-Down Valuation

At the simplest level, understanding the value of your incentive stock holdings using a top-down approach involves three pieces of data.

1. How many shares you own

2. How many total shares are outstanding in the company

3. The valuation of the company

With these three pieces of data, you can calculate the gross value of your options or RSUs at any given time using the following formula:

$$(\text{Your shares} / \text{Total outstanding shares}) * \text{the company's valuation} = \text{gross value}$$

For example, if you have 10,000 shares and there are 5 million total shares outstanding, your ownership percentage is 0.2 percent (i.e., 10,000 divided by 5,000,000). If the company's most recent funding round valued the company at $50 million, then, ignoring vesting for the moment, the gross value of your total grant is $50 million times 0.2 percent (0.002), which equals $100,000.

If you have restricted stock units (RSUs), then that's the current value of those RSUs. If you have options, that represents the gross value of the stock you would have if you exercised all of your options. You need to subtract the exercise price to understand the net value of the options at the moment.

How do you get the data to calculate the value of your holdings? Most companies use an equity management system (such as ShareWorks). Request access to it and register to use the system. Many employees never register or log into their system, which is a mistake. Log in and get familiar with the system and your holdings and ask your human resources or finance teams if anything you see is unclear.

You can view your grants and determine your vesting schedule through the equity management system. The system should also tell you what your holdings are as a percent of total shares in the company. From there, you can do some sleuthing to determine the company valuation from the last funding round. Sometimes that information is publicly available. Sometimes you need to unearth it by poking around inside the company with people in the know. Either way, with those two pieces of data, you are much closer to knowing the value of what you have.

Bottom-Up Valuation

You can also calculate the current value of your grant by multiplying the number of shares in your grant by the current stock price. This gets tricky because the price of the common stock, as determined by the 409A valuation, is different from the prevailing price of the preferred stock. You probably do not have access to the latest price of the preferred stock. To get it, you may need to make friends with someone in the finance department and persuade them to tell you.

To arrive at a reasonable approximation of the top-line value of your holdings, use the following formula:

(Current preferred stock price - your option exercise price) * (number of shares in your grant)

With RSUs, your exercise price is $0. If you have multiple grants, perform the calculation separately for each grant and then add the results to get the estimated value of your total holdings.

Let's consider an example. Assume you receive options at an exercise price of $1 per share, and the last financing round was $5 per share. Roughly speaking, the value of each option would be $4 per share ($5 per share minus the $1 exercise price). Multiply that by the number of options you have. That tells you the current bargain element (or net value) of your options at that point in time, excluding taxes.

Weighing your options means determining the value of your options at a point in time and using that information to help you make informed decisions to manage your career choices. The top-down approach starts with overall company valuation. It is a relative measure versus total ownership, which then begs the question of who has how much and whether that is a fair allocation of the overall equity in the company. Bottom-up valuation is more of an absolute valuation. Irrespective of what others have, it calculates what your options are worth today.

Watch Out for Waterfalls

A critical consideration in determining the value of your holdings is the waterfall of cash distributions. The company's funding history determines the waterfall and the valuation of the company relative to prior capital raised. Debtholders and outside investors have priority claims on cash distributions. Outstanding debt must be paid off. Preferred shareholders' liquidation preferences come into play if the company's valuation isn't high enough to motivate them to convert their preferred shares into common shares. The price per share the investors paid when they invested determines the liquidation preferences. It also matters whether they have participating or non-participating preferred shares.

Calculating the waterfall's effect on common shareholders' proceeds is easier said than done, as different investors convert to common shares at different sale prices. However, you should be able to get a rough handle on whether the company's valuation is significantly higher than the amount of capital raised in prior funding rounds. If not, there won't be much left over for the common shareholders and employees after the priority claims are paid.

The Ups and Downs of Equity Grant Pricing

Understanding the value of your holdings requires knowing the price of your grant at the time it was issued. From there you can gauge the changes in the value of your holdings as the company's stock price moves. Let's spend a few minutes on how the option or RSU price is set.

When you receive an equity grant, it contains several key features, including the number of options or RSUs, the exercise price in the case of options, the grant date, the vesting start date, and the vesting schedule (including any accelerated vesting). In Chapter 10 (Vested Interest), I discussed the grant size and how vesting works. Here I focus on the exercise price or strike price.

The basic formula to make money with stock is "buy low and sell high." The most important element influencing the potential value of the grant is the price of the common stock when the grant is issued. This is the "buy low" part of the equation.

A low exercise price allows you to benefit from a rise in the company's valuation reflected in a higher price per share at the time of exit (the "sell high" part of the equation). The other benefit is that if you want to exercise your option, it requires a smaller cash outlay.

The reverse scenario can also happen. A stock of a high-flying startup may have a lofty valuation, leading to an option strike price that is high and expensive to exercise. If the company hits snags along the way or the market takes a downturn, its valuation may go down, and the value of a share of common stock may end up below the option exercise price. This is called being **underwater**. At that point, you would never exercise the option; doing so would force you to pay more for the stock than its value at the time. You would just hold onto it and hope the stock price goes back up.

If the company were to be sold when the value of the stock is below the strike price, the bargain element of the option would technically be negative—though, practically speaking, it is worth $0. Exercising the option at a high price only to turn around and sell it at a lower price would lose you money. In this scenario, you would let the option go unexercised, and you would receive no payout from the proceeds of the sale.

Without a public market where stock prices are set, how do private companies determine the value of the stock they issue in equity grants? Decades ago, company management and boards would simply make up a valuation. The assumption was that the board would protect the interests of shareholders and that a fair and orderly price-setting process would occur. But with minimal restrictions on the process, this often proved not to be true.

To motivate their teams (and reward themselves), boards and management could set the strike price on options as low as they wanted to create the maximum possible incentives. With the board often in the back pocket of the founder or CEO of a company, this enabled a conspiratorial dynamic where the management and board could collude to transfer wealth from shareholders to insiders. The CEO set the course, and the board would rubber-stamp it.

In this scenario, as the valuation of the company continued to rise, the company could issue options to insiders (including board members to get them to go along) at very low prices, allowing them to reap huge rewards when the company went public or was acquired. This practice was rampant during the Dotcom era and came to a head during the Enron scandal.

As discussed in Chapter 9 (What Are Your Options?), in 2004, as part of broader legislation, a new provision of the Internal Revenue Code, Section 409A, was adopted to address this problematic dynamic. Section 409A regulates the price at which employees can buy equity in companies using deferred compensation programs, for example, incentive stock plans. In short, companies can no longer make up the strike price of options to suit their purposes. They must instead have a valuation performed at least once every twelve months by an independent third party to set the price.

The process of conducting the 409A valuation not only sets the price for the common stock but also provides management and board members a safe harbor (i.e., legal protections) when issuing equity grants. The board must officially adopt the price from the 409A report as the established value of the common stock underlying all equity grants. As long as any grants are issued with a common stock price at or above the 409A valuation, directors and officers of the company are insulated from claims that they lowballed the price to benefit insiders or employees. This helps protect them from shareholder lawsuits.

There are differences between preferred and common stock that are worth keeping in mind. Startup capitalization tables have both preferred and common stock. The prevailing price per share of the preferred stock is established (or marked to market) based on the price from the last funding round. If the company has not had a funding round for a while, the intrinsic value of the preferred shares may have changed due to outside market conditions or the company making progress. But the price may not have been adjusted, as most companies don't generally perform formal valuations of their preferred stock.

The 409A valuation sets the price of common stock. The outside firm conducting the valuation uses information from recent funding rounds and a variety of other information about the company's status and prospects. The 409A report usually contains several methodologies for coming up with a valuation, most of which are black-box approaches that make very little logical sense to the average person.

Regardless of methodology, the value of the common stock generally ends up being between 10 and 50 percent of the price of preferred stock in a venture-backed startup. To determine the difference between preferred and common stock prices, the valuation firm considers the liquidation preferences for preferred shares that take priority over common shares. Preferred shares are worth more than common mainly because their built-in liquidation preferences provide downside risk protection, as discussed in Chapter 11 (Equity and Inequity).

The variation between the low and high end of the range of common stock value is primarily based on how far away an exit event is and how favorable the liquidation preferences are for the preferred stock. The more favorable the preferences, the lower the common stock price is as a percentage of the preferred stock price. This is the key mechanism in the process through which incentive equity grants can be issued at low prices. Ironically, the very fact that common stock is valued far less than preferred stock is what creates the greatest potential value in the incentive stock grant for the recipient.

Let me explain. If the price of preferred stock in the last funding round was $3 per share, the 409A could result in a common stock valuation of $1 per share or 33 percent of the preferred price.

Assuming the company ultimately gets sold for $10 per share and the preferred shareholders choose to convert to common, all shareholders would receive the same amount per share—$10. Option holders issued options with a $1 exercise price would therefore receive a profit of $9 per share. The preferred shareholders who paid $3 per share would receive only $7 in profit per share.

This outcome may seem counterintuitive given all the advantages preferred shareholders have over common shareholders. Wouldn't you assume preferred shareholders should make more? In absolute, preferred shareholders may own more of the company and will receive higher overall proceeds. However, on a per-share basis, preferred shareholders would realize profits that are less than the earnings the options holders get. That extra $2 per share that option holders receive is a direct result of the 409A valuation process that valued the common stock lower than the preferred when setting the exercise price. When the preferred shares convert to common, all shares converge to the same valuation, and the price gap is closed, with common shares gaining a $2 per share step up in value.[42]

Once the 409A report is in place, the board can approve stock grants. The 409A report is statutorily valid for twelve months with some exceptions. Suppose material events happen, for example, a financing round. In that case, companies complete a new 409A valuation to ensure the board and management have a common stock valuation reflecting the company's current status. Until the 409A analysis is done, the board has no legal safe harbor to protect it when setting the exercise price, so no options should be issued. If you find yourself waiting a bit for your grant to be issued, this could be why.

---

[42] This is only true if the acquisition price is high enough to cause preferred share-holders to convert their shares to common shares and if their preferred shares are not participating preferred. In situations where the price is lower or there are participating preferred, the preferred shareholders will have preferential claims on cash flows that reduce the payout to common shareholders dollar-for-dollar.

The Future Value of Your Options

Thinking about the absolute valuation of your holdings at a given time is a way to calculate how much value you have accrued from investing your time in your company. It provides a reality check on whether your time invested over months or years will likely provide a meaningful payoff beyond the salary and bonuses you may have received. Savvy investors monitor the progress of their portfolios, and you should periodically try to get a handle on what your equity grants are worth to ensure you are making progress. Just don't obsess about it.

The long-term value of an option or RSU, however, is not so simple. It is not just the calculation of value at a point in time but the value that accrues in those holdings over time. Employee grants accrue value in two ways. First, the grants continue to vest. Second, the continued rise in the valuation of the company drives the stock price higher.

The uncertainty of the future value of the company makes option valuation difficult; it is so difficult that the complex mathematical formula used earned its creators a Nobel prize. If you are an options trader at a major financial institution, you would use the Black-Scholes Option Pricing model developed in 1973 to value your options position at a given time.[43]

As a startup employee, you might try to use Black-Scholes to value your options (I have tried!) But practically speaking, it gives you an answer that is likely inaccurate and won't help you make critical decisions. Whether to exercise your options or whether to stay or leave your company are not short-term trading decisions that require split-second analysis and precise calculations of

---

[43] "Derived by economists Myron Scholes, Robert Merton, and the late Fischer Black, the Black-Scholes Formula is a way to determine how much a call option is worth at any given time." *The Formula That Shook the World*, pbs.org, https://www.pbs.org/wgbh/nova/stockmarket/formula.html (accessed July 7, 2023)

the option value. Making those decisions demands a directional understanding of whether your options will gain or lose value over time. Just like long-term investors in stocks shouldn't worry about day-to-day price fluctuations in their portfolio, as an option or RSU holder, your perspective should be long-term. Remembering the "buy low, sell high" paradigm, you need to understand a few things:

- How the issue price of your RSUs or the exercise price of options is determined

- Where your company sits on the proof continuum and how fast it is making progress

- What the sources of value are in the company (technology, management, market leadership, customer base, etc.)

- The likelihood that your company reaches a successful exit (IPO or sale), including conditions in the financial markets

- The composition of the company's waterfall

Once you assess these fundamentals, you are in a better position to evaluate how quickly the company is growing and the effect that has on whether your equity will be worth something meaningful in the future.

Exhibit 14-1 shows the effect on option valuations as a company progresses through the proof continuum and attracts capital at higher and higher valuations. Assume the company's operating progress coincides with funding at increasing valuations (i.e., the company does not experience a reduction in valuation through a recapitalization or down round). The closer to a successful exit you receive your options, the higher the exercise price and the less value they will accrue before the company sells. For example, in the exhibit, options issued at the Proof of Technology stage would have a lower exercise price than options issued at the Proof of Scale stage, giving the earlier options more opportunity to rise in value above the exercise price.

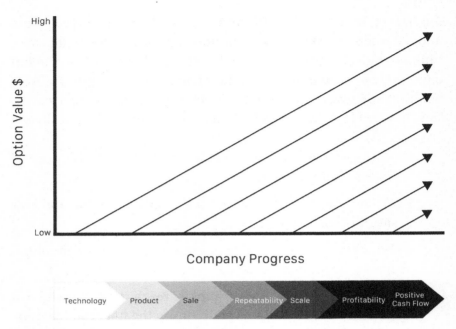

Exhibit 14-1: Effect of Company Progress on Option Value

The Bottom Line

Whether you have options or RSUs, the value of your holdings and the percentage those holdings are vested affect your decision-making. Failing to understand the value of your holdings may cause you to make uninformed decisions that you may regret later. Recognize that valuing your grants is somewhat challenging and do your best to get a rough idea of their worth; then think critically about what it means to your current situation and potential future opportunities.

Consider the value of your grants today and how they will grow from additional vesting. Assess whether your company is on a growth trajectory, treading water, or even going downhill. Evaluate what impact that trajectory will have on its stock price. Think about the company's waterfall and its effect on your option value.

Determine how those considerations affect your decision to stay or explore other options. You may find that walking away could be very costly as you leave a lot of embedded value from your options behind. Or you may find that the value of your grants is not that great or even underwater and not much of a tie that binds you to your company.

If you choose to walk away from your company, how you keep what's yours depends on whether you have options or RSUs. Vested RSUs are yours, and they can't be taken away. They are shares you own that you can hold until the company is sold or goes public. Options, however, are a different story. If you leave, you forfeit all your unvested options. To preserve the value of your vested options, you need to exercise them.

Regardless of whether you hold RSUs or exercise your options to acquire stock, for you to realize their value, the company must go through a liquidity event. That could be years down the road. For you to get paid, the company must be able to find you. Even if you leave, keep the company updated with your contact information—email and cell phone number. They may send you paperwork to sign to get your payout. If they can't find you or you don't respond, you risk never getting your due.

CHAPTER 15

The Price is Right

In December 1999, my wife Amena left her job at MCI WorldCom to take an executive role at OTG Software, a high-flying small software company about to go public. OTG had just taken in a pre-IPO funding round from several prestigious late-stage investors. Exciting times for sure.

OTG went public on the NASDAQ on March 10, 2000, just three months after Amena joined. On the initial day of trading, the company's stock soared 195 percent, riding the wave of the Internet boom. On paper, her options were worth nearly $4 million dollars. We were ecstatic.

Unfortunately, we had no way to capture that upside. Amena hadn't vested into any of her options yet. Furthermore, as an employee, she was subject to a **lock-up period,** which prevents insiders such as executives, employees, and early investors from selling stock in an IPO for typically 180 days. So, she would not have been able to cash out even if her options had been vested. All we could do was wait and hope that the stock would stay high.

Less than a month later, on April 5, 2000, the NASDAQ dropped 575 points. The Internet bubble had burst. Public and private valuations in the tech sector plummeted, and our millions of dollars of paper gains evaporated. Had she joined the company early on, her options would have been issued at very low exercise prices and would still have had significant value. But given the bottom falling out of the financial markets, joining just before the IPO was terrible timing.

Valuing your equity grants can drive key decisions about your job. The challenge is that the price of a startup's stock is a moving target. It is affected not only by how well the company is doing but also by outside market forces. When the overall tech markets are hot, VCs invest at overblown valuations. In market downturns, VCs pull back, and their caution drives valuations down.

This market dynamic drives the value you derive from your equity grants. Everyone wants to see their company's valuation rise. But a high valuation translates to a high stock price and increases the option exercise price for newly issued options. Since valuations in private companies are anchored on funding events, an **up round,** in which investors buy shares at a higher price than in previous rounds, triggers a new 409A valuation that causes the board to raise the exercise price.

People want to join hot startups that are gaining traction. It is exciting when top-shelf VCs decide to back a company, investing piles of cash at high valuations. But it's a double-edged sword. Reaping significant rewards from options with a high exercise price requires the company's valuation to keep rising, which is never guaranteed.

With valuations moving up and down, the timing of when you receive your options grant matters. Options issued when valuations are high reap significantly less upside if the company is sold or goes public. The reverse is also true. Down rounds, during which funders invest at lower valuations, can drive option exercise prices down.

The bursting of the Internet bubble in 2000, the financial crisis of 2008, and the tech market meltdown of 2022 all wreaked havoc on startup valuations. Employees holding previously issued options in high-flying companies during those periods watched billions in paper wealth disappear. Similar downturns will inevitably happen in your startup career.

During downturns, public tech company valuations decline precipitously, sometimes by more than fifty or seventy percent. The window for private companies to go public closes. Unable to raise funds through IPOs, later-stage companies turn to the private funding markets, and funders tend to move upmarket, investing in more mature companies with lower perceived risk. This crowds out investment in early-stage, less proven companies.

Many startups, like my company USLaw.com in 2000, are unable to raise money and quietly fade away, leaving their employees out of work. Many companies that can raise funds do so at depressed valuations, often with onerous preferential terms for investors, which come at the expense of the common shareholders and employees.

Option Prices Lag Declining Valuations

Most options are issued when employees first join their companies. If you join when the company valuation is high, your exercise prices may be inflated, limiting your potential upside. After you are there for a while, if your company raises money at a reduced valuation through a down round, the 409A analysis that follows should eventually drive a reset of the exercise price for new options. This can be good news if you receive new options at a lower price.

But follow-on grants tend to be modest relative to initial grants. While you may get some additional options at a lower exercise price, the bulk of your options would still have a high exercise price and may not be worth much after the downward movement in the valuation.

The other issue employees face is that option exercise prices tend to stay artificially high, as there is a structural bias against reducing them. First, management may fear that a significant reduction in option prices may alarm current employees holding options previously issued at higher prices. Realizing that your prior options may be worth far less than you thought can be demotivating, especially if you have worked for several years to vest into them.

Second, given that the options represent a wealth transfer to employees from the shareholders, the board of directors may balk at setting a new option price too low. The board has the prerogative to set the option price above the 409A valuation if they deem that valuation to be too generous. In one of my companies, after a significant down round, the board chose to issue options at a price forty percent higher than the 409A valuation—they simply felt that the 409A was too low.

The upward pressure on options pricing is even stronger when there is no funding round. 409A valuations are good for a year, and market conditions can shift dramatically over those twelve months. Without a recent funding transaction, most companies do not perform a new 409A valuation analysis until the prior one is about to expire. This leaves the company with no basis for lowering the exercise price, and new options continue to be issued using the inflated, old exercise price.

Declining Option Values: Threat or Opportunity?

When companies face declining valuations and funding challenges, employee options plummet in value. Unlike company stock, which typically does not fall to zero unless the company goes bust, your options can easily go underwater. Worse yet, if the valuation remains depressed when your company exits, there may be no payout on your options at all. You may end up with nothing to show for your years of hard work after investors take their cut.

A decline in the value of your options is bad for you, but it is also bad for your employer. The whole purpose of options is to allow employees to participate in the company's upside. They are a key retention tool, designed to keep employees at the company while the options vest over a three or four-year period. Without the prospect of realizing significant gains from your equity, what is your incentive to stay at the company?

It depends on what your company chooses to do in the short term. As companies face tough market conditions and skittish investors reluctant to fund them, the last thing they need is to see their teams splinter apart, which would destroy the value of the company. If the company recognizes how bad the deterioration in the value of options is for the team, this could present a golden golden opportunity to reap great rewards over the long term, assuming the company takes action to address the issue by adjusting the exercise price.

Just as VCs have an opportunity to invest in companies at reduced valuations when market conditions turn sour, employees who receive lower-priced options during a downturn also stand to realize significant upside. Over the years, my wife and I have experienced several instances when our companies reissued or repriced options. In fact, that is what happened to my wife at OTG Software and to me at Fugue.

This is not a decision companies make lightly. But tactically, recognizing that equity-based employee incentives have been undermined is critical for startups to keep staff from leaving. In our cases, when those companies rebounded and were ultimately sold, it was the lower-priced options we had been issued that accounted for most of our upside.

In the face of declining valuations, company management and the board are likely to do one of three things:

- Nothing. This is the path of least resistance and what most companies do. Working under the assumption that most employees don't fully understand their options and given the resistance of boards to sweetening the pot, it is easiest to maintain the status quo. Employees retain their existing underwater grants, and leadership hopes employees hang on for the ride without realizing what they have lost.
- Reprice Options. Some companies modify existing options with a lower exercise price. This requires approval from the

board but is easy to implement. The benefit of repricing is that the options retain the same features and vesting schedule as the originally issued options. Companies must explain that they are reissuing options because the company's valuation is down. This is not a great message, but most employees should view the reissuance as a sign that the company is considering how to keep the employees on board.

One caveat is that if you have exercised options before repricing and still hold the stock, the company won't reissue the options you exercised. You are stuck having paid the higher price (and any applicable taxes) for the exercise, and your stock is worth less than what you paid. I have experienced this scenario.

- Issue New Options. Companies may issue new grants at lower strike prices. These grants are generally smaller than the previous grants. Employees keep their prior grants, providing some psychic value, even though they may never get back "in the money" (meaning that the price of the company's stock grows once again to exceed the option exercise price). While most employees gladly accept new options at a lower strike price, the vesting clock on these grants starts ticking from zero.

Receiving a smaller option issuance at the new lower price may not be as attractive as having existing options repriced. But it is a compromise solution the board and company may find easier to justify than repricing all previously issued options. Either way, having your options repriced or receiving new options at a lower strike price presents a good opportunity to buy low and reap great rewards if your company's valuation rebounds.

The Bottom Line

As an employee in a startup, you have no control over the strike price of your options or the timing of their issuance. But if you are concerned about the potential impact of lower valuations on your stock options, you may want to consider several actions.

- **First, get the facts.** Find out what the current 409A valuation is and compare it to the exercise price of the grants you currently hold. Ask your CEO, CFO, or HR leader when the last 409A valuation was completed and when the next one is scheduled.

- **Evaluate your options**. Are your options "in the money" or "underwater" relative to the current 409A price; that is, is the current 409A value higher or lower than your exercise price? While the value of your options may have declined, they may still be worth something depending on when you got them and how low the issue price was. You may also have multiple grants at different prices, so evaluate the full picture.

- **Consider your company's momentum**. This is a much larger topic, but ultimately the value of your options is driven by a successful outcome for your company. Is your company gaining market traction? Has it attracted sufficient capital to ride out the current market uncertainty, or is it struggling with funding? Even if your options are underwater today, what matters is what the company's stock is worth when the company is sold. Use your judgment to consider whether it's moving in the right direction and if it's worth it for you to continue on the journey or jump ship.

- **Ask management about option repricing or reissuance**. Assuming you want to stick it out, can you influence or encourage management to reset options at a more favorable exercise price? If enough employees realize their equity has lost significant value or become worthless, the company may have no choice. Management and the board must be convinced that the move is necessary, and they generally don't like being backed into a corner. Repricing or reissuance are likely one-time events, so the timing matters, especially in a market that continues to decline. The good news is that other employees, including senior managers, are in the same boat as you—their option value would also have declined. Your incentives are aligned, which can create a groundswell to prompt the company to act.

If you are considering joining a new startup, you may have a great opportunity to take advantage of the downturn in valuations. But you want to know that the options you receive as part of your offer are properly priced to reflect the company's current situation and market conditions.

- **Again, get the facts**. Find out when the company's last 409A analysis took place and when the company last had a funding round. Ask about the trend in option pricing to see if the company has accounted for the downturn in its incentive equity grants. If they haven't, the options you receive may be overpriced and could clip your upside down the road.

- **Consider the company's runway**. Look at the company's funding history on Crunchbase. Did they raise money recently? Try to determine if the company has enough cash to last at least 18 to 24 months. If not, it may need to raise money soon in a challenging environment, possibly in a down round. If you receive options before that happens, your options may end up underwater right out of the gate.

Part of the allure of working for a startup is the potential upside of the equity you receive. In difficult funding environments, there's a good possibility you are working for or considering joining a company where the option pricing does not accurately reflect the current market reality.

You wouldn't buy public market equities at prices higher than what they are trading for. Try to avoid the same trap with private company equity. Hopefully, your company's management is cognizant of the impact falling valuations have on employee equity and is considering corrective action. If your options are overpriced and the company doesn't have plans to correct that, you may find yourself just working for a salary.

CHAPTER 16

Trigger Happy

For most employees in startups, the vesting schedule is what it is. You get an option grant and your right to exercise the option vests over a three- or four-year period. Maybe 25 percent vests on the first anniversary of the grant. Then the remainder vests monthly for the remaining period of the vesting schedule. In rare cases, grants can vest more quickly through a feature known as **acceleration**. Acceleration of options or RSUs is one of the most valuable features you can have in an equity grant. Along with receiving a low price for your grant as discussed in the last chapter, acceleration can have the greatest impact on the overall worth of your grant at the time of exit.

Acceleration

What is acceleration or accelerated vesting? It is the process by which unvested incentive options or RSUs become vested immediately when predefined events happen. The immediacy of the vesting means that you do not have to wait for the vesting schedule clock to run out. Whatever rights you have related to vested grants are automatically activated upon acceleration. When you consider that the economic value of an option or RSU grant is not valid until that grant vests, acceleration is a big deal.

The most common event that causes accelerated vesting of grants is the sale of the company. In legal speak, this is known as a **change of control**. Technically speaking, change of control means that new owners have taken control of more than 50 percent of the voting stock of the company, and the prior shareholders are no longer in charge.

If you have a stock grant with full (100 percent) acceleration based on a change of control, your entire grant vests in conjunction with the sale of the company. When a company is purchased in a cash transaction, you get paid the full value of your stock if you have RSUs or the bargain element of your entire option grant at the time of the sale.

Let's consider an example. You join a company and receive 10,000 options to purchase common stock at $1 per share. Your vesting schedule is standard, with 25 percent of the options vesting after one year and the remaining 75 percent vesting in equal monthly installments over the following three years. You have 100 percent acceleration of unvested options upon change of control. If the company sells before the four years of your vesting schedule are up, all your unvested options vest.

Six months after joining, your company is purchased for $5 per share. Technically, the day before the deal closes, all your options would vest, and you would have the right to be paid out of the sale proceeds. The amount of the payout would be $40,000 (your bargain element). That is 10,000 shares times the difference between $5 per share (the purchase price) and $1 per share (the option exercise price).

In this scenario, the acceleration results in a $40,000 payout. Without acceleration, none of your options would have vested—you had not been with the company the full year needed to vest even the first 25 percent, and unvested options are not entitled to any payout. The payout on your equity from six months of service would have been $0 at the time of the sale.

As with most compensation-related requests, the best time to ask for acceleration is at the time of hire. The disappointing news for most employees is that acceleration is not a standard feature of most grants. It is typically reserved for senior executives and board members. If you are someone with rare talents, you may have leverage to negotiate for acceleration. Highly prized employees who may pose flight risks from the company may also be able to ask for accelerated vesting.[44] Besides these two examples, few employees have sufficient bargaining leverage to demand special treatment. Even if you are among those with the leverage, you must know enough to ask.

A company and its board rarely offer acceleration without being backed into a corner. Most companies do not provide acceleration to their regular staff and bristle at offering it even to executives. From the company's perspective, acceleration is a superpowered feature of an offer to a new employee. The company must weigh the risk that an employee whose grants fully accelerate upon a change of control no longer sees value in staying at the company. At that point, the buyer has to offer them new financial incentives to keep them from walking away.

This is a critical consideration. Startup investors and senior managers need to keep their employees happy and motivated. They also want to avoid actions that make the sale of the company more difficult or expensive. Acquirers look to buy companies based on the value of their technology and products, their customer base, and their team.

If key team members have little incentive to stay, the buyer may rightfully fear that the team they are buying is a house of cards that falls apart after the sale closes. Or they might be forced to offer rich incentives to retain key employees, making the deal more expensive and less attractive. The buyer will closely examine employment terms for key employees. Concerns regarding

---

[44] It is possible, but not common, for existing option grants to be modified to add acceleration. As with any change to an option's terms, this change requires board approval, which management will be reluctant to ask for unless pressed.

post-transaction retention may derail the deal or result in some employment terms getting modified before the deal closes.

Partial Acceleration

One way employers thread this needle is offering **partial acceleration** on change of control instead of full acceleration. Acceleration is not an all-or-nothing feature of equity grants. The employer can offer any amount of acceleration from zero (the most common) to 100 percent (the rarest). C-suite executives and board members may get full acceleration, VP-level executives may get 50 percent (or maybe 25 percent) acceleration, and employees below VP level get no acceleration at all.

The thing to remember is that the acceleration applies only to the remaining unvested portion of the grant. If you have been with a company for three years, your initial grant with a four-year vesting schedule is already 75 percent vested. If you have 50 percent acceleration, the incremental portion of your grant that vests is just 12.5 percent (50 percent of the remaining unvested 25 percent). Getting that 12.5 percent acceleration is nothing to sneeze at, but as a retention tool, that amount of acceleration can be marginal.

Triggers

Change of control is the most common catalyst for the acceleration of vesting, but it is not the only type of event that can cause equity grants to accelerate. Vesting can be time-based, or milestone based. Time-based vesting is straightforward—the grant vests according to a set schedule. Milestone-based vesting is tied to company or individual performance goals. It may be a standalone basis for vesting or may be overlaid on time-based vesting to accelerate vesting if the milestone is met.

For example, a VP of Sales may be brought into a company with the objective of reaching certain revenue milestones laid out in the company's operating plans. The executive receives an incentive equity grant with the standard vesting schedule. However, the grant could have a feature that accelerates some or all of the grant if the company's performance meets or exceeds agreed-upon targets. The acceleration provides added incentive for the executive to meet the goals.

A commonly used term for an event that results in accelerated vesting is **trigger**. Trigger is not a legal term but rather a colloquial reference to the catalyst that leads to partial or full acceleration. When the board of directors is considering the structure of equity grants, triggers are always a heated topic of conversation.

As fiduciaries, the board must preserve value in the company for the shareholders. With accelerated vesting, any additional payouts to employees come directly from the pockets of shareholders, who, in most cases, are the investors. While everyone wants the company to succeed and grow, discussions centering on how the pie is divided reveal the conflicting incentives between employees and shareholders. The more equity grants accelerate, the more money employees get, and the less shareholders get. It is a zero-sum game.

Discussions about partial or full acceleration pit the interests of shareholders against the interests of employees. The senior management team is the intermediary. Depending on their point of view, they may lean toward being more or less generous to the staff. That orientation influences how hard they fight the board for terms advantageous to the staff.

A standalone event such as the sale of a company that results in the acceleration of equity grants is known as **single-trigger** acceleration. From an employee's perspective, that is the best possible formulation of acceleration. Single-trigger acceleration is exceedingly rare, which goes back to what I said earlier. If the options accelerate, employees have little incentive to stay after they get fully paid on the option value.

Full (i.e., 100 percent), single-trigger acceleration is usually offered only to board members and advisors. Those groups do not stay on after a transaction, and single-trigger acceleration recognizes they will not be around to continue vesting into their grants. Rather than having to negotiate for added acceleration at the time of the sale when tensions are running high, board members and advisors have single-trigger full acceleration baked into their grants from the outset. They get paid and exit the stage. Once the deal is done, they are never heard from again, except when they report on LinkedIn or their websites about their participation in the successful exit.

Companies may not want to give single-trigger acceleration to key employees, but neither do employees want to lose out on the value of their unvested options in case of a sale. To balance the risk between employer and employee, options can contain an acceleration provision that kicks in if the employee is terminated after a change of control. This joint contingency—sale followed by termination—is known as **double-trigger** acceleration.

The theory of double-trigger acceleration is to protect an employee who stays on after an acquisition from losing their unvested options if the company terminates them. You can imagine a scenario where a company completes an acquisition, and all the shareholders get paid. Then some employees are fired so the acquiring company can recapture their options. Depending on how critical they deem the employees, this could be an economically rational decision for the buyer. They could reduce cash burn while also saving millions of dollars in employee compensation down the road. Double-trigger acceleration mitigates that risk for the employee.

A common formulation of double-trigger accelerated vesting states that if the employee is **terminated without cause** within twelve months following an acquisition, their equity grants fully (or partially) accelerate. The feature can be negotiated when an employee joins the company or after, and it is included as a provision when the options are issued or can be added later with board approval.

Although double-trigger acceleration is better than no acceleration, it is not a perfect way to avoid risk. While you might take comfort in having this acceleration clause in your contract or offer letters, double-trigger acceleration has several drawbacks, especially if another private company or private equity firm acquires your company.

First, an acquirer does not have to accept the transfer of your options. The acquirer's compensation and stock plans may differ from that of the acquired, and meshing the two may be complicated. This mismatch could create imbalances in the incentives between the acquirer's existing employees and the team they absorb through the transaction. So, the acquirer may decide to terminate all remaining unvested options as a pre-condition of closing on the transaction, causing existing employees to lose the value of their unvested options. In this case, the buyer will create new incentive plans for the incoming employees, which may be less generous and will likely result in vesting starting over from scratch.

Second, even if the acquirer agrees to roll your options into their plan, you will not be paid on the value of your vested options if you are terminated without cause. Your previously unvested options accelerate after the second trigger (termination), but you are still left holding vested options that must be exercised within 90 days of when you leave, or they are forfeited. If you are suddenly out of work, you may not want to write a check to the company that just fired you to exercise options that you are not sure will be worth anything down the road. So, despite the acceleration clause, you may still lose the value of your vested options.

Third, most double-trigger features only kick in if you are terminated without cause within the specified period, usually no longer than 12 months. Your employer could wait until after 12 months to take action. You would get the additional 12 months of vesting post-acquisition but lose your remaining unvested options upon termination. So double-trigger acceleration is not a panacea to ensure you receive full value from your options.

After Fugue brought on new investors in the spring of 2021, the entire option plan for the company was reconstituted. All the employees at the VP level and above received some amount of accelerated vesting as a retention tool—in most cases double-trigger. This was critical at the time because the company had a limited window to realize a successful exit. Holding the entire team together was of paramount importance. However, when the company was sold, the buyer refused to adopt the unvested employees' options, and all unvested options were terminated.

It turned out to be a game of Russian Roulette. Those few individuals with single-trigger acceleration, including board members, realized the full value of their options. Everyone else watched their unvested options get shot dead, despite the double-trigger feature embedded in their grants.

Finally, if you are forced to exercise within 90 days of termination, you face a real dilemma. After exercising your options, you may have to wait years to realize a financial benefit from an exit, assuming it ever comes. While you are holding the stock and unable to turn it into cash by selling it, you risk the stock's value going down, maybe even to zero.

The Bottom Line

Depending on your position and leverage in your company, you may be able to negotiate for accelerated vesting. It can happen when you join. It can happen once you have proven yourself to be indispensable. It might take threatening to leave for management and the board to agree to provide it. The two levers to negotiate are single- versus double-trigger and what percentage of your unvested options the acceleration applies to.

If you are able to negotiate for acceleration, start by asking for 100 percent acceleration with a single trigger and work your way down from there. You may not be able to get single-trigger acceleration on 100 percent of your unvested options but getting it on 50 or even 25 percent of your options can be highly valuable.

If you end up with double-trigger acceleration, you are much better off than the average option or RSU holder. In some cases, employees are terminated at the time of acquisition. This is especially true if you are in administrative functions, such as finance and human resources, that a buyer might find redundant. If that happens, double-trigger has the same practical effect on vesting as single-trigger acceleration. Just recognize that there are numerous ways the buyer's actions may end up undermining the value of double-trigger acceleration.

CHAPTER 17

Is Exercising Good for You?

Financial advisors recommend that clients working for public companies limit the amount of their company's stock held in their retirement accounts. The reason is simple. They depend on the success of their company for their jobs. Holding a substantial part of their portfolio in company stock compounds that dependence and creates too much concentration of risk.

The same is true of startups, even more so given how risky startups are. Every day you go to work for a startup is an investment decision. Putting capital into the company by exercising your options is a substantial leap of faith in an already risky undertaking. That doesn't necessarily mean you shouldn't do it. It just means you need to consider the decision carefully before you do.

Realizing value from exercising options depends on several steps all going right. Exhibit 17-1 lays out the climb from when you first take your job and receive your options grant and ends when your company exits and your options are cashed out. As you ascend the stairs, your progress toward realizing the value of your options may stall. You may leave the company and not exercise your vested options in time. Your company may be left in limbo and never consummate a sale. Or, as we have discussed, it may sell for a price that doesn't clear the preferred shareholders' liquidation preferences. Whatever the reason, the result is the same—no payout.

The turning point is whether you stay at your company until the exit or leave. Choosing to leave is the only time you are forced to decide whether to exercise your options or lose them. At any other point in your journey with your company, you can ride the wave, leave your options unexercised, and wait to see what happens.

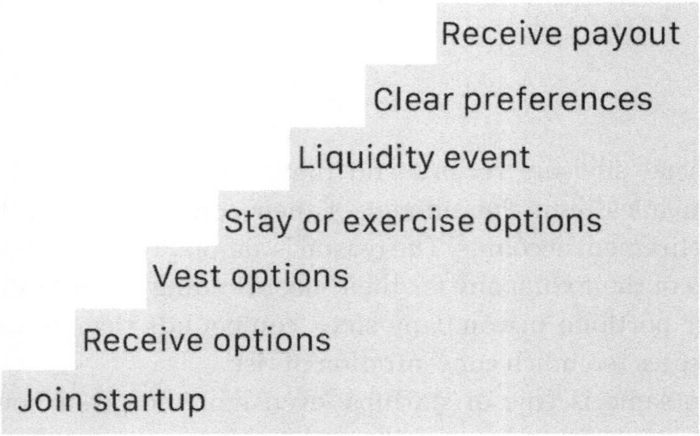

Receive payout

Clear preferences

Liquidity event

Stay or exercise options

Vest options

Receive options

Join startup

Exhibit 17-1: The Stairway to Options Payout

Why Employees Don't Exercise Options

Throughout my career, I have observed that few private company employees proactively exercise their options. During my time as CFO at Fugue, we hired about 150 people. When the company was bought, our employee count was just under fifty. Of the hundred or so employees who came and went before Fugue was acquired, fewer than ten ever exercised their options.

There are several good reasons employees don't exercise options:

1. Options vest over time, so exercising requires multiple active decisions during the period they are vesting.

2. Options have value even if they remain unexercised.

3. Exercising requires investing hard-earned cash and paying the tax bill.

4. Private company stock does not provide liquidity, and its value is uncertain.

5. When people leave a company, they are not predisposed to invest in that company.

6. Inertia is a powerful force.

Let's explore each of these in more detail.

Options Vest Over Time

With cliff and monthly vesting, an option grant may have more than 35 vesting events. It is reasonable to assume that grantees would consider exercising options after a year when the first 25 percent vests. It is a different story once options start vesting monthly. Each exercise transaction requires completing paperwork, writing a check, and waiting for the issuance of a stock certificate. Very few employees want to go through that hassle, especially if their grants are relatively small. So, they just let their options ride.

Unexercised Options Have Value

Once your options vest, if the company is sold, the bargain element of your option is paid out to you as part of the sale proceeds. You don't need to exercise the option proactively to get paid. The mechanics are simple. The day the sale closes, your vested options are deemed to be exercised, the company calculates your bargain element and pays you out in cash, net of taxes.

The downside of waiting with your options unexercised until the company sells is that the proceeds are taxed at ordinary income tax rates. Other than a bigger tax hit, you risk nothing by holding unexercised options while you remain at the company. So most people leave well enough alone and don't exercise.

Exercising Requires Hard-earned Cash (and Paying the Tax Bill)

The other side of the coin is if you decide to exercise, you have to come up with the cash to do so.[45] Many people don't have the liquid assets to invest in their company's stock. Part of this decision depends on how many shares you have and the exercise price. The cost might be manageable if the options were issued early in the company's life when the valuation was relatively low.

In addition to requiring cash to purchase the stock, the transaction is taxed as ordinary income on the bargain element, the difference between the then-current stock valuation and the exercise price. If the price of your company's stock has increased prior to you exercising options, you incur tax liability without receiving any cash to cover it. In fact, just the opposite—your company will deduct the taxes from your payroll upon exercise.

The Value of Private Company Stock Is Uncertain and Illiquid

Unlike investing in the stock market, when you exercise your options in a private company, you are stuck with the shares until the company is sold. There is no liquid market for the shares, so you are making a bet that there will be a positive return on your investment. Either way, you cannot capture your gains or mitigate your losses based on the company's fortunes. You're along for the ride no matter what.

The exception to this is if the company becomes a rocket ship and a secondary market for the shares develops. As an individual

---

[45] In certain circumstances, option holders may be able to access third-party lenders to finance for options exercises. These financing sources typically only require pledging the underlying stock as collateral for the loan, so do not pose any additional risk on the borrower other than the loss of the stock if its value falls below the size of the loan.

small shareholder, you probably won't have access to those opportunities unless you are part of a larger group selling shares. In addition, secondary market buyers prefer to buy preferred shares. So as a common shareholder, you may still be out of luck until the company has a liquidity event.

If You're Leaving, Why Invest?

When people leave a company, it is either voluntary or involuntary. They may choose to leave for greener pastures. They might resign because they are unhappy. Or they may be forced to leave because they are fired or laid off. In any of these cases, they are usually disinclined to exercise their options. It's human nature.

When you leave a company for bigger and better opportunities, you have determined that your current company does not provide the path for growth or gain that makes it worth sticking around. If you are no longer interested in investing your time in the company, why would you turn around and invest your money? Usually, investing time and money go hand in hand.

If you are terminated and suddenly find yourself out of a job, it is unlikely that you want to take a portion of your savings and plow it back into the company that let you go. Given the uncertainty of being without a job, prudence dictates that you preserve your resources as a hedge against difficult times ahead.

Even if you have the money, the emotional trauma of losing your job may make you reluctant to exercise your options. Most people who have lost their jobs—whether through firing or layoffs—harbor resentment toward their former employers. Who would turn around and write a check to someone who just told you they don't want you around?

Inertia is a Powerful Force

In the catalog of reasons people don't exercise options, inertia may be the most powerful. Exercising options requires thinking about it, deciding, and doing it. The tendency to stick with the status quo, the requirement to invest cash, and the widespread lack of understanding among employees about the value of options and company stock combine to create powerful deterrents to action. Even when exercising may serve the option holder's financial interest, overcoming inertia is a significant obstacle.

The closest analogy to option exercises may be employee behavior regarding 401(k) retirement plans. In a 2022 study conducted by T. Rowe Price and MIT Sloan School of Management, 401(k) programs that included autoenrollment features had more than double the employee participation rates than those that didn't—85 percent versus 39 percent.[46] The closest thing to autoenrollment in incentive stock compensation is the issuance of restricted stock units (RSUs) rather than options. Granting RSUs eliminates the need for employees to exercise options and gives them actual share ownership. Once the RSUs vest, the employee owns them without having to decide to exercise.

Inertia, in my view, is the most disappointing reason people don't exercise their options. If you go through your analysis and decide, with good reason, not to exercise your options, that's fine. But don't let lack of initiative derail you. This is too important a decision.

The Results of Exercising

If most startup employees don't exercise their options, does that mean exercising options may not be such a good idea? People tend

---

[46] Joshua Dietch and Taha Choukhmani, "Automatic enrollment's long-term effect on retirement savings," *T. Rowe Price Insights on Retirement*, https://trowe.com/3JRhxHw, June 2022.

to vote with their wallets and have great incentives to look out for their best interests. Nevertheless, rather than blindly following the crowd, you should think carefully about this decision.

There are four possible outcomes based on whether you exercise or not and what happens to the company as shown in Exhibit 17-2. In some cases, you win. In some, you lose. If you exercise and your company fails, you will wish you hadn't. If your company succeeds, you can cash in on your vested options without exercising, but you will pay higher taxes. And if you have left your company before that successful outcome and didn't exercise, you would have missed out.

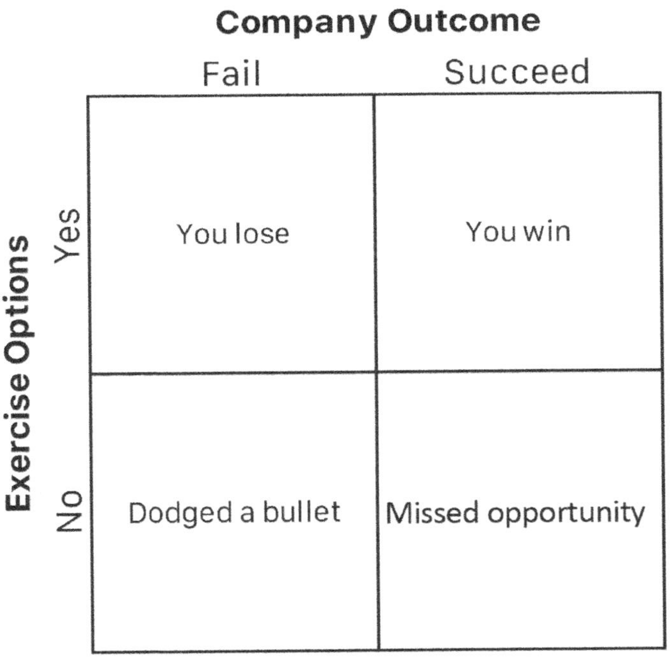

Company Outcome

	Fail	Succeed
Yes	You lose	You win
No	Dodged a bullet	Missed opportunity

Exercise Options

Exhibit 17-2: Options Exercise Possible Outcomes

Your job when considering exercising is to assess whether you think your company will succeed and whether the common stock will be worth more than the exercise price you pay for that stock. That higher common stock price is driven by the company's progress and whether and by how much the sale proceeds exceed the preference stack. Assessing the company's prospects is an ongoing effort and relies on much of the same research and analysis (i.e., due diligence) that we discussed in earlier chapters when we talked about whether you should join a startup in the first place.

Some Real-Life Examples

You need to think like an investor and consider all the possibilities before pulling the trigger on your option exercise. The results associated with exercising options can vary widely. As career startup veterans, my wife and I have experienced "the thrill of victory and the agony of defeat"[47] of all the scenarios represented in Exhibit 17-2.

Exercise, and the company fails. In the early years of Fugue, the company was gaining momentum in terms of investor interest and valuation. That upward trajectory led me to believe that Fugue's stock would continue to rise significantly. As a result, I chose to exercise options on a couple of occasions, investing more than $100,000 in the company. I was excited about the company's prospects and wanted the capital gains clock to start ticking to get the best possible tax treatment when the company eventually sold.

Unfortunately, the company ran into significant operational headwinds a few years later. In the midst of those struggles, we completed a challenging funding round, including a recapitalization

---

[47] The famous words of Jim McKay in the opening sequence to the television series _Wide World of Sports_. _Wide World of Sports_, 1961 through 1998, ABC.

(see Chapter 12). Because the new capital came in at a very low valuation relative to prior rounds, the ownership stake of common stockholders, such as me, became massively diluted. The stock that I was so excited about purchasing through my earlier option exercises lost more than 90 percent of its value.

Although Fugue realized a successful exit, as an option holder who exercised and then watched the company ride the rollercoaster down before going back up, I lost a significant amount of money on those exercised options. Though the company's value went back up, the value of my stock never recovered its prior value. I exercised and lost.

Exercise, and the company succeeds. Right after the completion of the Series A-1 recapitalization round in which the investors paid $0.60 per share for preferred shares, the Fugue board recognized that having employees whose options were now worthless was a recipe for massive staff attrition. So, the company issued new options to all employees at a much lower exercise price ($0.10 per share) after completing a 409A valuation based on the recently completed financing. Note that the exercise price on the options was only 16.7 percent of the price paid by the investors for the preferred shares (because the preferred shares were participating preferred with a two times liquidation preference).

Once again, I had an opportunity to exercise options, this time at the very low price of $0.10 per share. Believing the company was likely to be acquired within the next couple of years, I concluded it was a great time to invest. The cost of exercising was modest, so the risk to me was low. As in the early days of the company, once again, I chose to exercise my options.

This time, the outcome turned out quite differently. A few months after the recapitalization and down round, the company launched a new product that captured the attention of a strategic buyer. Within six months, the company was sold, and I received

$3 per share, 30 times what I had paid to exercise the options. This time, I exercised and won.

Don't exercise, and the company succeeds. My wife was a marketing executive in a software company for approximately seven years. When she was recruited to a new position, she was faced with whether to exercise her fully vested options, knowing she would otherwise forfeit them within 90 days of her departure. We discussed the decision at length, considering that we would have to invest $100,000 in a company with uncertain prospects and a waterfall with more than $65 million in priority payouts to outside investors.

We concluded that the company would likely not be purchased for a high enough price to clear the preference stack and deliver significant returns to common shareholders. We passed on exercising the options, and my wife forfeited fully vested options on two percent of the company. Two and a half years later, the company sold for over $150 million. Had we decided to exercise her options, her common stock would have been worth about $3 million, netting her a $2.9 million pre-tax gain after the $100,000 exercise costs. We didn't exercise and missed a golden opportunity.

Don't exercise, and the company fails. In addition to these three examples, we have both been part of companies where we left positions and didn't exercise. The companies didn't succeed in having meaningful outcomes for the common shareholders. Those were good outcomes for us because we would have lost any money we invested by exercising our options. This is by far the most common scenario, considering that most employees never exercise their options when they leave, and most startup ventures do not reach financially successful outcomes.

It is extremely difficult to decide whether to exercise options in the face of so much uncertainty and how easy it can be to get it wrong. The stakes are high, and the outcome often turns out differently from how we anticipate.

When Can You Exercise Your Options?_

There are two main points when options vest and become exercisable: when a portion of your option vests and when an option is subject to an early exercise provision.

You are not obligated to exercise your options at any given time while you remain with a company. Options have a ten-year life from the date of issue, giving you the choice to just sit tight. You can exercise your vested options until they expire or until the company is sold. Assuming your options are in the money (the valuation of the underlying stock exceeds the exercise price) and you plan to stay at the company, the difference between exercising or not mainly comes down to optimizing taxes at the time the company has a liquidity event. You still gain from the positive value of the options.

Early exercise rights allow you to exercise your options before they vest. While incentive stock plans usually allow for early exercise provisions, this feature is rarely offered on individual grants to regular employees. Senior executives may negotiate early exercise rights as part of their employment package before they come on board. If your options have early exercise rights, there can be significant tax advantages to pulling the trigger and exercising well before they vest.

The one time you are forced to decide whether to exercise is when you leave the company, voluntarily or involuntarily. At that point, the stakes are much higher. In most cases, you have only 90 days to exercise your options, or you forfeit them. That's not a decision you should take lightly.

In rare instances, particularly if you are a senior executive whose employment has been terminated, you may be able to negotiate for an extended exercise period, which could be two or three years. There is a great benefit to holding onto your options after termination for a couple of years to see what happens with the company.

Pros and Cons of Exercising

Every investment decision involves risk, including choosing to exercise your options. Failing to exercise your options before they expire or are forfeited could cost you the upside you worked so hard for. On the other hand, putting up cash to exercise options comes with the risk that the company doesn't succeed, and you lose the investment.

The key is to assess the expected value of your options and the underlying common stock over time and evaluate it against the potential downside. Every company and option grant is different. Whether to exercise depends on the situation and the timing. You must consider your financial position, how much risk you can take, and if you believe the company will achieve a successful exit.

Understanding the waterfall and capitalization table is also critical. Exercising your options leaves you with common stock, which sits below company debt and preferred shareholders on the capitalization table in terms of cash distribution priority. You may not see a significant payout even if the company has a positive liquidity event.

If you were certain the company would be successful, you would want to exercise your options as soon as they are vested (or early exercise) to lock in the favorable tax treatment we discussed in Chapter 10 (Vested Interest). On the other hand, if you knew your company would languish or fail, you would never exercise your options. The challenge is that most companies sit somewhere in the middle. Even if your company is on a positive trajectory, there is no guarantee of an attractive exit with a meaningful payout to the common shareholders.

The Case for Exercising

You have worked hard to earn your options and put in the time for them to vest. You want to make sure you make the most of them when the company succeeds. By exercising your options, you are claiming your ownership of the company, ownership that cannot be taken away from you, even if you leave or are terminated.

The arguments for exercising are relatively straightforward. They mostly revolve around tax benefits, although there are a couple of emotional and practical considerations as well:

1. Options, even vested options, are subject to forfeiture when you leave. Stock owned outright is not. Once you own it, nobody can take it from you. It can get diluted or devalued over time, but it is yours.

2. Once you exercise, additional appreciation in the stock is subject to capital gains taxes, not ordinary income taxes or payroll taxes. Those capital gains taxes could save you a lot of money at the time of a sale. Once you get the clock ticking on ownership, if you hold the stock for more than a year, you pay long-term capital gains taxes at the time of sale, which is much lower than either short-term capital gains or ordinary income tax. Under certain circumstances, if you hold the stock for more than five years, you may be able to avoid federal capital gains taxes altogether.[48]

3. If you have Incentive Stock Options (ISOs), your tax benefit from exercising is even greater, as capital gains tax rates may apply to all the gains above your exercise price if you hold the stock for the required period.

4. When you leave your company, you are less likely to exercise your options, so exercising while you are still at the company removes the emotional friction that can deter exercising upon your departure.

---

[48] The IRS has created a Qualified Small Business exclusion, commonly referred to as the Section 1202 Exclusion, that exempts certain shareholders who hold stock for more than 5 years in qualifying companies from paying federal capital gains taxes on the gains realized from a sale.

5. Most importantly, you believe the company is on a path to a successful exit, and the stock will be worth substantially more in the future than the price you would pay for it upon exercise.

The Case for Early Exercising

All the reasons for exercising options apply equally to options with the early exercise feature. In addition, option grants that come with an early exercise feature have a special advantage. Because you can exercise right away, you can take advantage of the fact that the exercise price is the same as the current 409A valuation of the common stock. This is typically not true for regular options.

Exercising at the same price as the current 409A valuation means you incur no ordinary income taxes at the time of exercise. The bargain element (or gain) of the option at the time of exercise is $0, meaning there's no tax owed.[49]

This is a meaningful distinction from options without the early exercise feature. Common stock valuations are refreshed annually through the 409A valuation process. By the time your regular options have partially or fully vested at least a year after you receive them, the valuation may have changed, usually upward, triggering an income tax liability if you exercise later.

One critical technical note about exercising early is that if you choose to do so, you need to file a Form **83(b)** with the IRS registering the transaction to ensure that you lock in the basis of your restricted stock at the exercise price. If you fail to file the 83(b) election, you are subject to ordinary income taxes each time a portion of the grant vests, similarly to how restricted stock unit (RSU) grants are treated. Consult a tax advisor and your company's finance department to ensure you follow the procedure correctly.

---

[49] Options exercised right after issuance incur no ordinary income tax, because the company's 409A valuation per share of common stock remains the same as the exercise price per share and there is no built-in gain from stock appreciation.

The Case for Not Exercising

While there are good and compelling reasons to exercise your options, there are also convincing reasons not to. If you plan to stay at your company for the long term, nothing is forcing you to pull the trigger. As I pointed out earlier, the decision to exercise is one very few employees make.

So why might you choose not to exercise?

1. You could realize the upside from a company sale even without exercising.

2. You may not have excess cash available to invest.

3. Investing leaves you with an illiquid investment and no way to sell it later.

4. You don't want to run the risk that the value of the stock you bought goes down.

5. The company may never achieve an exit or may shutdown.

6. There is a significant difference between your exercise price and the current 409A stock valuation, which creates an immediate ordinary income tax bill upon exercise.

7. If your options are ISOs, there is a possibility that exercising could push you into a situation where you must pay Alternative Minimum Tax when you file.[50]

8. You don't have enough information to assess whether the company will be successful, or worse, you know that the company is struggling to make progress or raise financing.

---

[50] Calculating the Alternative Minimum Tax is complicated. If you hold ISOs that you are considering exercising, consult with a tax professional before doing so as the resulting tax bill could be substantial with no incoming cash to cover it.

9. There is a large liquidity preference stack from debt holders and preferred shareholders (investors), making it unclear how well common shareholders would do in a liquidity event.

Any or all of these reasons could give you pause and cause you to hold off. Remember what my VC friend Jonathan Silver told me: VCs ask 100 questions, and it takes only one "no" for them not to invest. The same is true of exercising your options.

The upside of exercising has to do with maximizing gains by minimizing taxes. The downside is that exercising could cost you hard-earned cash. Depending on how risk-averse you are, you might prefer to forego tax optimization rather than risk your capital, especially since your eggs are in one basket with your day-to-day livelihood dependent on your company's continued success.

Should You Exercise Your Options?

As you weigh the pros and cons of exercising your options, there are a couple of categories of questions to ask yourself. First, consider whether your situation and risk tolerance make you comfortable committing resources to the exercise. Second, look at the exercise as an investment and consider its merits.

Before you choose to exercise your options, you should be able to answer yes to the following questions:

- Can I afford to lose the money I plan to use to exercise the options?
- Can I handle the tax bill that results from exercising the options? The taxes owed are deducted from your paycheck by your employer, so they eat into your take-home pay at the time of the deduction.
- Am I willing to risk that the value of the common stock goes down, possibly even to zero?

- Do I have enough cash to cover other obligations and goals? (daily expenses, home purchases, college expenses, medical expenses, emergency fund, etc.)

- Does holding illiquid stock fit within my overall financial plan?

- Have I consulted a financial advisor or trusted and knowledgeable resource to discuss these issues?

Assuming you can answer yes to these questions, you still need to determine if exercising your options is a good investment. In Chapter 7 (Look the Horse in the Mouth), I provided a detailed set of due diligence questions you should review to make your evaluation. Here are some high-level questions you should ask to determine whether the company is making good progress, assess risk, and gauge whether and when the company may have a liquidity event:

- **How long has the company been around?** As a benchmark, most VCs expect their companies to reach a successful exit or go public within five to seven years. It can be faster or slower. It could be a red flag if the company has been around for years and hasn't achieved meaningful market success.

- **Where is the company on the Proof Continuum?** Consistent with the last point, companies should make steady progress through the stages of the proof continuum. If the company appears to be stuck at any stage, try to figure out why. Lack of resources? Poor execution? Unclear product-market fit? Dysfunctional culture? Poor leadership? Concerns about any of these may be a good reason to refrain from exercising your options.

- **How fast have the company's revenues grown over the prior 2 to 3 years?** Successful startups should experience rapid revenue growth, especially early on. If the company is not achieving topline revenue growth rates of at least 50 to 100 percent annually, there may be an issue with the product or the go-to-market approach. Slow growth in a startup spells trouble. The company may encounter difficulty obtaining follow-on funding on favorable terms, and at the very least the company's valuation may stall, limiting the upside on your equity.

- **How successfully does the company retain its customers?** Many companies proudly report metrics such as their net revenue retention (NRR or Net Dollar Retention, NDR) and customer satisfaction ratings (for example Net Promoter Score or NPS[51]) as indications of their healthy customer relationships. These metrics are something management should readily provide to employees. Try to get those numbers and benchmark them against industry standards. A company struggling to retain customers probably won't turn out to be a great investment.

- **How consistently does the company meet its quarterly or annual targets?** Pay close attention to management briefings about company performance, especially as compared to goals. Go back and look at prior company presentations if available. Consider if bonuses are being fully paid or withheld as an indication of the company's performance and overall health. Companies that consistently fail to meet targets, especially sales targets, get hammered on valuation. If bonuses aren't paid consistently, that's a telltale sign of trouble.

- **Where is the company's future growth going to come from?** When companies are bought, the buyer

---

[51] Net Promoter Score or NPS is a measure of customer satisfaction based on customer surveys that identify the likelihood of customers to promote a company or its products and services to others. *"The History of Net Promoteer"*, Bain & Co., https://www.netpromotersystem.com/about/history-of-net-promoter/

is interested in some combination of the team, the technology, and the future potential. Big exits happen when there is potential for future revenue growth. That means new products, new customers, and new markets. If you can identify clear areas for rapid growth, there may be significant upside in the company's valuation. If the company has great technology that an acquirer may be able to sell to its large stable of customers, that has the makings of a highly successful exit.

- **Does the company have debt, and how much outside equity capital has the company raised since inception?** If the company has raised a ton of capital, there is certainly a large liquidity preference stack ahead of the common stock. Try to figure out how high an exit price would be required for your shares to be worth something. Then determine if reaching or exceeding that hurdle is realistic based on market valuation metrics, using recent acquisitions and public company valuations in your sector as comparables.

- **What is the implied valuation of your exercise price in addition to any current tax liability you incur when exercising?** If you want to buy low and sell high, you must be confident that the price you are paying for the stock by exercising is reasonable. Factor in taxes and calculate your total cost of exercising. Then consider how much the company would have to sell for to deliver a meaningful return on your investment. Compare that to the liquidity preferences on the capitalization table if you can. If you received options early when the company's value was low, the chances that you'll reap large rewards are higher as long as the liquidity preferences are exceeded. If the strike price of your options is already high, there is less upside, and you might even lose money.

- **What are the prospects for a successful exit?**
  Realizing a positive outcome on your investment in your options exercise requires a liquidity event, without which, you are just holding worthless paper. While some companies achieve liquidity for their shareholders through an initial public offering (IPO) of their stock, most companies that successfully exit do so through a merger or acquisition. Consider whether your company has a clear path to a liquidity event. Are there natural buyers for whom acquiring your company would be strategic? Is the company performing well enough that private equity buyers might want to take it over?

Act like an investor and do your due diligence. Try not to make your decision based on emotions or impressions. Instead, seeking concrete answers to the preceding questions will help determine the attractiveness of exercising your options. Answering these questions may not be particularly easy. It partly depends on how transparent senior management is. It also depends on how quickly things change in the company or your industry, as the historical data you can gather may not reflect the current reality.

Startup markets move very quickly. You need to pay attention to all the information shared by your company in meetings and communications and try to stay on top of industry developments. Don't just look at a snapshot. Try to assess the trends in your industry and your company's progress. Hopefully, your company maintains archives of presentations and briefings. Pull them up and review them. Review company goals and performance against those goals over time. Look at third-party reviews and analyst reports about the company's products and prospects. Read articles and analyst reports about your sector.

Your peers in the company may also be tracking what's happening with customers and competitors. Talk to them about what they are seeing and hearing. Your colleagues in sales, marketing, and product management have their fingers on the pulse of the market and can provide valuable insights. The more you know about the market your company competes in, the better able you are to assess the wisdom of exercising your options.

As a rule, the employees most informed about financial questions around the company's stock are the CEO and CFO. In a small company, they should be relatively accessible to you if you just reach out and ask to speak with them. During my tenure as a CFO at Fugue, many employees came to me asking for information and advice regarding the company's financial position and prospects.

The most pointed conversations I had were with employees leaving the company. I was in the delicate position of trying to avoid providing direct financial advice (which would have been inappropriate) but offering as much insight as possible regarding the company's prospects. My aim was to help people make informed decisions regarding their options before they were forced to forfeit them after 90 days post-departure.

Create Your Exercise Plan

If you have decided that your company's stock is a good investment, it's time to work through the mechanics. Contact your company's finance or human resources department and let them know you plan to exercise your options. They will ensure that you complete the proper paperwork and confirm the amount of the check you need to write. They should also help you assess the taxes you will owe upon exercise.

Once you've reached this point, remember exercising your options is not an all-or-nothing decision. You can hedge your bets by exercising only a portion of your options. If the company succeeds, you will participate in the upside; if they don't, you won't have risked as much. That is true whether you intend to remain with the company or are on your way out. Of the few people I have seen who exercise options, most didn't exercise their full grants. If they had multiple grants, they exercised the ones with the lowest exercise prices.

If you only exercise part of your options, no matter what you do, your decision will be wrong in hindsight. The problem is that you don't know in which direction. If your company is successful, you'll wish you had exercised all your options. If it's not, you'll beat yourself up for exercising any of them.

Once you complete the exercise process and pay for your new stock, you should take a couple of final steps. Make sure the new stock gets issued. You might get physical stock certificates, or increasingly likely, your ownership will be recorded in your company's online equity management system. Either way, ensure your ownership is properly documented and registered on the company's capitalization table. If you are invited to register for the equity management system, do it immediately and keep track of your login credentials. I can't tell you how many people don't pay attention to this critical source of information.

Finally, keep an accurate and accessible record of the purchase transaction, including your basis in the stock. Several years later, when your company is sold and you receive a 1099 for the proceeds you receive, you have to use your basis to calculate your gains, so you don't end up paying taxes on the entire amount you receive.

Cashless Exercise and Outside Financing Sources

One intriguing alternative that may be available to capture value from your options is the **cashless exercise**. In public companies that still issue options (as opposed to RSUs), there is a mechanism for exercising vested options without putting out cash known as a cashless exercise. Briefly, this allows the option holder to use the proceeds from a portion of the exercise transaction to pay for the exercise of the balance of the options. The result is that the employee ends up with a smaller number of shares than the number exercised but doesn't have to put out cash to do so.

Unfortunately, this is not an option in private companies. There is no ready market to cash out the shares you acquired through the exercise and raise cash to pay for the exercise of the remaining options. There are, however, companies that specialize in financing employee exercise of stock options. Assuming they deem your company worthy of financing, they can provide the funds needed to exercise employee stock options, using the underlying stock as collateral.

Typically, these loans represent **non-recourse financing**. That means if the stock is worth more than the loan when it is sold, the loan is repaid from the proceeds and the stockholder keeps the difference. But if the stock is worth less than the loan amount, the stockholder is not responsible for paying back the shortfall. The only collateral for the loan is the stock itself.

Companies providing these loans take a substantial piece of the upside of the stock for providing the funds to exercise, sometimes as much as 25 to 50 percent.[52] However, for employees who prefer not to risk their own cash and are willing to give up some of the upside, using a third party to finance the option exercise can be an attractive solution.

The Bottom Line

You have already made a significant investment in your company by working there. Doubling down by exercising options and investing your cash is a major vote of confidence but also bears risk. If you are going to stay with your company, you can ride the wave and just let your options accrue value. You will realize that value when the company is sold. You may pay higher taxes, but that may be worth it to avoid the risk of losing your investment.

---

[52] For a more comprehensive description of stock option financing, refer to Bruce Brumberg, "Financing Stock Option Exercises in Private Companies: Insights From a Top Financial Advisor," *Forbes*, September 20, 2021, https://bit.ly/3pDAWEQ

The decision whether to exercise your options is often made based on emotions or by default. You should instead make it clinically and unemotionally. Assess to the best of your ability the probable outcome for your company when making this decision. You need to have a process and decision framework for making the decision. Gather as much information as possible, carefully assess the upside and risks, and make the best decision given your situation and the information at your disposal.

If you are confident the company is on a path to a successful exit, it may benefit you to exercise your options as soon as possible to minimize payroll taxes (Social Security and Medicare taxes) at the time of exercise and get the long-term capital gains clock ticking. In that case, you could save as much as 15 or 20 percentage points on your taxes.

On the other hand, without a crystal ball to predict the future, exercising options may feel like a crapshoot. Before you risk your hard-earned money exercising your options, make sure it is money that you can afford to lose. If not, accept the situation, hold onto your options, and take the tax hit.

The rubber hits the road when you leave the company. At that point, exercising is the only way to preserve your upside without forfeiting your options (or negotiating for an extended exercise period). You will no longer be present to influence the company's success or gain an insider's insights into what is happening that affects the value of your shares. If you don't have a clear indication your investment will grow in value, it may be emotionally easier and more practical to let your options lapse. If you think there's some chance of success, hedge by doing a partial exercise. That allows you to retain participation in the company's upside and gives you a reason to cheer your former colleagues on to success.

PART IV

❧

SHOULD YOU STAY
OR SHOULD YOU GO?

CHAPTER 18

Tragedy, Drama, or Comedy

In Chapter 3 (Prove It!), we discussed the proof continuum milestones a startup must achieve to reach its final act–a successful exit. There's no guarantee it can get there. No script pre-determines the outcome. The whole experience is an improv show, where the actors make it up as they go along.

There are, however, archetypal stories in the world of startups. The tragedies of visionary founders with great technology whose companies lose out to faster, nimbler competition and slowly die on stage. The dramas of companies that struggle for years to find product-market fit, undertake multiple pivots, management changes, and must endure increasing pressure from investors. And the comedies where all's well that ends well, and the team and investors laugh all the way to the bank.

The proof continuum outlines the main acts in the startup play. The framework helps you assess not only how far along a company is when you join but also if it is making reasonable progress. If a company spends too long at a given stage of the continuum without moving on to the next act, it may be a sign that the play will flop. On the other hand, progress is not always linear, so you must consider if the company will be able to overcome the obstacles holding it back. If not, the show's patrons–the investors–will eventually grow tired of funding the production.

Conventional wisdom among venture capital investors is that a small percentage of their portfolio companies *make* their funds. A few bets–the comedies–deliver great returns and offset losses that plague the other companies in the portfolio. Likely a third or more–the tragedies–will go under. The rest–the dramas–will languish indefinitely in limbo consuming the lives of the team and the attention of investors with little to show for their efforts. For VCs, any given company going out of business is a blip on the radar. It may create uncomfortable moments for the sponsoring partner in their investment committee. But one startup going out of business is not a make-or-break occurrence for a VC firm.

This creates a self-fulfilling dynamic for startups. Like theater critics, VCs continually assess the health of their portfolio companies, showering praise and funding on perceived winners and panning losers. A few companies folding is an expected part of portfolio investing. An individual VC with a few failed investments might see their path to advancement within their firms affected, so they will try to keep the show running until they determine whether a given company will succeed or die. They double down with greater investment and support for companies gaining traction and pull back funding and support from laggards, all but ensuring they flop. For startup founders and employees, unlike for the investors, that failure is a life-altering event.

OKRs Are Your Company's Script

The closest thing that a company may have to a script is an operating plan and a set of corporate objectives. One of the best systems I have seen for setting and operating toward company goals is OKRs, which stands for Objectives and Key Results.[53] When our new CEO joined Fugue in 2018, he immediately instituted OKRs throughout the company. Each quarter, the senior management had an offsite to review our past quarter's performance and confirm or reset the company's long- and medium-term objectives. Once the objectives were confirmed, we established the key results we needed to achieve that quarter to ensure we were on track and reviewed our progress toward those results every month.

The value of the OKR system to employees was that all the objectives and key results were made available for the whole company to see. Not only were they public, but each department and member of the team was expected to establish their own OKRs that would feed into the company-level OKRs. The system was designed to establish visibility and alignment throughout the organization. The positive by-product of the exercise was that it provided full transparency each quarter to the entire staff regarding how the company was faring against its objectives.

Anyone paying attention to the OKRs after the company's product pivot in early 2019 would have seen it making significant progress on its product goals. We moved from Proof of Technology to Proof of Product steadily. However, the company's go-to-market progress was far less impressive. Quarter in and quarter out, the company failed to achieve its sales and marketing targets, sometimes by wide margins. Those results were shared with the staff. Diligent observers would certainly have realized the company was struggling.

As an employee in a startup, you have very little control over how the show turns out. You play your part and make your

---

[53] OKRs were developed in the early 1970s by Andy Grove at Intel Corporation as a way to keep management at the company on track in achieving its goals. For a more detailed explanation of OKRs, refer to: John Doerr, *Measure What Matters*, (New York: Portfolio/Penguin, 2018).

contributions. The one thing you do have control over is reading the signs to see if they foreshadow the outcome for the company. While there may be no script to follow, there are enough clues available if you read between the lines of company communications. Ignore them at your peril.

Think Like a Critic

Just as venture investors are continually evaluating their portfolio companies, you need to keep monitoring the health and progress of your company. Just as investors decide whether to keep investing and supporting their companies, you need to decide how long to keep investing your career in your company.

Making those decisions requires you to think like a critic, not just like an actor in the show. Certainly, you hope your company is successful. You put in your best performances day in and day out. But you must also step back and assess whether the play hangs together and delivers on its promise.

Every day you show up for work, you make another investment, hoping it will deliver a positive return. You could choose to make that investment in any number of places. But there is a lot of inertia in our day-to-day habit of going to work at a given job, collecting a paycheck, and continuing to do that over and over for months and years. The switching cost is high, and as the saying goes, "if it ain't broke, don't fix it."

Giving in to inertia and ignoring the signs can be costly. When a startup breaks, it is usually because it runs out of money. The circumstances that lead to that point don't come with flashing red lights and sirens. It is generally a slow unraveling coupled with much reassurance from the senior management team. The worse things are, the less information the bosses are inclined to share. They don't want the staff to get spooked and start leaving. If your startup goes broke, you may be suddenly left out in the cold with little warning and no job.

Watch the action closely. Assess and reassess how open and honest the culture is in your company. Take note if your company has historically been reasonably transparent and communications start to dwindle. In companies I have been involved in, we regularly weighed how much information to share and what to keep on a need-to-know basis.

Ask yourself if you are getting the straight scoop about how the company is doing. When things are going well, management shares information because it motivates staff. When things are not going as well, the test of management's relationship with and faith in the staff shows. That's when you find out whom you can trust and believe.

Before our last round of funding at Fugue, when the company was struggling to attract investors, our CEO continued trying to share as much information as possible. We didn't come out directly and say that there was a possibility that the company could run out of money, but we made it clear that the funding process was taking longer and was more difficult than expected. We assured staff we were working diligently to find investors and close the round, but the process wasn't yielding the desired results.

It was a calculated risk on the part of the leadership to try to be open and an even more calculated risk on the part of the staff to stick it out. Not everyone did. We had a couple of departures as people weighed their personal risk tolerance and decided they needed more certainty than we could provide.

What we did not share with the staff was that, after promising for nearly six months that they would participate in our funding round, two of our investors bailed out when the time came to commit to funding the company. Having the rug pulled out from under the company at the last minute was a real gut-check moment. We weren't sure if the company would survive, and we could not share that news with the staff without potentially causing a mass panic.

The fact that we closed on our funding and the company sold less than a year later was nothing short of miraculous. When we closed the funding round, we had less than two months of cash in the bank. Had the round not closed, we would have had to go into fire-sale or shutdown mode, and the staff would have had almost no warning.

Fortunately, it didn't come to that, but it shows how a startup can sit on the knife's edge. Despite being turned down by more than forty VCs, we were lucky to find a willing investor who saw our vision and jumped in with both feet, although with onerous terms on the financing. Though costly, we lived to fight on. Not all startups are so lucky.

The Bottom Line

Your ability to predict how the plot turns out for your startup depends on how attentive you are to the foreshadowing provided by management as the play unfolds. When things are going well, management happily showers staff and investors with good news. When they aren't, you may see a subtle or not-so-subtle shift in the nature, frequency, and comprehensiveness of information being shared. When you start to see signs of trouble coming or management closing ranks, you need to decide whether you are willing to stay and risk being left standing in an empty theater in the dark when the stage lights go to black.

CHAPTER 19

The Point of No Returns

Venture capital firms are structured as partnerships that manage multiple investment funds. Each fund has a typical life of up to ten years and is expected to deliver high returns to the fund's limited partners (the outside sources of capital that invest in the fund) within that time frame. VC firms thrive by raising successive funds, and the returns realized by earlier funds are critical in establishing their track record to attract investors into later funds. So how do they generate those returns?

VC firms generally operate on what is called the "2 and 20" model. They receive a small percentage (usually 2 percent per year) of the committed investor capital as management fees. But they make most of their money when their portfolio companies have successful exits. Most of the proceeds from those exits go to the funds' limited partners, with the VC firm participating in the upside through **carried interest** (20 percent of the gains on profits from company exits). The more quickly returns are realized through company exits, the more appealing the VC firm's subsequent funds are to prospective investors in the fund. This dynamic puts a lot of pressure on the general partners of the VC firm managing the funds to deliver returns quickly.[54]

---

[54] Venture capital firms attract investment from limited partners, who are outside institutional investors or high net worth individuals. Limited partners want to invest in VC funds run by firms with successful track records in their prior funds.

VCs May Stop Funding Your Company

The pressure VCs face to deliver returns rapidly adds to the challenge investors face when deciding whether to keep investing in a given company. If a company is floundering, putting more money into it may only postpone its inevitable failure and siphon the VC's funds away from other more promising opportunities. But there is also the chance that the company will have a breakthrough if it has an extra six to twelve months of life. VCs must make hard judgment calls about continuing to support a company, and they may decide to pull the plug at any point for any number of reasons.

With the pressures at work in VC firms, time is not a startup's friend. Companies that aren't rapidly progressing toward a successful exit within an acceptable time window (three to five years) become a nuisance to their investors. Even though these companies are not on a path to deliver attractive returns, the VC still needs to track and report on the companies to their limited partners. Additionally, if the firm's partner remains on the board, they must still fulfill their responsibilities.

This pressure for portfolio companies to thrive quickly is further complicated in several ways because VC funds have limited investment periods. First, the typical fund life is ten years, and the investment period to deploy fresh capital may only be five years, after which the VC is focused on helping its more successful companies to achieve an exit. If a company needs capital outside of the VC's investment period, it may be out of luck. VCs reviewing deals outside of their investment period may choose to pass on participating, sometimes because they have no more capital to commit.

Second, if a VC firm chooses to invest from a later fund in its active investment period, there are complicated political dynamics at work. The VC partners on the investment committee in the later fund may be different from the individuals in the original fund that invested or served on the board. This can result in VC partners within the same firm having to negotiate against each other on deal terms, which VCs usually prefer to avoid.

Finally, partners in the original fund that invested may have retired or moved on to investing in companies out of subsequent funds and have grown impatient with the "living dead"[55] companies remaining in the prior fund that have limited prospects to achieve successful exits.

My wife, Amena Ali, headed up marketing at a company constantly grasping at straws to raise capital to keep going. The offerings from the 20-year-old company had become commoditized. To make matters worse, it lost more than 20 percent of its revenues when the contract with its largest customer was terminated. The early investors, and most VCs in general, who had historically funded companies in that space, were well past their investment periods.

Despite the company's Herculean efforts to develop innovative new products, its sheer age made potential investors wonder whether the company would ever deliver attractive returns. After fighting these battles for several years at the company with limited success, Amena opted to leave.

Given the pressure for fast returns, VCs press company management to exhibit urgency, build their market presence quickly, and position themselves for an attractive exit. Or worse, if progress is too slow, they may push the company into a fire sale. In the case of Fugue, our principal champion at NEA, the formidable Harry Weller, who was named a "Midas List VC" nine times by *Forbes* magazine, passed away as we were closing our Series D

---

[55] Companies that are not moving quickly toward an attractive exit but are also not likely to fail anytime soon are referred to as "living dead" or "zombies." They continue to exist but are perceived by investors to be going nowhere.

round.[56] Harry's shocking, sudden death at the age of 46 opened a gaping hole in the DC venture community and left companies like ours struggling to maintain relationships with NEA. While NEA followed through and closed on the Series D round to honor Harry's commitment, we never again had the same relationship with the NEA partnership, and they stopped supporting the company financially.

After a few years, when Fugue needed another round of financing to go to market with a promising cloud security offering, the new NEA partner on our board pushed hard for a quick sale rather than agreeing to advocate to his firm's investment committee to provide further investment. Without his support, the investment committee would not approve even a small investment, which left Fugue scrambling to find investors to bridge the company to its ultimate sale.

Good Money After Bad?

It is easy to understand why a VC firm might pull the plug. Once a company has been around for a while and has not proven that it can make material progress through the stages of the proof continuum, investors lose faith. While history is not always a guide to the future, the odds are that a management team that hasn't produced results in the past may continue to fail going forward. This is the "point of no returns."

Investors gauge whether incremental investment and time may yield a positive outcome. Building and investing in startups requires what I often refer to as pathological optimism. But there comes a point when the evidence is compelling that the company may be heading nowhere. The prudent response by investors is to call it

---

[56] Loizos, Connie, "Harry Weller, a 'Midas List' VC and the head of NEA's East Coast practice, has passed away", TechCrunch, https://bit.ly/3JMOViE, November 20, 2016.

a day. I have found myself in that situation not only as a startup executive but also as an angel investor.

In 2008, as the principal investor in a high-end office coffee service called Barista on Demand, I realized that, with the financial crisis in full force, companies were not likely to be spending money on high-end perks for their employees anytime soon. Having failed to gain significant traction a couple of years after it was founded, the company still needed regular infusions of cash. It reached a point where I, as the principal investor, had to draw the line and say, "No more." While I agonized over the decision for a few weeks, the need to stop throwing good money after bad was clear. Without additional funding, the company shut down.

The challenge in these situations is that the founders and management team rely on continued funding to keep the lights on and pay salaries (including their own). While the investors are able to take a more unemotional view of the situation, those running the company are slower to admit to themselves that the company is dead. They have too much wrapped up in the deal to give up, too much at stake, including their livelihoods. They continue to hope.

Joining a company at this crisis stage is a waste of your time and effort, especially if you could have pursued other opportunities. You would think companies struggling to complete their next funding round would not be able to hire, but that can be deceiving. In its last-ditch effort to prove the company is worthy of investment, management may hire new employees to work on important initiatives or bring on salespeople to try to close a few key deals. They may also have had staff departures as people recognize the company's status and may need to fill critical gaps.

If you are currently working in a company that has reached the point of no returns, recognizing this dynamic is critical to your financial and professional well-being. You are in the unenviable position of continuing to invest your efforts when there is no upside. The question is whether you realize the dire straits the company is in. If you do, look for a lifeboat and try to exit gracefully and professionally before the ship sinks.

There may be no definitive way to know that a company is in trouble unless you hear it directly from the management or employees who have left. However, there are a few telltale signs that should raise alarm bells.

- Consistent failure to reach stated company goals such as OKRs

- Senior management departures

- Multiple junior staff departures in a short period

- Layoffs (especially more than one round)

- More than two or three years since the company closed a funding round

- Few or no job postings

- Minimal new product releases or new product features

- Multiple customer defections or lack of new customer wins

Pay attention and keep an eye out for these signs. It is easy to sweep concerns under the rug or feel that you are being paranoid. But if you suspect your company may be in trouble, you owe it to yourself to try to confirm your suspicion.

The Bottom Line

Startups are regularly in need of additional funding rounds. Venture capital investors must constantly monitor the health of their portfolio companies and make tough calls regarding continuing to fund their companies. When a VC decides that a company can no longer deliver positive returns, it may cease funding it or may provide a small bridge loan just to keep it going long enough for a quick exit.

As an employee, you face the risk that the company you work for reaches the point of no returns. Just as you need to evaluate the health and likely success of a company before you join, you need to make regular assessments as to whether your current company is worth continuing to invest your time in.

When a company is in trouble, management tends to pull in its horns and go quiet. It's instinctive. They don't want to draw attention to themselves and bring on excessive scrutiny. And they don't want to alarm the staff. Your antenna should go up if you notice any telltale signs of a company in trouble. If you do, consider whether it makes sense to continue your involvement with the company or to start making an exit plan.

CHAPTER 20

Exiting the Stage

According to a 2022 report from the Bureau of Labor Statistics, the average person could change jobs as many as eight to ten times over a four-decade career. The report puts average job tenure in the US at a little over four years. For workers aged 25 to 34, that job tenure is even shorter, at 2.8 years.[57]

When you go to a theater production, one of the first things you'll hear is an announcement pointing to the exits. Under normal circumstances, you don't need to know where the exits are until the show is over. But it's useful to be prepared for emergencies.

Most people don't think about their exit plan when starting a new position. Why should you? You are excited about your new company and the possibilities seem endless. In fact, most people don't think about an exit plan until it's time to exit. But how can you expect to optimize your next career move if you wait until the last minute?

Numerous circumstances may lead you to head for the exit sooner than you anticipated, whether voluntarily or involuntarily.

---

[57] "Employee Tenure Summary", U.S Bureau of Labor Statistics, https://www.bls.gov/news.release/tenure.nr0.htm, September 22, 2022.

1. Your company may be acquired. Once that happens, all bets are off as to what the acquirer does with the newly acquired company's employees, especially non-technical staff.

2. Your company may struggle to find traction and could run out of cash and shut down.

3. Before a shutdown occurs, the board and management may take measures to cut cash burn, and you could get laid off, even if you consider yourself essential to the company.

4. You may find that you don't love your job or that the company isn't able to offer you the advancement or experience you are looking for.

5. If you have taken my advice throughout this book, you may have evaluated the prospects for your company and determined working there is not an investment worth continuing to make.

6. And there's always the possibility of getting terminated for performance reasons. It happens.

If you have joined a two-year-old startup, the odds are you'll find yourself looking for work within three to five years, if not sooner, as the company works through its lifecycle. We prepare to apply to college for at least four years of high school. We plot our internship strategy and prepare to apply for our first jobs and plan for graduate school throughout college. Why don't people approach their careers similarly when the reality of job change is inevitable?

Preparing for Your Exit

The day you join your new company, you should start preparing for your exit. That doesn't mean you write a resignation letter and stow it away for the day you'll need it. It does mean consistently investing in your future to prepare for your next career move when the time comes.

Think about it like tending a garden. You can't expect to drop seeds in the ground, pour gallons of water and a bag of fertilizer on them, and instantly have a garden full of beautiful flowers. They take time to grow, and you must nurture them consistently. Similarly, the ingredients required to advance your career—skills and experience, track record and credentials, and professional networks—take time to gather.

The building blocks of your career grow over time, even if you aren't purposeful about nurturing them. The more years you work, the more projects you work on, the more people you work with, the more each of those flowers starts to bloom.

The alternative is to simply keep your nose to the grindstone, work hard, be a good colleague, and get your job done. Eventually, if you're lucky, an interesting new job might come along. Some people happen to be in the right place at the right time when opportunities fall in their laps. But that's rare.

Why leave your career to chance? Why not create your own luck? A systematic approach to career management with modest regular effort optimizes your ability to take advantage of opportunities that arise. If you do have to move fast because your company starts to fail, you will be more prepared to harvest the fruits of your preparations and sustain yourself until you find more fertile soil.

Before you experience the pressure of having to switch jobs suddenly, systematically focus on a few key areas such as building skills and experience, advocating for advancement, finding a mentor, taking advantage of professional development opportunities, documenting what you accomplish, building your networks, and preparing financially.

Build Skills and Experience

One of the appealing aspects of startup life is the chance to take on different kinds of assignments. There is never a lack of projects, and if you are ambitious and take the initiative, you can build a wealth of skills and experiences that make you a go-to person within your current company, positioning you for your next job.

Given the fast pace of startups, being eager to take on new assignments is a prerequisite. There is an important caveat to bear in mind, however. Building trust with your colleagues means successfully doing the work assigned to you first. Constantly looking around and volunteering to do something else that sounds more interesting or important can signal that you are unhappy with your current job or not willing to roll up your sleeves and do what's needed, even if it's somewhat mundane.

I have seen this dynamic play out quite a few times, particularly with employees early in their careers. Out of inexperience, they may take a position that seems interesting or because they need the money. Then reality sets in, and they discover that the day-to-day content of the job is not what they expected or hoped for. They are doing more grunt work than anticipated or find that their skills or interests are not aligned with their role.

Looking around, they see others doing work that appears more interesting. There is nothing wrong with learning about other kinds of jobs and deciding you want to pursue a different path. But if coveting the jobs of others means you're not giving your full attention to your job, don't be surprised if before long, you find yourself on a Performance Improvement Plan (PIP) or without a job at all.

Once you master your position, taking on more responsibilities allows you to create a stepping stone for a lateral or upward move inside or outside your company. It is logical that many employees wait until they get promoted before looking for a new job. It's easier to move into a position at another company for a job you are already doing than to convince a new employer to hire a junior person for a higher-level position. For most employers, especially small companies with limited training resources, bringing on new employees is risky enough without taking a flyer on unproven talent.

Advocate For Your Advancement

The two primary means of building your skills and experience are by doing more technically challenging work individually and by taking on increasing managerial responsibilities. This reflects the two major paths to advancement in a startup.

As an individual contributor, you are primarily responsible for delivering on your own projects. You have minimal supervisory responsibilities but are expected to execute effectively on more and more complex projects. As a manager, by contrast, you advance by managing increasingly more staff and bigger and more important projects or departments.

One of the challenges that arise in startups is that the expertise required to develop software or new drugs, for example, is highly technical. Technical talent is precious. But individual contributors may hit a ceiling. If the only path to advancement is moving into management positions, companies may have to promote their best technical staff members into management positions where their greatest talents are lost or underutilized. There is also no guarantee that a talented technical contributor desires to move into management or will even be a good manager.

To address this structural flaw, some startups create dual advancement tracks. Employees can follow the traditional path of climbing the ladder to more senior managerial positions. Or they can follow a track that recognizes the increasing value of individual contributors, especially in engineering and product development.

Whether on the management track or progressing as an individual contributor, you may find yourself operating at a level higher than your job title or compensation would suggest. Startups are less hierarchical than larger companies and are often less systematic about requiring managers to complete performance evaluations, which can delay your advancement. There's also downward pressure on costs that permeates many startups operating in the red.

To ensure you are well-positioned to move jobs when you need or want to, regularly assess whether you are being adequately recognized, compensated, and, when appropriate, promoted. Your job title and compensation should reflect your contributions to the company and serve as a marker to future employers as to where you would fit best in their organization.

Self-advocacy is critical in this regard, especially given the tendency of startup management to focus relatively little attention on personnel issues until they become problems. If you don't tend to your career advancement, you may become stalled and resentful, which could affect your job performance or cause you to leave the company before you have gotten the most out of the experience.

Find a Mentor

One of the most valuable things you can do to help navigate opportunities and advancement is to find a mentor or two, ideally one within your department or team and someone senior outside of your group who is knowledgeable and influential in the company. Developing professional relationships with senior managers is far easier in a startup than in large companies, especially since most startups maintain an open-door policy for staff to engage with leadership. Take advantage of this dynamic.

Personal relationships often determine access to opportunities. Having mentors who know you well and are vested in your advancement may tip the scales when senior management decides whom to tap for new opportunities. Don't hesitate to consult them on how to manage your career progression, including what assignments to pursue, how to navigate challenging supervisors, or when to consider asking for a raise or a promotion.

Just recognize that your mentors' investment in helping you grow is tied to their desire for you to make greater contributions to your company. You should go into the mentoring relationship with a clear understanding that it may be largely transactional. While you may hope the relationship transcends your tenure at the same company, it may not. My relationships with my mentors during my early years as a consultant at Bain & Company faded into the background when I decided not to return to the firm after business school.

Depending on the circumstances, when the day comes that you choose to leave the company, your mentor or mentors may feel disappointed or betrayed, and the nature of the relationship could suddenly change or grow cold. Anticipate that this is possible and make the most of the relationship while it lasts. If you are lucky, your mentor will continue to support you after you leave the company. If the relationship becomes strained or fades upon your departure, appreciate what the mentor was able to do for you and move on.

Leverage Professional Development Resources

Even if startups don't have formal training programs, some may offer access to outside training resources and reimbursement programs for professional development. This is one of the most underutilized benefits available. When you join a firm, or better yet, are discussing joining, find out what kind of professional development resources the company offers. The most common include:

- Access to firmwide subscriptions for educational resources (such as LinkedIn Learning)

- Reimbursement for classes taken to advance your skills (assuming you pass) or to work toward professional designations such as a CPA

- Support for certifications programs from recognized outside sources such as competency designations from the major tech companies like Amazon Web Services or Microsoft

- Paid time off and sponsorship to attend industry or technical conferences

- Subsidy for membership in professional organizations such as the Society of Human Resources Managers (SHRM) for HR professionals

It is easy to get sucked into the day-to-day rhythms of your job and ignore the resources the company makes available. In some ways, the company is counting on the fact that most employees don't take advantage of these perks because if everyone did, it could be a huge line item in the budget. But don't let inertia win. Pursuing professional development is a career-enhancing move.

One of our developers at Fugue took advantage of the company's resources to develop expertise in cybersecurity practices and ended up as the firm's Director of Security. This was not coincidental. The company needed a point person to fill the role, and our CEO asked him if he would be interested. As you consider how to enhance your skills through professional development, aligning your interests with the company's needs is a powerful combination that can accelerate your professional ascent.

Failing to take opportunities seriously can backfire. When considering how to leverage professional development resources, understand the commitment and requirements and manage expectations with your company. Reimbursement may be tied to passing a course or achieving a certain grade, so take it seriously.

Finally, there may be restrictions on how you use company resources, and you might need advance approval. Consider your request carefully and be prepared to justify why your proposal makes sense. Most importantly, ensure that pursuing professional development opportunities does not interfere with your day job. Manage expectations with your supervisors carefully if you need to spend time studying or need to be out of the office for an exam.

Document Your Journey

The day you start your new job, you start building on your track record of accomplishments. Over time, it is easy to lose track of everything you worked on and the milestones you achieved. From day one, it is beneficial to keep a log of what you worked on, when, with whom, and what the outcome of that work was in concrete terms.

Keeping a log enables you to refer to the specifics in the months and years that follow. Quantify specific accomplishments in terms of dollar impact, customers acquired, projects completed, products launched, etc. A detailed record helps you populate your resume and LinkedIn profile with the highlights of your tenure. Having these specifics organized at your fingertips proves invaluable when interviewing for new positions. Sharing your success stories with prospective employers, using the facts and figures you have recorded, adds depth and credibility to your narrative.

In addition to logging your professional track record, keep copies of your performance reviews. Pull out quotations highlighting your key accomplishments or positive messages about your contributions. Pulling together a compendium of highlights from your prior performance reviews can help you distill a positive professional picture of how your supervisors have viewed you as an employee over time. It also helps you identify any weaknesses you may need to work on.

Finally, keep a record of your salary and incentive compensation changes and percent attainment against goals over time. By regularly tracking your compensation, you can see concretely how quickly you are progressing and whether your compensation is keeping up with the market. A track record of rapid promotions and significant pay increases is evidence for future employers that you are a high-performing contributor and someone they really want on their team. Tracking attainment against company or individual goals (i.e., OKRs) is a powerful way to show professional success.

If your career progress is slower than you think it should be, keeping track of the details helps you decide quickly whether your company is failing to recognize your contributions adequately. This can serve as the basis for HR discussions regarding right-sizing your compensation or figuring out what you need to do to advance more quickly. Either way, information is power.

Build Your Networks

Once you have landed that dream job, you might be tempted to throttle back on networking. Don't. Professional networking is a job that is never done. Rather than marking the end of networking, joining a new company presents a great opportunity to enhance your networks inside and outside the company.

A common way startup employees find new jobs is through referrals from former co-workers and bosses. Someone leaves for greener pastures. Naturally, if their new employer is hiring, they may want to bring along their respected colleagues. When my daughter left her first PR agency job for a competitor, within less than a year, she had referred two of her former co-workers, helping her friends find new opportunities while earning referral bonuses from her new employer.

It is in your interest to develop positive relationships with others who work for your company as soon as possible, especially given the short tenure that most people have in a given job. Some of this happens organically with the people you work most closely with. But try to branch out beyond your immediate colleagues—invest in developing broader relationships throughout the company.

A few of the ways you can build your network include:

- Set up coffees or lunches with colleagues to get to know them.
- Attend company parties and gatherings.

- Take advantage of one-on-ones with senior executives whenever they are offered, and make sure you prepare thoughtful questions in advance.

- Participate enthusiastically in company activities like information sessions, game nights, sporting events, volunteering activities, and happy hours.

- Invite your colleagues to connect on LinkedIn and share relevant content with them.

Not only do these actions help you professionally, but developing friendships and relationships makes the workplace more enjoyable and productive. Having those relationships to rely on as needed will also make you more effective in your job.

In addition to networking internally, solidifying and building your external network is valuable. Leaving a prior company can sometimes create ill will. But if you left on good terms, capitalize on the relationships you built. Reach out to former colleagues and let them know where you landed. Ask former supervisors to write endorsements on your LinkedIn page or confirm if they would be willing to serve as professional references in the future.

Beyond former colleagues, start to consider how to expand your network in your industry. Consider joining professional associations, or identify conferences focused on your job function or industry. Look at the companies in your investors' portfolio and reach out to peers in those companies who are in positions like yours. Not only might that offer the opportunity to compare notes on best practices, but eventually, it may lead to them wanting to recruit you or vice versa.

Networking is a never-ending and nearly infinite task, so you need to consider how much time, effort, and money you want to invest in the process. The network you build may be the key to unearthing your next opportunity or helping you land on your feet if your company finds itself in challenging circumstances. At the very least, it is a great source of camaraderie, advice, and guidance.

Raise Your Professional Profile

Beyond simply building your networks, it is valuable to establish yourself in your field. There's a saying that it's not what you know but who you know. That is true, but it is even more potent to consider who knows you. Having lived for several decades in Washington, DC, I know this dynamic all too well. Everyone knows who the powerful and influential are. But that doesn't mean they know you. Raising your professional profile to the point where influential people in your space know and respect you will pay dividends.

There are many ways to enhance your professional standing depending on your skills and what you are trying to accomplish. You can volunteer for leadership positions in your industry associations. Or develop an active voice on relevant social media platforms in your sector. You can contribute to important open-source projects that highlight your technical skills. Or seek opportunities to speak at industry conferences on your company's behalf.

Most people in the networking game are trying to sell something or get something from their contacts. Building your professional profile by volunteering, speaking, educating, and contributing your time and talents will provide you with an opportunity to raise your visibility and build a positive professional reputation among important people without having to ask them for anything in return.

Prepare Financially

What if you had to go for six months without a salary? What about a year? Given how quickly startups can find their backs against the wall, you must be as prepared as possible. This is doubly true in uncertain economic times. Startups benefit greatly when the markets are roaring— investment dollars flow freely, and hiring abounds. But the reverse is also true. When economic downturns happen, startups, especially early-stage startups, are often the hardest hit. Funding dries up. The board turns the screws by forcing budget cuts, and management teams are forced to make difficult decisions to let staff go, sometimes on short notice.

You don't want to get blindsided. Put aside emergency funds to mitigate risk, consider in advance how you can reduce your living expenses, and buy time to find your next opportunity. Explore contracting opportunities directly with your network and through outsourcing companies that promote freelancers, especially if you have technical skills.

When It's Time to Go

How you approach your departure from your company depends on the circumstances. If you are leaving to take another job, provide as much notice as possible and depart graciously. Work diligently to create a smooth transition. Offer any constructive suggestions you can in your exit interview. Be gracious throughout the transition—thank your bosses and colleagues for the opportunity you had to work there. Keep the door open for a future relationship. Life is long, and you never know when you might end up back at the company or working with former colleagues. Don't burn your bridges.

If you are terminated, look out for yourself, and ensure you get everything due to you. Negotiate for the most severance possible. Ask for a longer period to exercise your options after your departure. Ask the company to cover the cost of your benefits for a period. Understand your options for retaining your benefits, especially your health insurance, even if you must pay for them. See if the firm would pay for outplacement services to help you find another job. It also helps to stay positive and avoid bitterness despite the unpleasant circumstances. Again, you never know when you may need a reference or you have the opportunity to be rehired.

In January 2019, Fugue laid off approximately 40 percent of our staff due to a change in business strategy. The senior management committed to networking on behalf of all departing employees. Given the strong relationships between the team and senior management, the company did everything possible to help everyone land on their feet. We offered everyone four weeks of compensation. We extended health benefits for a couple of months beyond the termination date.

Within a few weeks of the layoffs, all but one of the employees had found new positions, many as a result of introductions made by senior leadership. That was an unusual effort put forth by the company. It reflected the strong sense of community built on bonds forged among the employees and company leadership over the years.

Whether you leave voluntarily or involuntarily, you must address critical financial details, such as keeping your 401(k) in the company plan or rolling it over to your IRA or new employer's retirement plan. Arguably the most important is deciding whether to exercise your stock options. You typically have 90 days to pull the trigger. Don't ignore this important financial decision. Consider the lessons from this book and determine whether it makes sense to exercise all, some, or none of your options.

The Bottom Line

In one of the most well-known business books of all time, *Dig Your Well Before You're Thirsty*[58], the consummate networking guru Harvey Mackay encourages readers to build their network of

---

[58] Harvey Mackay, *Dig Your Well Before You're Thirsty* (New York: Crown Business, 1997).

contacts long before they need them. This lesson applies equally to all aspects of preparing to exit from your company. Waiting until you decide to leave to plan for your next move leaves you behind the curve.

Preparing in advance provides you with greater flexibility, makes you a more attractive candidate, helps you sell yourself more effectively, and puts you in a position to move quickly and confidently. Building your exit plan all along the way requires a systematic investment in numerous areas:

- Consistently build your skills and experience.
- Advocate for yourself to secure raises and promotions.
- Find and nurture relationships with mentors inside and outside your company.
- Leverage professional development opportunities whenever you can.
- Document your accomplishments.
- Build your professional network inside and outside your company.
- Raise your professional profile.
- Provide yourself with as much financial flexibility as possible to weather the storm.

Mission Possible

What do you call an organization that:

- Is led by a charismatic leader with the vision and drive to "make the world a better place"?

- Is trying to achieve the near-impossible despite being chronically underfunded, under-resourced, and understaffed?

- Is completely dependent on outside funding for its survival and growth?

- Is filled with passionate, committed staff working long hours on tight deadlines, often for below-market wages?

Outside the business world, those characteristics describe the typical nonprofit organization. They attract a special breed of person willing to sacrifice personal financial gain to do mission-driven work. People who go to work for nonprofits are under no illusion they will get rich. They do it because of a desire to solve critical societal problems or benefit their communities.

Startups bear a striking resemblance to small nonprofit organizations. All the characteristics in the list could fairly describe a typical startup. Most startup founders would argue that their purpose is their mission. What motivated them to start their companies was believing they could solve a problem that was not being solved adequately. This notion of startup founders claiming they are "making the world a better place" is so common that the hit HBO series *Silicon Valley* included a hilarious sequence of startup pitches where every founder used the phrase to describe their offering.[59]

Like nonprofit leaders, startup founders must have a vision and passionately promote it to attract funders and employees to join them in their journey. The main difference between nonprofits and startups is that in a nonprofit, the mission is the sole purpose. There is no expectation the organization will make money, go public or get acquired, or enrich shareholders.

In most cases, the profit motive is antithetical to the essence of a nonprofit. Running a surplus at a nonprofit often leads it to consider how to grow the delivery of its services, expand its mission, or build an endowment to help sustain the organization for the long run. There is little chance that the leadership or employees will become wealthy unless there is significant fraud or self-dealing, which sadly does happen in the nonprofit world.

A Startup is a Nonprofit Attached to a Lottery Ticket

While a startup may also be mission-driven, the underlying objective of the company is to provide shareholders with financial returns. Notice I didn't say employees. Paying employees is a means to an end. If employees happen to make money in the service of making the investors wealthy, that's a bonus.

Most investors pay their employees only what they must to retain them and keep them motivated. This is especially true given that startups seldom run a profit. Startups continually burn investor

---

[59] "Third Party Insourcing," *Silicon Valley*, Season 1, Episode 6, directed by Mike Judge, written by John Altschuler, Dave Krinsky, and Mike Judge, HBO, 2014

cash, so the lower the company can keep its expenses, the longer it can hold off until it needs to raise additional funds.

As long as a company shows significant progress on the proof continuum, it can continue tapping the capital markets to fuel growth. Through the first five stages, a startup exhibits negative cash flow and losses. Even once they reach profitability, many high-growth companies continue to invest in research and development (R&D), sales, and marketing to keep growing market share. In pursuit of continued innovation and market leadership, they keep burning cash.

Over the years, we jokingly (or maybe wistfully) referred to Fugue as a "nonprofit." Like many venture-backed startups, from the day the company was founded until the day it was sold, it never came close to turning a profit. In fact, our balance sheet accrued tens of millions of dollars of operating losses. That didn't stop us from raising more than $80 million of venture capital, ultimately selling the company, and making a select group of our investors a substantial amount of money.

Given the focus of startups on making money for investors, how do they attract and retain employees? By selling their vision and mission, just like nonprofits. The mission may be for operational efficiency, industry disruption, or social good. Whatever it is, startups play on the fact that they are cool, disruptive, innovative, and mission-oriented to woo employees.

For employees, the prospect of gaining material wealth by working at a startup may also be an essential part of the motivation for joining. The equity they receive conveys a sense of being part of something larger than themselves and provides ownership in both the literal and figurative senses. But in economic terms, an equity grant is essentially a lottery ticket. In a small number of cases, it may pay off handsomely. Like most lottery tickets, though, the odds of winning big are low.

Many employees joined Fugue because of the extraordinary vision of our principal founder, Josh Stella. In 2011, Josh saw the future of distributed computing through the cloud and the need for a way to secure it more effectively. People joined the team by the dozens to share in the journey. It was the company's vision and the sense of shared purpose and mission that not only attracted the team but held it together through the ups and downs until the company was sold.

As a result of Fugue's sale, some employees' lottery tickets paid off. For most, the payoff was more akin to a scratch-off game than to Powerball or Mega Millions. Relative to the investors, the employees who did all the work earned a small fraction of the proceeds from the sale. The co-founders who left the company before its exit were left with little to show for having helped birth the company. Even the two co-founders who remained with the company for ten years walked away with payouts that paled in comparison to what the investors received.

Why Join a Startup?

Despite Fugue's roller-coaster journey, the company sold for approximately $120 million, which puts it in the ranks of successful venture-backed startups. Even with the company's relative success, most employees who stuck it out made a lot less money than they could have had they pursued careers in big tech companies. Still, if you ask them, knowing what they know now, whether they would do it again, I suspect the answer for many would be yes.

Throughout this book, much of my focus has been on the economic aspects of working for startups. If you look at the equation through a purely financial lens, going to work for most startups may not make sense. They generally can't pay as well as big companies. The benefits are not as good. There's less stability and unclear opportunity for promotion and career advancement. Equity that you may receive can get diluted, devalued, lost, or forfeited.

So how can you justify going to work for a startup? Career choices are rarely one-dimensional. If economics were the only consideration, who would ever work for a nonprofit? Or become a teacher or a nurse? Or a firefighter or college professor?

Working for a startup is different from working at a big company. Over my startup career, my contributions felt highly tangible and impactful. Startups offer endless opportunities to take initiative, gain responsibility, engage in creative problem-solving, and collaborate with passionate, innovative, brilliant colleagues working to realize a company's vision.

Certainly, I hoped the companies I started or worked for would be successful and my stock would be worth a lot of money. But even the best ideas don't always lead to great financial outcomes. I have come to recognize over the years that so much of the success of startups depends on luck, timing, and even geography.

But money wasn't my principal motivation. If I had desired a more straightforward path to financial gain, I would have stayed in management consulting or gone to work on Wall Street or in private equity. Startups became my passion. The opportunity to help build mission-driven organizations with smart, hard-working, committed individuals was far more important to me than the size of my weekly paycheck or the ultimate equity payout.

The Bottom Line

When my daughter was starting as a first-year student at Wesleyan University in Connecticut, the president of the University, Michael Roth, welcomed the families to campus. He encouraged incoming students to look at their college years and beyond as an opportunity to do three things: find their passion, get good at it, and then determine how to share it with the world. He didn't say go out and make as much money as possible. Setting financial considerations aside, if you want to follow President Roth's advice, the startup experience offers a great opportunity to do all three.

There is a lot to recommend going down the startup path. It's great to be excited by a company's mission and the visionary leaders you'd follow to the gates of hell and back. Startups offer tremendous opportunities for varied experiences with lots of responsibility. They provide significant access to senior leaders and the opportunity to work closely with colleagues seeking innovative solutions to as-yet unsolved problems.

Just go in with your eyes open. Consider the opportunity costs of the years you may invest in building someone else's vision and the investors' wealth, not necessarily your own. Ask yourself if it's the right time in your career or life to jump in.

Assess the risks. Consider that the company may not deliver an adequate return on your time invested and may even go out of business. Evaluate your risk tolerance and ask yourself, "What's the worst thing that could happen if the company ceased operating?" If that outcome is something you can live with, then the risk may be acceptable.

After doing your homework and evaluating the opportunity carefully and unemotionally, if you believe the risk is worth it and the fit is good, go for it. You may or may not find the financial success you hope for. Even if you don't, you will likely find a sense of purpose in working to solve interesting and important problems. You will meet and forge lasting bonds with a band of comrades and have plenty of battle scars and war stories to prepare you for the next phases of your career.

The decision to join is only the beginning. Every day you go to work, you make an additional investment in your company. Learn to be a smart investor with your most precious assets—your time and career. Regularly assess your chosen path and read the signs along the way. You cannot count on your company to look out for your best interests. At every stage of your startup journey, you need to look out for yourself.

Glossary of Key Terms[60]

83(b) election - A filing made by an employee with the Internal Revenue Service at the time restricted stock is issued either directly by the company or as a result of the early exercise of a stock option. The filing, which must be made within 30 days of receipt of the restricted stock, is designed to ensure that the stock receives capital gains treatment at the time of sale.

409A valuation - Refers to Section 409A of the Internal Revenue Code, which governs how incentive stock grants are issued. The value of a company's stock (usually common stock) at a given time that forms the basis for the company to set the exercise price for stock options. Must be conducted by an independent third party at least every 12 months or when a material event happens to the company that would affect the value of the company's common stock.

acceleration - The process by which stock options, restricted stock, and restricted stock units (RSUs) become vested more quickly than the underlying vesting schedule. The process is associated with specific events such as a company sale or change of control. See also trigger.

---

[60] Special thanks to Randy Domolky of PAN Investments for sharing some of his firm's definitions which are incorporated into this glossary.

active angel - An individual investor who takes an active role in helping an early-stage company by providing strategic or technical advice, coaching the management team, and making introductions to prospective customers and other investors. Also see angel.

advisory board - A group of experienced businesspeople who support the company with strategic advice, provide credibility, especially to pre-seed, seed, and early-stage companies, but have no governance power over the company's affairs. Also called board of advisors.

angel - An individual providing a relatively small amount of capital—typically less than $250,000—to a startup for an equity stake in the company. Angels are most active in companies that are early stage and pre-revenue. Also see active angel.

annual recurring revenue (ARR) - The point-in-time snapshot of the annualized revenue associated with all currently active customer contracts. Often associated with SaaS companies.

anti-dilution provision - a feature of preferred shares that calls for the issuance of additional preferred shares to the holders if the company sells shares in a later funding round at a price per share lower than the price at which the preferred shares in question were purchased. Can result in significant dilution for common shareholders. See down round and recapitalization.

at-will employment - The right by an employer to terminate an employee at any time for any reason. A standard feature of most employment arrangements.

bargain element - The spread between the value of a share of common stock (for example, at the time of a company sale) and the exercise price at which an option holder may purchase the common stock. Represents the nominal value of the stock option at a given time.

basis - The price of a share of stock used to determine capital gains or losses when the stock is sold or written off.

board of advisors - See advisory board.

board approval - The process whereby the board of directors approves corporate actions, such as the issuance of incentive equity grants, by an affirmative vote of its members.

board of directors (BOD) - A group of influential individuals, elected by stockholders, chosen to oversee the affairs of a company. A board typically includes investors, mentors, and industry experts as well as members of the management team such as the CEO. Not all startups have a board, but larger institutional investors (i.e., venture capital firms) typically require a board seat in exchange for investment in a company.

bridge - A round of financing meant to provide enough capital to a company to allow it to operate until it can raise a full round or consummate a sale. Often funded by company insiders through convertible debt or a SAFE. Also called bridge round. Also see convertible debt and SAFE.

burn rate - The amount of net cash a company spends monthly to fund its operations.

capitalization - The collective funding a company has received over its life since inception. Usually refers to equity funding but can also include debt.

capitalization table – A spreadsheet listing the ownership of company stock by owner and class of stock. Includes shares outstanding overall and by class as well as the available shares in the option pool. Also called cap table.

carried interest - The mechanism through which venture capital firms profit from exits by their portfolio companies. A percentage (usually 20 percent) of profits venture capital firms retain as compensation for managing investments in their funds using capital from outside limited partners, with the remaining percentage (80 percent) being distributed to the limited partners.

cashless exercise - A process for exercising stock whereby a portion of the exercised stock is forfeited to pay the exercise price in lieu of the option holder paying cash to acquire the stock. Most typically happens in public companies. Also see non-recourse financing.

change of control - The sale of more than 50 percent of the stock of a company, giving the buyer governance control over the company. An event that may trigger accelerated vesting of options.

churn - the loss of customers. A metric tracked to gauge how well a company is retaining customers and meeting market needs.

cliff vesting - A feature of the vesting schedule for incentive equity grants whereby a portion of the grant vests all at once after an extended period, typically a year, rather than on a monthly or quarterly basis. See also options and vesting.

common stock - the lowest class of stock representing ownership in a corporation. Usually, the class of stock held by founders and employees and the equity type underlying incentive grants such as stock options and RSUs.

conversion price - The price at which convertible debt or a SAFE converts into company shares (usually preferred shares). The conversion price is set by the terms of the convertible security, which typically provides a discount to the share price set in a financing round following the issuance of the convertible debt or SAFE. See also convertible debt and simplified agreement for future equity.

convertible debt - A loan made by an investor to a company with the right at the investor's option to convert the face value of the loan (plus accrued interest) into shares in the company. Usually issued in the early stages of a startup in advance of an equity funding round and converted into equity at a discounted price per share when the equity funding round is completed. Also called a convertible note.

customer acquisition costs (CAC) - A metric used to calculate the cost-efficiency with which a company acquires additional customers and revenue. Often evaluated by VCs relative to the expected lifetime value of a customer to determine whether the economics of a business are viable or progressing toward viability.

dilution - The reduction in a shareholder's percentage ownership in a company caused by the sale of additional stock or the issuance of stock options to other parties. See also fully diluted.

double trigger - The accelerated vesting of an equity grant contingent on two events happening. Most commonly associated with the combination of a change of control of a company followed by termination of the option holder within a specific period (i.e., 12 months). See also single trigger and trigger.

down round - A funding round through which investors buy shares at a valuation lower than the previous funding round. Generally considered a negative occurrence for the company as it can trigger anti-dilution provisions in preferred stock, leading to significant dilution for existing shareholders, especially common shareholders, along with a negative impact on the value of employee stock options. See also recapitalization, round, and up round.

due diligence - The process of validating the worthiness of a company for investment, purchase, or merger. Includes broad investigation and analysis of all aspects of the company, including legal status and compliance, financial results, operational stability, technology, and personnel. Conducted using company-provided information and internal and external interviews and research. Typically takes place prior to the closing of a transaction. Also, a general term for using proper effort and research to evaluate an opportunity.

early exercise - The process of exercising a stock option prior to the option being vested. A provision offered in select cases, usually to executives, to optimize tax treatment of stock ownership from incentive equity grants.

early stage - A general term used to categorize a startup in the early phases of its lifecycle. Typically, will include companies that have yet to achieve substantial revenue or profitability. Term also used by VCs to identify the maturity of companies in which they invest.

equity - General term referring to all classes of stock or ownership interests in a company.

exercise - The purchase by an option holder of stock associated with a vested stock option. Involves the purchaser (option holder) paying the exercise price in cash to the company and receiving the stock in exchange. The process may trigger taxable income to the purchaser.

exercise price - The price at which the holder of a stock option may purchase a share of stock under an option agreement. The price is set based on the company's 409A valuation and ratified by the board of directors for inclusion in stock option grants. Also called strike price.

exit - The sale or initial public offering of a company. The method by which an investor and/or entrepreneur monetize their holding in a company.

exploding offer - A job offer with a short window (from a day up to a week) for the offeree to accept it, after which the offer is rescinded. Used by companies as a pressure tactic to get prospective employees to commit quickly.

follower - In a syndicate of investors, an entity that commits capital to a funding round while relying on the lead investor to negotiate terms with the company and conduct due diligence.

fully diluted - A calculation of stockholder ownership percentages that includes unissued shares held in the option pool in the denominator of the calculation. Fully diluted percent ownership equals shares held divided by (shares issued and outstanding plus the option pool). See also dilution.

general partner - a member of a venture capital or private equity firm responsible for sourcing, investing in companies and overseeing the firm's portfolio of investments. Often a member of the firm's investment committee and a board member for individual portfolio companies. See limited partner.

generally accepted accounting principles (GAAP) - A set of standards and guidelines established by the Financial Accounting Standards Board (FASB) and the Securities and Exchange Commission (SEC) governing how company financial transactions are accounted for and recorded.

growth stage - the stage of a startup's development after early stage. Characterized by rapidly growing revenue, often exceeding 100 percent per year. Includes companies with annual revenues exceeding $3 to 5 million.

incentive equity - A form of direct or derivative stock ownership in a company, usually issued to employees, contractors, advisors, and board members. Includes stock options, restricted stock, restricted stock units, and warrants.

incentive stock options (ISO) - A form of stock option issued only to employees that provides tax advantages (such as capital gains treatment) if exercised and held for more than a year. Issuance amounts are subject to limitations of no more than $100,000 of such options vesting annually.

incentive stock plan - The document issued by the company and approved by the board of directors governing the issuance of incentive stock grants such as options and restricted stock. The document sets terms such as standard vesting schedules, procedures for grant issuance, ISO and non-qual issuance, and forfeiture and repurchase procedures.

insider round - A funding round in which all the capital is provided by previous investors in the company without participation from new investors.

intellectual property - Intangible assets of a company such as patents, trademarks, copyrights, and trade secrets.

issued and outstanding - A term used when calculating ownership percentages of stockholders. Excludes any unissued shares held in the option pool from the denominator of the calculation. Percent ownership equals shares held divided by shares issued and outstanding.

land and expand - A strategy used by companies to grow revenue. The approach entails closing small deals with customers and then working to increase the dollar value of the customer relationship over time by selling more products or services or selling into different departments or divisions within the same customer.

late stage - the stage of a startup's development after growth stage. Characterized by operations with significant revenue exceeding $10 million with companies at this stage able to attract investment interest from private equity firms.

lead investor - In a funding round for a company, the investor who takes responsibility for negotiating the terms of the round, leading due diligence, and working with investor counsel on behalf of the syndicate of investors in the round. Often but not always the largest investor in the round, also known as "leading the round." When the investor is a venture capital firm, also called the lead VC.

lead VC - See lead investor.

lifestyle business - A company, usually a small business, that provides income and lifestyle flexibility to the owner(s). Typically, not a business that outside investors fund as the goal of such a business is not to maximize growth and returns to investors.

limited partner (LP) - an investor who commits capital to a venture capital or private equity fund. May be a high net worth individual or an institutional investor such as an insurance company, pension fund, or other asset manager. Usually, a passive investor who relies on the venture capital or private equity firm to select companies to invest in and manage the portfolio of investments on the LP's behalf.

liquidation preference - The right to receive priority distribution of proceeds from a sale or liquidation of a company. Usually associated with preferred stock.

liquidity event - A financial transaction, such as a merger or acquisition, that provides shareholders of a company with a payout of cash or other forms of compensation for the sale of their stock.

lock-up period - The time, usually 180 days but can vary, after an initial public offering of company stock during which insiders in the company (executives, employees, board members, private investors, and advisors such as lawyers, etc.) may not sell their stock. This practice is designed to provide stability to the stock price and keep large inside shareholders from dumping their stock and running after the IPO.

management carve-out - An agreement by the board of directors to reward specific employees for results, such as the successful sale of a company. Generally paid prior to investors receiving the proceeds from the sale. Often used if the sale will result in minimal or no payment to common shareholders and option holders to keep management focused on completing the transaction.

net revenue retention rate - A metric used by companies to track customer loyalty and churn. Takes into account loss of customers as well as expansion of customer revenue through increased sales. Also called net dollar retention rate. See land and expand.

nondisclosure agreement (NDA) - A legal agreement between two entities, whether individuals or corporations, that restricts how confidential information provided by the parties to each other may be used and shared with third parties.

non-participating preferred - A form of preferred stock that offers shareholders the right to receive their liquidity preference payout (usually 1 time their investment) or convert into common shares and participate *pro rata* in the proceeds to common shareholders. This form of preferred stock is less investor friendly and more company friendly than participating preferred. Also see participating preferred.

non-qualified stock options - A form of non-cash compensation that provides employees, advisors, contractors, and board members the right to purchase the stock of a company at a specified exercise price. Usually subject to a vesting schedule. "Non-qualified" refers to the tax treatment of the option, which receives no special tax treatment, unlike incentive stock options. Also called non-quals, NSOs, or NQSOs. See incentive stock options.

non-recourse financing - A loan provided by a third-party source to enable the exercise of stock options by an option holder without using their own cash. The third party accepts the purchased stock as full collateral for the loan, and repayment takes place at the time the stock is sold. The third party takes a portion of the upside when the stock is sold as compensation for providing the financing.

on-target earnings (**OTE**) - The total dollar amount, including salary plus incentive cash compensation such as bonuses or commissions, an employee should expect to earn if they meet their goals (including company goals if a portion of the bonus is driven by company performance).

option — The right granted by a company to employees, contractors, advisors, and board members to purchase shares of the company's stock (usually common stock) at a set exercise or strike price. Typically contains a time-based vesting schedule requiring a period of service by the grantee to the company before that right becomes active. Also called stock option.

option pool - The common shares allocated on a company's capitalization table and held in reserve for the issuance of incentive stock grants such as options. Represents unissued shares that do not receive proceeds in the event of a company merger or sale. See also issued and outstanding and fully diluted.

partial acceleration - The process by which a portion of the unvested stock options, restricted stock, or restricted stock unit (RSU) grants become vested more quickly than the underlying vesting schedule. The process is associated with specific events such as a company sale or change of control. See also acceleration and trigger.

participating preferred - An investor-friendly form of preferred stock that offers preferred shareholders a preferential payout of proceeds from a liquidity event *plus* the subsequent right to convert into common shares and participate pro rata in the proceeds to common shareholders. The participation feature typically calls for a priority payout of 1 time the invested capital but can also be a higher multiple of the investment depending on what is negotiated in the funding round. See non-participating preferred.

penny warrant - The right granted by a company, usually to banks or other vendors, to purchase shares of the company's stock (usually common stock) at a negligible exercise or strike price (sometimes $0). Used as a sweetener to induce the recipient to do business with the company.

post-money valuation - The valuation of the company immediately following the injection of new capital in a funding round, consisting of adding the capital invested to the pre-money valuation and accounting for the issuance of new shares to the investors. See also pre-money valuation and valuation.

preference stack - The total amount of consideration that must be paid to preferred shareholders before payment can be made to common shareholders and incentive equity grant holders (i.e., employees). Usually equals or exceeds the amount of capital raised in all prior rounds. See also liquidity and waterfall.

preferred shares - See preferred stock.

preferred stock - A class of stock with liquidation preferences regarding the distribution of proceeds from a liquidity event. Often comes with corporate governance rights such as special voting and representation on the board of directors. Also called preferred shares.

pre-money valuation - The valuation of a company as determined by negotiation between the lead investor and the company prior to the injection of new capital. A key term in a term sheet offered by a prospective investor. See also post-money valuation and valuation.

pre-seed stage - The earliest stage of a startup, often before a company has raised outside capital. Sometimes used interchangeably with seed stage to emphasize how young the company is.

private equity - a broad category of investors focused on taking majority or full ownership stakes in mature private companies that have achieved substantial revenue and profitability. Generally focused on later-stage private companies than early-stage companies funded by venture capital firms. An important source of exits for startups.

product management - The function within a company that coordinates the activities of product development/engineering with the sales and marketing teams. Assesses market needs for a product or service and translates market feedback into development plans for the offering while also helping shape sales and marketing strategies and messaging. .

proof continuum - A seven-stage construct that reflects the full lifecycle of a startup from inception to sale or initial public offering. Reflects the key milestones companies must achieve to continue to demonstrate momentum and attract investment capital.

pro rata - From the Latin 'in proportion.' Refers to the right of investors to receive cash proceeds from the company in accordance with their percent ownership. Also refers to the right to invest in future funding rounds in proportion to prior ownership or previous investment.

proprietary information and inventions agreement - An agreement required by employers specifying restrictions on employees' use of and disclosure of a company's intellectual property (IP), ownership of IP developed by employees while at the company, and other key provisions and restrictions, including but not limited to nondisclosure of confidential information, nonsolicitation of company employees and customers after employees' departure, and non-competition provisions (as permitted under the law).

recapitalization - A funding round completed at a lower valuation than prior rounds, usually when a company is in a distressed position. Sometimes accompanied by a restructuring of the capitalization table and the activation of anti-dilution provisions for preferred shares. See also down round.

regreen - The practice of providing new incentive equity grants to employees whose prior grants are reaching high levels of vesting. A tactic used by employers to create employee retention incentives.

restricted stock - A type of stock grant, usually common stock, issued as incentive compensation. The grant vests over time, and the unvested portion is subject to forfeiture upon the recipient's departure from the company. Also, stock acquired through the early exercise of options that have not yet vested. This form of incentive compensation maintains certain favorable tax treatment relative to restricted stock units and is usually issued to senior staff in a company. See 83(b) election and early exercise.

restricted stock unit (RSU) - A form of stock grant, usually common stock, issued as incentive compensation. The grant vests over time, and the unvested portion is subject to forfeiture upon the recipient's departure from the company. Similar to restricted stock but lacks the favorable capital gains tax treatment associated with restricted stock. Subject to ordinary income taxes upon vesting.

reverse merger - The process whereby a shell public company with no business operations merges with an operating company for the purpose of creating an operational publicly traded company.

round - A financing event during which a company raises capital from a group of investors. Startups raise funds from venture capital firms in individual rounds of funding, depending on the stage of the company. The sequence of rounds typically consists of a seed round followed by Series A, B, C, and D rounds, etc.

runway - The time frame usually expressed in the number of months until a company runs out of money, given its current cash reserves and burn rate. See burn rate.

simplified agreement for future equity (SAFE) — An agreement used by early-stage companies to accept investment in advance of a later funding round. Usually issued in the early stages of a startup in advance of an equity funding round and converted into preferred shares at a discounted price per share when the subsequent funding round is completed. Developed by Y Combinator as a more company-friendly alternative to the issuance of convertible debt.

seed - The first official round of financing for a startup. Typically used to fund hiring of early employees and development of a prototype. See also seed stage.

seed round - See seed.

seed stage - The stage of a pre-revenue company shortly after inception when its focus is on raising funds for proof of concept and building a prototype.

series preferred - A general term referring to stock from all funding rounds where preferred stock has been issued (e.g., Series A, Series B, etc.).

severance - Payment of continued compensation for a fixed period after the termination of an employee's employment by the company. May be paid out to any employee terminated but is often associated with a negotiated term in the employment agreement of executives.

single trigger - A feature of an incentive equity grant that provides acceleration of the unvested portion of the grant upon the occurrence of a singular event such as a change of control. See also change of control, double trigger, and trigger.

special purpose acquisition company (SPAC) - A blank-check company or shell corporation with no operations, listed on a stock exchange for the purpose of merging with a private operating company. The SPAC enables a private company to go public without going through the traditional initial public offering (IPO) process.

stage - A phase of development of a startup company. Startups are categorized as seed stage, early stage, growth stage, and late stage. Also a focus of a venture capital firm's investment strategy defining the level of maturity of companies it seeks to fund.

stock - Ownership interest in an entity as represented by shares or ownership percentages. Terms associated with this general term include common stock, convertible preferred stock, non-participating preferred stock, participating preferred stock, preferred stock or preferred shares, restricted stock, restricted stock unit (RSU), and series preferred. Also can be referred to as shares.

strategic buyer/investor - A non-financial company that purchases or invests in a startup to enhance the buyer/investor's product offerings or customer base. Usually an operating company.

strike price - See exercise price.

term sheet - An agreement between a company and prospective investor(s) that outlines the major aspects of an investment to be made in the company. Typically issued by a venture capital or other lead investor in a round. Sets the groundwork for creation of detailed legal documents necessary to close the round. It is typically non-binding and contingent on successful completion of due diligence.

termination - The act of a company discontinuing the employment of a staff member.

termination for cause - Termination based on the employee's violation of their employment agreement. May involve fraud, gross negligence, or commission of a crime, among other conditions. Also called termination with cause. See termination.

termination without cause - Termination of employment by the employer without specific justification such as the employee's violation of the employment agreement or company policies. The subject of a clause in the employment agreement that triggers severance obligations due from the company to the employee. In the case of double trigger acceleration, also the second trigger to cause acceleration of vesting of unvested equity incentive grants. See acceleration, severance, and trigger,

trigger - An event that causes the full or partial acceleration of vesting associated with an incentive equity grant such as a stock option. Most commonly associated with a change of control of the company.

underwater - The status of a stock option in which the exercise price of the option is below the value of the underlying common stock that would be purchased if the option were to be exercised. Also referred to as out of the money.

unicorn - A startup whose valuation exceeds $1 billion based on its most recent funding round or valuation.

unvested - The status of options or restricted equity subject to a vesting schedule in which the holder does not currently have the economic or other rights associated with the holding. The unvested holding is subject to forfeiture upon the holder's departure from the company. See also option and restricted stock units.

up round - A funding round where the price per share paid by investors is higher than in the previous round or rounds, resulting in an increased valuation of the company being funded. See also down round and round.

valuation - The market capitalization of a company derived from multiplying the share price times the number of shares in the company. Also, the process by which a company's worth or value is determined or the actual stated monetary value. In a private company, it can be a subjective number determined by the company or outside investors or valuation firms that analyze capital structure, financial performance, management team, customer base, and market opportunities, among other factors, to determine the worth of the company. See also 409A valuation.

venture capital (VC) - The industry comprises firms investing in early, growth, and late-stage private companies. Also, the actual funding provided by the firms in the industry.

venture capitalist - A firm or individual engaged in the business of investing capital from third parties in high-growth potential private companies, usually in their early stages of development. See also venture capital and limited partners.

vest - The process by which an incentive equity grant holder obtains the economic rights associated with their grant. In the case of options, once the grants or a portion thereof is vested, the holder has the right to exercise the options. In the case of restricted stock units, once vested, the holder owns the shares outright.

vesting schedule - A time-based protocol whereby the exercise rights of incentive equity grants such as options and restricted stock units are activated. Usually, a three to four-year period. See options, exercise, restricted stock, vest, and unvested.

warrant A form of option to purchase a company's stock usually issued to another company as a sweetener for a commercial transaction, such as a bank loan or an important customer contract or to enhance the attractiveness of an investment in conjunction with a funding round.

waterfall - The order of priority by which proceeds from a liquidity event are distributed to creditors, shareholders, advisors (such as lawyers and investment bankers who help with the sale transaction), employees, and other interested parties.

Index

About the Author

Gus Bessalel is a serial entrepreneur and author of *The Startup Lottery: Your Guide to Navigating Risk and Reward,* as well as a collection of articles on startup life and entrepreneurship available at thestartuplottery.com and LinkedIn.

During his 30-year startup career, Gus founded, managed, and invested in over a dozen early-stage ventures and raised over $100 million in capital. He is a Harvard MBA and Inc. 500 CEO who advises startups through CONNECTPreneur, Georgetown University Venture Lab, East Carolina University, and SEEDSpot.

He has guest lectured to business students at American University, Johns Hopkins, and Georgetown and served as a startup pitch mentor for the Harvard Business School Alumni New Venture contest. Gus is also a co-founder of Compass Pro Bono, which provides free consulting services to nonprofits.

Gus resides in Bethesda, Maryland, with his wife Amena Ali, a three-time tech CEO.

For additional information including more of Mr. Bessalel's writing on startups and additional resources, visit:
TheStartupLottery.com

Made in United States
North Haven, CT
10 January 2024

47284266R00214